The Dove that Returns,
The Dove that Vanishes

The nature of psychoanalysis seems contradictory – deeply personal, subjective and intuitive, yet requiring systematic theory and principles of technique. The objective quality of psychoanalytic knowledge is paradoxically dependent on the personal engagement of the knower with what is known.

In *The Dove that Returns, The Dove that Vanishes*, Michael Parsons explores the tension of this paradox. As they respond to it, and struggle to sustain it creatively, analysts discover their individual identities. The work of outstanding clinicians such as Marion Milner and John Klauber is examined in detail. The reader also encounters oriental martial arts, Greek tragedy, the landscape painting of John Constable, a Winnicottian theory of creativity and a discussion of the significance of play in psychoanalysis. From such varied topics there evolves a deepening apprehension of the nature of clinical experience.

Illustrated throughout with clinical examples, *The Dove that Returns, The Dove that Vanishes* will prove valuable both to those in the field of psychoanalysis, and to those in the arts and humanities who are interested in contemporary psychoanalytic thinking.

Michael Parsons is a training analyst of the British Psycho-Analytical Society and a member of the International Psychoanalytical Association. He works in private practice in London.

THE NEW LIBRARY OF PSYCHOANALYSIS

The New Library of Psychoanalysis was launched in 1987 in association with the Institute of Psycho-Analysis, London. Its purpose is to facilitate a greater and more widespread appreciation of what psychoanalysis is really about and to provide a forum for increasing mutual understanding between psychoanalysts and those working in other disciplines such as history, linguistics, literature, medicine, philosophy, psychology and the social sciences. It is intended that the titles selected for publication in the series should deepen and develop psychoanalytic thinking and technique, contribute to psychoanalysis from outside, or contribute to other disciplines from a psychoanalytical perspective.

The Institute, together with the British Psycho-Analytical Society, runs a low-fee psychoanalytic clinic, organises lectures and scientific events concerned with psychoanalysis, publishes the *International Journal of Psycho-Analysis* (which now incorporates the *International Review of Psycho-Analysis*), and runs the only training course in the UK in psychoanalysis, leading to membership of the International Psychoanalytical Association – the body which preserves internationally agreed standards of training, of professional entry, and of professional ethics and practice for psychoanalysis as initiated and developed by Sigmund Freud. Distinguished members of the Institute have included Michael Balint, Wilfred Bion, Ronald Fairbairn, Anna Freud, Ernest Jones, Melanie Klein, John Rickman and Donald Winnicott.

Volumes 1–11 in the series have been prepared under the general editorship of David Tuckett, with Ronald Britton and Eglé Laufer as associate editors. Subsequent volumes are under the general editorship of Elizabeth Bott Spillius, with, from Volume 17, Donald Campbell, Michael Parsons, Rosine Jozef Perelberg and David Taylor as associate editors.

ALSO IN THIS SERIES

THE NEW LIBRARY OF PSYCHOANALYSIS
39

The Dove that Returns, The Dove that Vanishes

PARADOX AND CREATIVITY IN PSYCHOANALYSIS

MICHAEL PARSONS

London and Philadelphia

First published 2000
by Routledge
11 New Fetter Lane, London EC4P 4EE

Simultaneously published in the USA and Canada
by Taylor & Francis Inc.,
325 Chestnut Street, Philadelphia, PA 19106

Routledge is an imprint of the Taylor & Francis Group

Typeset in Bembo by Graphicraft Limited, Hong Kong
Printed and bound in Great Britain by TJ International Ltd,
Padstow, Cornwall

British Library Cataloguing in Publication Data
A catalogue record for this book is available from the British Library

Library of Congress Cataloging in Publication Data
Parsons, Michael, 1941–
 The dove that returns, the dove that vanishes / Michael Parsons.
  p. cm. — (The new library of psychoanalysis ; 39)
 "Published simultaneously in the USA and Canada."
 Includes bibliographical references and index.
 ISBN 0-415-21181-6 (hbk) — ISBN 0-415-21182-4 (pbk.)
 1. Psychoanalytic counseling. 2. Psychoanalysis. I. Title. II. Series.
 BF175.4.C68 P37 2000
 150.19′5—dc21   99-046205

ISBN 0-415-21181-6 (hbk)
ISBN 0-415-21182-4 (pbk)

And the ark rested in the seventh month, in the seventeenth day of the month, upon the mountains of Ararat.

And the waters decreased continually until the tenth month: in the tenth month, on the first day of the month, were the tops of the mountains seen.

And it came to pass at the end of forty days, that Noah opened the window of the ark which he had made:

And he sent forth a raven, which went forth to and fro, until the waters were dried up from off the earth.

Also he sent forth a dove from him, to see if the waters were abated from off the face of the ground;

But the dove found no rest for the sole of her foot, and she returned unto him into the ark, for the waters were on the face of the whole earth: then he put forth his hand, and took her, and pulled her in unto him into the ark.

And he stayed yet other seven days; and again he sent forth the dove out of the ark;

And the dove came in to him in the evening; and lo, in her mouth was an olive leaf pluckt off: so Noah knew that the waters were abated from off the earth.

And he stayed yet other seven days; and sent forth the dove; which returned not again unto him any more.

Genesis 8: 4–12

*This book is dedicated
with thanks for all they have given me
to my parents and my children*

Terence, Betty, Zoë, Harriet

Contents

Figures

Acknowledgements

When a book has been as long in the making as this one, it has more co-authors than could fit on the title page.

My patients, for a start. They are the ones who have made this work possible, and I hope the clinical descriptions give some idea of what I owe them. Those mentioned and those who are not, have all, by what they brought to their analyses, played their part in these ideas.

The British Psycho-Analytical Society and its accompanying Institute provide a training and a professional companionship which, warts and all, are second to none. Some of these chapters grew out of work I began as a student, and those who taught me are present here. Other chapters come from lectures or papers that colleagues asked me for, and I am grateful for the stimulus of those sometimes challenging requests. The papers by Klauber, Bion and Bernardi, referred to in Chapters 5 and 11, formed part of a course I gave at the Institute of Psycho-Analysis, and the aliveness of the students in those seminars has contributed to the book as well. In one way and another (not least at the Spanish Club), all these chapters have been enriched by discussion with friends and colleagues.

It was my good fortune to have a training in the classics. I do not know what my tutors of long ago would make of Chapters 6 and 7, but I remain grateful for their teaching. My debt to E.R. Dodds' edition of *Bacchae* is evident throughout Chapter 6. P.E. Easterling's edition of *Trachiniae* was equally invaluable in Chapter 7.

The writing itself has been encouraged and supported by many people. Analytic spouses have a lot to put up with, and much that is here would have been impossible without Sarah Parsons' patient acceptance of my work. Special thanks are due to Elizabeth Spillius. As General Editor of the New Library of Psychoanalysis she went on believing, however long nothing seemed to be happening, that the book would one day exist. Her tactful silences, and occasional enquiries about progress, were just the required mix of freedom and rigour. I am also grateful to her anonymous readers for their thoughtful comments on the manuscript. Thanks too to the New Library's other General Editors: David Tuckett who, years ago, commissioned a completely different book from this, and Susan Budd for her active support when it was needed; also to Joanne Forshaw at Routledge and Mandy Collison, Senior Production Editor at Psychology Press, for her help in the transitional space between manuscript and book. Melanie Hart read and re-read the manuscript, urging me to clarify my ideas and helping to improve their expression. I, and the reader, owe her a great deal.

As I say in the Introduction, being an analyst is a particular way of being a person. The book is also in gratitude to those, both within and outside the world of psychoanalysis, who have helped me towards that.

For permission to reproduce the paintings in Chapter 9 I am grateful to the following: Ipswich Borough Council Museums and Galleries (Figure 1); The Master, Fellows and Scholars of Downing College in the University of Cambridge (Figure 2); W.H. Proby, Elton Hall (Figure 3); Tate Gallery, London 1999 (Figure 4); V&A Picture Library (Figure 5); National Gallery, London (Figure 6).

I am also grateful for permission to reproduce copyright material as follows: an extract from the Authorised Version of the Bible (The King James Bible), the rights in which are vested in the Crown, by permission of the Crown's Patentee, Cambridge University Press; extracts from *Moving Zen: Karate as a Way to Gentleness* by permission of the author and Paul H. Crompton Ltd; an extract from *T'ai Chi Ch'uan for Health and Self-Defence* by permission of Random House Inc.; an extract from 'East Coker' in *Four Quartets*, Copyright 1940 by T.S. Eliot and renewed 1968 by Esme Valerie Eliot, by permission of Faber & Faber and of Harcourt Inc.; an extract from *Report to Greco* by Nikos Kazantzakis by permission of Faber & Faber; extracts from poems by W.B. Yeats by permission of A.P. Watt Ltd on behalf of Michael B. Yeats, and of Simon and Schuster (Copyright 1940 by Georgie Yeats, renewed 1968 by Bertha Georgie Yeats, Michael Butler Yeats and Anne Yeats); an extract from *Winnie-the-Pooh* by permission of Methuen, an imprint of Egmont Children's Books Ltd, London, and of Dutton Children's Books, a division of Penguin Putnam Inc. (Copyright 1926 by E.P. Dutton, renewed 1954 by A.A. Milne); an extract from *Tales of Love* by Julia Kristeva by permission of Columbia University Press; extracts from the *Bhagavad Gita* and *Tao Te Ching* by permission of Penguin Books Ltd; lines by Elizabeth Jennings by permission of the author and of Carcanet New Press; lines by C.P. Cavafy by permission of Thames and Hudson Ltd; extracts from Sophocles' *Trachiniae* by permission of the University of Chicago Press; extracts from *The Standard Edition of the Complete Psychological Works of Sigmund Freud, translated and edited by James Strachey* by permission of Sigmund Freud Copyrights, The Institute of Psycho-

Analysis, The Hogarth Press, Alfred A. Knopf (a division of Random House Inc.), W.W. Norton & Co. Inc. and Liveright Publishing Corporation; extracts from *The Collected Papers, Volume 4* by Sigmund Freud. Authorised translation under the supervision of Joan Riviere. Published by Basic Books, Inc. by arrangement with The Hogarth Press, Ltd. and The Institute of Psycho-Analysis, London. Reprinted by permission of Basic Books, a member of Perseus Books, L.L.C.; extracts from *The Future of an Illusion* by Sigmund Freud, translated by James Strachey. Copyright © 1961 by James Strachey, renewed 1989 by Alix Strachey. Used by permission of W.W. Norton & Company, Inc.; extracts from *New Introductory Lectures on Psycho-Analysis* by Sigmund Freud, translated by James Strachey. Copyright © 1965, 1964 by James Strachey. Used by permission of W.W. Norton & Company Inc.; extracts from *Introductory Lectures on Psycho-Analysis* by Sigmund Freud, translated by James Strachey. Copyright © 1965, 1964, 1963 by James Strachey. Used by permission of Liveright Publishing Corporation; extracts from *Civilization and its Discontent* by Sigmund Freud, translated by James Strachey. Copyright © 1961 by James Strachey, renewed 1989 by Alix Strachey. Used by permission of W.W. Norton & Company, Inc.; extracts from *The Ego and the Id* by Sigmund Freud, translated by James Strachey. Copyright © 1960 by James Strachey, renewed 1988 by Alix Strachey. Used by permission of W.W. Norton & Company, Inc.; extracts from *An Autobiographical Study* by Sigmund Freud, translated by James Strachey. Copyright 1952 by W.W. Norton & Company, Inc., renewed © 1980 by Alix Strachey. Copyright 1935 by Sigmund Freud, renewed © 1963 by James Strachey. Used by permission of W.W. Norton & Company, Inc. Material from some of my own papers, originally published in the *International Journal* and *International Review of Psychoanalysis*, is reproduced by permission of the *International Journal of Psychoanalysis*.

Introduction

Psychoanalysts who are primarily immersed in clinical work have to do their writing piecemeal. This book is based on articles I have written, and lectures and seminars I have given, over the last 15 years. Ideas develop over time, and a variety of audiences makes for variations in style and complexity, so by its nature such a book cannot be uniform. At the same time unexpected connections and continuities reveal themselves, and I have reworked the original material with an eye to tracing these out and clarifying them. Having begun life separately the chapters can be read independently of each other, but that reworking has also turned them into a kind of extended meditation on themes which recur and interweave.

The book is divided into two parts with a concluding chapter, but this structure is a loose one. Topics important in the chapters of Part II are already turning up in Part I, and the questions which belong to Part I echo through Part II. Despite such overlaps, two themes are central to Part I. One is a tension that lies at the heart of psychoanalysis, between elements which are intrinsic to its nature but stand in apparent opposition to each other. There is the deeply personal, subjective and intuitive aspect of psychoanalysis, and there is the need for objectivity, theory-building and technical discipline. The chapters of Part I look at the many different ways in which this polarity reveals itself, and the temptation to sacrifice one aspect of psychoanalysis to the other.

The second main theme of Part I is the question of identity. Being a psychoanalyst is a particular way of being a person. There is no such thing as an analyst, or a person, in the abstract. There is only whatever unique psychoanalyst, whatever unique person, someone arrives at being, through his or her own particular process of becoming. This idea emerges gradually in the course of Part I. Its consequences for analytic training are somewhat problematic, and it also has implications for the theory of personality development.

Psychoanalysis began as a medical treatment but immediately showed itself to be, in the same activity, an instrument of personal growth as well. This double identity of the discipline is explored in Chapter 1, 'Vocation and martial art'. Psychoanalysis is both a thing done and a mode of being. It is the uniquely appropriate choice by which the analyst expresses who he is, so that when he is doing analysis he is being that.[1] The subjectivity and individualism of this, however, seem at odds with the need for analysis to be grounded in general principles of theory and clinical technique. Balancing psychoanalysis as a vocation against psychoanalysis as a discipline is not easy, and Otto Rank and Jacques Lacan, who were remarkably close in their views of what it is to be an analyst, exemplify how one side of this equilibrium may suffer.

It might seem surprising to turn, for illumination about the nature of psychoanalysis, to the Chinese and Japanese martial arts. But the question of how something can be, at the same time, a technical procedure to be correctly performed, and a mode of being that expresses and develops a person's inmost nature, has been much thought and written about in those traditions. T'ai Chi, archery, swordsmanship and karate all have examples to offer.

Marion Milner was someone who examined with clarity and determination what being an analyst meant for her, and how it reflected who she was. Her work is remarkable for its cross-referencing and integration between profound subjective experience and psychoanalytic conceptualising. Chapter 2 considers in detail her three autobiographical books, which may be less read, at least by analysts, than her psychoanalytic writings. The chapter's title, 'The other in the self', relates to a certain kind of experience Milner describes, of encountering something which, while evidently belonging to our own inner worlds, at the same time seems other than ourselves. There is a sense of recognition, yet what this something produces comes from somewhere unknown. Dreaming can have this quality. Sudden moments of creativity are another instance of it. Milner discovered in herself an agency which she called her Answering Activity. It embodied a wisdom and perceptiveness beyond what was ordinarily available to her. Her sense of it as part of herself, but also something (or somebody) other, with which to make contact, was very distinct.

What made this possible for Milner was a special quality, in her self-inquiry, of openness to the unexpected, and Chapter 3, 'Suddenly finding it really matters', shows how valuable the same quality is in clinical work.

---

1 I have used 'he or she', and 'his or her', when the flow of a sentence allows it. Otherwise I have used 'he', and sometimes 'she', generically. Trying too dogmatically to eradicate this can produce clumsy repetitions which are more insensitive than the pronouns themselves.

How does an analyst stay open to seeing that what she thought she understood matters more than she realised, or matters in new and unexpected ways? Patient and analyst have to make their own discoveries of what really matters in an analysis, and for the patient to be able to do that the analyst needs to be open to it as well. Spiritual experience is suspect for many analysts, but this paradox, of simultaneous attachment and non-attachment in the analyst, has close parallels in spiritual tradition, particularly the Taoist and Zen Buddhist traditions which lie behind the martial arts.

Chapter 4, 'Refinding theory in clinical practice', considers the same need to find fresh meaning in what is already known, as it applies to theory. Theory has two aspects, both essential: an external, 'public' one that can be learnt, and an internal aspect that can only be found in lived experience. However experienced and knowledgeable they may be, analysts always need to discover psychoanalysis itself afresh within any individual analysis. An extended clinical example illustrates my own attempt at this, and a discussion of the philosophy of science shows that, however anti-subjective and rationalist one's view of the nature of knowledge, there is no escaping the need for it to be personal as well as objective.

Chapter 5, 'Psychoanalytic and personal identity', bulges a bit at the seams with all it has collected into itself. This may be because it not only ends Part I, but is also a bridge into Part II. Central to the identity of a psychoanalyst is an analyst's relationship to his or her own unconscious. An earlier working title for the chapter was 'Trusting the unconscious'. The analyst does need to be able to trust the unconscious processes between himself and the patient, so as to help the patient have more confidence in his own internal processes. But the unconscious, however well analysed, keeps areas of darkness and complexity, and trust depends on a willingness, at the same time, to mistrust the unconscious. Lacan's failed attempt to institutionalise this awareness without institutionalising it, is fascinating. It is also interesting when analysts give us the chance, like Milner, to watch the development of an identity over the years. John Klauber and Wilfred Bion both reveal in their writings how their analytic identities evolved towards a greater degree of trust in their own unconscious processes. A comparison between Freud and Sándor Ferenczi illustrates how differently the psychoanalytic vocation can act as an expression of the analyst's being.

The evolution of analytic identity is a particular case of how personal identity in general evolves. Human beings arrive at being who they are by a largely unconscious process of developmental choice. All forward movement involves loss, and while these developmental choices open new avenues of growth, in doing so they close off other possibilities. An important aspect of our identities lies in how we relate to the people we did not become. This view of personality development offers a fresh perspective on prejudiced states of mind, and the last part of Chapter 5 looks at prejudice as a 'normal psychosis'.

Through all these chapters of Part I runs the polarity between, on the one hand, spontaneity, the sense of mystery, openness to the unexpected and trust in unconscious processes; and on the other, rationality, adherence to fundamental principles, conceptual rigour and consistent, disciplined technique. These two aspects of psychoanalysis pull in opposite directions, and psychoanalysts become the analysts they are, by the ways they find of sustaining a creative tension between them.

Part II appears more diverse. But the inevitability of loss was declaring itself as an important theme at the end of Part I, and the capacity to bear loss wholeheartedly, without pushing the experience away, emerges, through the seemingly disparate chapters of Part II, as essential to being truly alive and engaged with the world.

The first two chapters, 'Self-knowledge refused and accepted' and 'The Oedipus complex as a lifelong developmental process', contain studies of three Greek tragedies: Euripides' *Bacchae* and Sophocles' *Oedipus at Colonus* in Chapter 6, and Sophocles' *Trachiniae* in Chapter 7. These chapters look at the text of the plays in considerable detail, but they do not need specialised knowledge. If they prompt readers to turn to the plays themselves, I shall be delighted. The readings of the plays are closely tied to analytic ideas, and because Chapter 6 is based on a seminar that was given for classicists, mixed in with the textual detail is a very basic presentation of certain aspects of psychoanalytic developmental theory.

The discussion of *Bacchae* and *Oedipus at Colonus* follows on from the end of Chapter 5. Pentheus in the former, and Theseus in the latter, can be seen as people confronted with alternate versions of themselves. The two plays represent opposite possible outcomes of this situation. Pentheus can react only with violent prejudice, and his 'normal' psychosis breaks down into outright madness. Theseus, on the other hand, when faced with the person he did not become, can offer his alternate self a home. *Trachiniae*, perhaps Sophocles' least known play, is permeated with Oedipal themes. There is an important distinction, where these are concerned, between triangular sexual relationships and triangularity in its own right as an aspect of psychic structure. Chapter 7 elaborates this and, through a reading of *Trachiniae*, reveals the Oedipus complex as a lifelong developmental challenge. Working through new kinds of Oedipal configuration that belong to later life, with the acceptance of loss that they involve, is essential for continued maturing into old age.

The idea of play as central to psychoanalysis gives rise to various responses. Some analysts seem to find no difficulty with it; others react rather strongly against it. 'The logic of play' (Chapter 8) tries to sort out what really is the role of play in psychoanalysis. The psychoanalytic process is able to take place because of a framework which defines a paradoxical reality. This is the reality of the play space in which, as with stage plays, things may be real and not real at the same time. This concept is a tougher one than some enthusiasts for the idea of psychoanalytic play may realise. There is room in an analysis for real playfulness, and the forward-looking, exciting aspect of play allows an imaginative exploration out of which choices may grow and identity evolve. But development also requires separation and mourning, and there is an intrinsic connection between play and loss. This is bound up with the tragic and ironic aspects of psychoanalysis. Gruelling and painful analytic situations in particular depend on the paradoxical reality of the play space to allow the analysis to continue.

The last two chapters of Part II, in the discussion of their own topics, carry some of these themes further. 'Creativity, psychoanalytic and artistic' puts forward a theory of creativity based on Winnicott's concept of potential space. The play space is an example of this, but it is only one form of it. Winnicott was describing an area of experience, intermediate between internal and external reality, which permeates the whole of life. Freud's view of creativity as a defence against neurotic breakdown had a powerful and lasting effect. Analytic ideas about creativity, and responses to those ideas, have been in dialogue with it ever since. The question of what need in any artist is met by creating a work of art is obviously important. But the theory put forward in this chapter is about the creative process itself, seen not as serving a function but as a natural expression of what being human means.

'Psychic reality' is an often, but often vaguely, used idea. It is implicit in these discussions of creativity, of play, and of the nature of dramatic reality. Chapter 10, 'Psychic reality, negation and the analytic setting', takes it up explicitly and tries to trace some of its ramifications. It may be a defensive avoidance of ordinary reality, but it is also the realm where psychic work, and psychoanalytic work, is done. This use depends on a different sort of separation from ordinary reality. The double function of psychic reality is linked to the double significance of negation, which may be used defensively, but also in a flexible, provisional way, to disengage from ordinary reality without contradicting it. Symbolism and play too depend on this non-defensive use of negation.

This chapter also develops the idea that the analytic setting represents, in its external structure, the internal structure of the mind. The negations of ordinary reality, which the setting embodies, represent the internal activity of negation by which psychic reality is constituted. The freedom and defensiveness with which patients make use of the negations embodied in the setting express how free or restricted they are internally in the use they can make of their own psychic realities.

The concluding chapter finds a metaphor for much that the book has attempted to explore, in the image of Noah's dove. The dove that returns to show Noah the olive leaf, and the dove that, by vanishing, shows him more, are the same bird. They represent opposite ends of a single dimension, corresponding to the opposites whose polarity was examined in Part I. The patient's material, the analyst's interventions, their silences, can emanate from different parts of this dimension. The character of an interpretation may depend much more on whereabouts within the analyst it originates from, than on the words it consists of. The analyst should be able to shift freely back and forth along this dimension, so as to help the patient develop a similar internal freedom of movement. It is sometimes hard to find a psychoanalytic vocabulary for these ideas, but Bion's concepts of alpha-function and reverie are valuable. The book ends by comparing analytic reverie to the state of mind of the martial artist, described in Chapter 1.

Part I
Rigour and freedom

Tradition is to receive past knowledge, break it down and use it in a creative way, and to hand down that knowledge again as a true history.
Toshio Ohi, eleventh generation pottery master
of the Ohi Chozaemon family (1997)

1

Vocation and martial art

If words be not . . . an incarnation of the thought but only a clothing for it, then surely will they prove an ill gift.

Wordsworth (1810: 84) *Essays upon Epitaphs III*

At karate training one evening we were practising with our partners a prearranged sequence of attack and defence when the instructor, a great karate master called Hirokazu Kanazawa, broke off the exercise and dismissed the class, well before the training session would normally have ended. At the next session someone asked why he had stopped the class early. 'Spirit no good!' came the reply. He said we had been making our attacks without real commitment or sincerity. He understood that we did not want to hurt our friends, but an empty attack was no expression of friendship. If we were true friends to our training partners, he said, we would strike with all the speed and power we had. The totally committed attack calls for total commitment from the defender to block it. Only by demanding that from our partners would we give them the chance to develop their karate properly. But our instructor's teaching demanded not only the right spirit. Speed and power means that attacks must also be delivered with discipline and control. The fuller and more sincere your commitment of spirit towards your partner, the more indispensable becomes a deeply founded and reliable technique. I began to learn that lesson as a student of karate. Years later, as a student of psychoanalysis, it took a while for me to recognise where my sense of *déjà-vu* was coming from.

Psychoanalysis started life as a medical treatment developed by a neurologist for disorders which did not respond to current therapeutic regimes. So viewed, it is the treatment of choice for certain types of patient in certain diagnostic categories. This carries implications about training, scientific attitude and therapeutic stance which relate the professional identity of the psychoanalyst closely to that of the physician. Sometimes, indeed,

9

it has been a contentious question whether anyone but a physician should be a psychoanalyst. Where the physician is concerned, and particularly, perhaps, the surgeon (Freud 1912: 115), his technique matters more to us than his spirit. We shall put up with some emotional ineptness if the diagnosis is correct and the operation well performed. It became clear early on, however, that, at the same time as being a treatment, psychoanalysis was an instrument for personal development. This carries quite different connotations. A person need not be ill to be entitled to it and there is no evident necessity to be trained in diagnosing and curing sickness in order to practise it. The professional identity of such a practitioner might be nearer to that of a creative artist, pastoral worker or historian than a physician or surgeon.

There is a tension here which lies at the heart of psychoanalysis. The originality of Freud's discovery is such that the identity of the psychoanalyst cannot be assimilated to other, more comfortably recognisable, roles. The psychoanalyst at work has to do two things at once. He must carry out a technical procedure as correctly as possible and also engage with another human being, with full respect for that person's spirit and commitment of his own. It would be problematic enough if these were separate things to be done in parallel. What characterises psychoanalysis is that the one activity has to be both at the same time. This fundamental polarity has been described in all sorts of ways. Is the analyst, for example, more like a repairman or a healer (Bakan 1967)? A repairman must be, first and foremost, technically competent. He investigates whatever he needs to, but without personal involvement. His aim is to assess what is wrong, put it right and tidy up afterwards. All that is certainly true of a surgeon, and Freud's picture of an analyst at work is sometimes like this. By contrast, it is the *person* of a healer that counts, and the healer's commitment to the sufferer as a person. A healer aims to help the sufferer find meaning in what is happening and, above all, seeks to liberate the sufferer's own impulse towards health. All that is also true of the psychoanalyst at work. Either picture on its own, though, is one-sided. The image of the repairman leaves out the analyst's concern for the patient as a person, the meaning of the patient's difficulties in a wider frame of reference, and the open-endedness of the analytic process. The image of the healer lacks the rational explanatory framework which is needed to build theories, to generalise or differentiate between patients, and to develop a clinical method that can be refined and passed on to others.

Some will prefer one model, some the other; but to argue the two against each other misses the point. Psychoanalysis is both, and the polarity between them is an essential part of its nature. This is difficult and paradoxical, and there is a temptation to escape into emphasising one aspect at the expense of the other. Critics of psychoanalysis also tend to focus on either aspect in isolation, and there are two broad strands of critical comment that this has generated.

The first of these portrays psychoanalysis as an artificial procedure, backed by a specialised training which gives the analyst expert status, where knowledge belongs to the analyst but not to the patient. Psychoanalysis applies this procedure to the patient using technical rules that are part of the analyst's expert knowledge. Freud's images of the analyst as a blank reflecting screen or an impassive surgeon may be invoked to support this picture: of technique used in a rigid and impersonal way at the expense of the patient's uniqueness and humanity. Such criticism sets this against a view of therapy as a symmetrical encounter between two individuals. Although the focus is on helping one of them, this does not mean the other has to be a different, special sort of person. Therapy depends on ordinary human qualities like warmth, tact and emotional sensitivity, and the therapist is simply someone with experience in using these to try and help another person (Lomas 1981).

It is possible to have specialised theoretical knowledge and a defined clinical technique, and still be a caring and understanding human being. To set these up as mutually exclusive is a false distinction. This kind of criticism is more radically challenged, however, by descriptions of the actual experience of analysis. An analyst who behaves in a firmly classical way, not giving information about himself or herself, examining difficulties rather than sympathising with them, might seem just the aloof and ungiving person at which such criticism is aimed. But through this apparent austerity, the quality of the analyst's attention can communicate to patients that they are in contact with someone to be trusted and who is deeply committed to their well-being. They may be baffled by their own feelings of appreciation. One such account, a remarkable description of an analytic journey of recovery from psychosis, ends like this:

> 'Good-bye, Doctor.'
> 'Good-bye, Madame. I'll be here if you need me. I will be happy to hear how you are doing if you consider it necessary to tell me.'
> Inviolable little man, so he's going to maintain the role to the end!
> The door closes behind me. In front of me the cul-de-sac, the city, the country and an appetite for life and for building as big as the earth itself.
> (Cardinal 1975: 212)

Formality or informality for its own sake is not important. Although Marie Cardinal found her analyst's formality immovable, she appreciated enormously what was expressed through it. What matters is how far the analyst's analytic identity is an expression of his personal identity. Harry Guntrip's (1975) comparison between his two analyses with Ronald Fairbairn and Donald Winnicott shows how crucial this can be. Fairbairn too adopted

11

a formal analytic stance, but Guntrip's experience of this was very different from that of Cardinal with her analyst. He wrote that it was only in talking with Fairbairn after the session that he could 'find the natural warm-hearted human being behind the exact interpreting analyst' (Guntrip 1975: 149). Guntrip contrasts this with Winnicott's naturalness, not just as a person but as an analyst in the session. He experienced a kind of harmony between Winnicott's gentleness and incisiveness, while Fairbairn's analytic work was in uneasy counterpoint with his personality. As with anyone describing his own analysis, Guntrip's account cannot be taken entirely at face value and it has itself been analysed (Padel 1996; Markillie 1996). None the less the sense of difference between the analysts remains. Guntrip appreciated Fairbairn's efforts on his behalf, and he did gain from them. But the fact that, for Winnicott, analysing had come to be a natural, organic function of his personality, allowed something to happen for Guntrip in that analysis that had not been possible with Fairbairn.[1]

All this goes beyond the rather obvious statement that being professional does not stop an analyst also being human. Cardinal's account of her analysis and Guntrip's description of Winnicott show that the application of professional knowledge with a specific technique and the sensitive caring which is an ordinary human attribute, far from being opposite kinds of therapeutic behaviour, can be fused together. Then it is not a question of how to mix two ingredients which are both necessary, let alone of having to choose between them. They are absorbed into each other so that the analytic work and the expression of the analyst's humanity become one and the same thing.

The second broad strand of criticism takes issue with psychoanalysis for lacking rigour and being too subjective. The reproach, in this case, is that clinical practice depends on intuitive observations that cannot be objectively validated, made in unique, individual situations that cannot be generalised. This sort of critique is clearly travelling in the opposite direction from the first. It makes the accuracy of interpretations into a central issue. B.A. Farrell (1981), for example, evaluates criteria by which analysts may claim to judge the truth of an interpretation: it may have been right in other similar cases; the patient himself may acknowledge the interpretation; or it may open up fresh material and move the analysis forward. Farrell argues firstly that, as a matter of logic, these criteria do not confirm an interpretation's truth. Then, using a transcript from a taped session, he considers which of the analyst's utterances constitute interpretations and concludes that it is not possible, in any case, reliably to determine whether the

---

1 Peter Rudnytsky (1991: 75) has also written of 'the inseparability of Winnicott's intellectual and personal qualities', and Masud Khan (1975: xi) said of him: 'I have not met another analyst who was more inevitably himself.'

patient's responses satisfy those criteria. Such arguments implicitly see the analyst's task as being to establish a set of propositions that comprise a true account of the patient, and to express that account in particular kinds of utterance called interpretations.

At the International Psychoanalytical Association Congress held in Edinburgh in 1961, the question of the analyst's 'human' as against his 'analytic' qualities, and the implications of this for interpretation, was a prominent issue. There was a symposium on 'The Curative Factors in Psycho-Analysis', whose three papers, by Maxwell Gitelson, Sacha Nacht and Hanna Segal, with the ensuing discussion, are revealing (Symposium 1962).

Gitelson (1962), writing particularly about establishing the psychoanalytic process in the early phase of analysis, was concerned to allow a place for interventions by the analyst which are not obviously interpretative but foster an atmosphere of security and encouragement for the patient. His point was that, because these arise out of the dynamics of an instinctually structured situation between patient and analyst, they are not a departure from the classical analytic framework. In particular, they are not a matter of suggestion as a substitute for interpretation. He says they can be seen as 'preparatory incomplete interpretations' (Gitelson 1962: 204) and come, just as complete interpretations do, from the analyst's 'diatrophic function' (Spitz 1956), which is his 'healing intention' (Gitelson 1962: 197) towards the patient.

Nacht's (1962) theme was that the way patients receive interpretations is inevitably coloured by their unconscious perception of the analyst's unconscious attitude towards them. He emphasises that it is not a question of the analyst's trying consciously to adopt a certain attitude for therapeutic purposes. What counts is his actual, unconscious, internal stance towards the patient and towards the whole work of analysis. He quotes Glover's (1937: 131) remark that 'a prerequisite of the efficiency of interpretation is the attitude, the true unconscious attitude, of the analyst'. Like Gitelson, Nacht tried to be clear that he was not departing from the ordinary analytic framework.

> It seems obvious to me that only a timely and technically appropriate attitude of gratification can allow the patient to accept his need to love and be loved, and to express it without fear. But this attitude must, of course, be expressed neither in words nor in gestures, but *solely by an inner state of being*. Here again, we see how the deep inner state of the analyst can be a decisive curative factor.
>
> (Nacht 1962: 209)

But 'gratification' is a word to set alarm bells ringing, and this attempt to head off misunderstanding was not successful. Comments in the discussion show that both Gitelson and Nacht were heard as failing to distinguish

13

between the analytic and an ordinary relationship, and as though they favoured gratifying rather than interpreting the patient's desires.

Segal ([1962] 1981) took a more unequivocal stance. For her, the only curative factor in psychoanalysis was insight as given by interpretation and, specifically, by interpretation in the transference. The analyst's tolerance and sensitivity may be needed in facilitating the development of the transference and in bearing what happens in it, but these attributes act only in the service of interpretation which is distinct from them. This unambiguous viewpoint escaped the criticism that Gitelson and Nacht encountered, but it is interesting that in Segal's (1979) own later reflections on her paper, she has come to see understanding as an expression of love.

Psychoanalysis is not simply a matter of the analyst's discovering truths about the patient and communicating them to him in the form of interpretations. Interpretation needs to leave space for the patient to take himself by surprise (Winnicott 1971: 51), and begin to notice for himself the person that he is. A patient once said to me that his analysis was like a Chinese painting, where the paper keeps whatever mark you make on it. If you make a mistake you cannot change it. It just has to become part of the picture. He sometimes felt he wasted a session, or that I failed to understand him. But even those times seemed to be all part of the way he was getting a new view of himself. Analysis is an attempt to set up conditions in which new knowledge of the patient can crystallise out between himself and the analyst. Interpretation is the continuing activity by which the analyst tries to provoke and sustain the crystallisation process. Saying the kinds of thing that are called 'interpretations' is a major part of this, and there is certainly such a thing as a wrong interpretation. But the process of interpretation should not be reduced simply to making those sorts of utterance. As Harold Stewart (1992: 127–8) has written: 'It is somewhat artificial to speak of interpretations or any other agents as the mediators of psychic change since they all usually arise gradually out of a complex matrix of interactions and not as complete and separate interventions.'

The two strands of criticism – that psychoanalysis is too impersonal on the one hand or too subjective on the other – seem at odds with each other. Despite this, the responses to them that have emerged from this discussion have something in common – the denial of separation between the technique of analysis (as shown, for example, in formulating a transference interpretation) and the rest of the analyst's activity. The act of analysing is identical with the caring of which the analyst is the embodiment, and interpretation is the vehicle for the analyst's continuing provision of himself, which helps the patient to discover a new view of his own self. There are not two sorts of thing happening but only one. It may not even be possible to separate out the analyst himself or herself from the thing that he or she is doing. This might seem strange, for we habitually distinguish between who someone is and what that person does. But to call somebody a good analyst refers both to what they do and who they are. I am suggesting that who an analyst is and the analysis that that analyst does, are not merely related but are actually the same thing.

To say that analysing is a mode of being, and not just a thing done, might seem a truism. Is not everything we do an expression of our being? In a trivial sense, perhaps so. 'Crossing the road is an expression of one's being' may not be a false statement; it just does not mean much. The question is whether our crossing the road expresses anything. (It may, of course, in particular circumstances.) But what about 'The way that man eats is an expression of his being'? We should take this to mean that the man's way of eating reveals a particular aspect of his character. This is not trivial. Still less of a truism would be 'The President's whole political career has been an expression of his being.' These examples indicate what increases the significance of an activity. First, intentionality. The eater might well be taken aback at having this said to him. But the President would probably reply 'Of course. It has to be. How else could I be an effective President?' The second element is specificity. The eater may reveal that aspect of his character in all sorts of other ways as well. The President probably sees his career as an expression of who he is that would not have been possible in any other way. To call psychoanalysis a vocation is to see it as the uniquely appropriate choice by which the analyst expresses who he is. When he is doing analysis he is being that.

Two major figures who would have agreed with this idea are Otto Rank and Jacques Lacan. But their responses to it illustrate how problematical is the polarity I am pointing to, and how difficult the equilibrium between opposites which it demands. For both Rank and Lacan, this perception of analysis as a mode of being became the occasion for abandoning, in their different ways, another, equally necessary, understanding of it.

The concept of Will was central to Rank's thinking. He saw man's will as the instrument by which he forms himself as a person. The average individual, according to Rank, manages this to a satisfactory degree and lives an ordinary, well-adjusted life. The 'creative' personality, however, uses his will in an exceptional way to elaborate his individuality. Rank's favourite example is the artist. 'When we intuitively admire some great work of art we say the whole artist is in it and expresses himself in it' (Rank 1932: 373). Such people's lives are imbued with a sense of meaning, and their actions arise more out of their grounding in their own identity than from a need to accommodate themselves to external demands. Alongside the average and creative types Rank also describes the 'neurotic' type. This is not someone who has failed in ordinary development but someone who, having rejected the average as unsatisfactory, has got stuck and not been

15

able to go on creatively to structure an autonomous self of his own. Rank (1932: 25) speaks of such people as *'artistes manqués'*.

Rank (1929–31) thought the therapist should be someone of the creative type. The therapist is there to foster the patient's use of his will in pursuing the creative effort whose failure, so far, has brought him into therapy. To do that, the therapeutic work needs to be an expression of the therapist's creative use of his or her own self. A psychologically average, unremarkably well-balanced person is probably not a psychoanalyst in the making. The analyst-to-be needs to need his own analysis, not simply undergo it for form's sake. In Rank's terms he must be trying to create meaning in his life to start with, and analysis (his own, and later his analysis of others) becomes his way of developing that meaning.

Lacan left the Paris Psychoanalytical Society because of a disagreement over exactly this issue. He thought the decision that one is ready to be an analyst was the responsibility of the individual, the expression of an identity which that person had made his own.[2] There is a close affinity in this with Rank's idea of the creative will which determines the growth of a person's self. Rank said, just as Lacan did about the analyst, that the artist appoints himself. His first creative act is the creation of his identity as an artist. 'He is now himself the work of art' (Rank 1932: 81). Lacan, being more concerned with the relation between psychoanalysis and language, likened becoming an analyst to deciding to be a poet. He says of himself that he is 'a poem, a poem that is being written' (Lacan 1977: viii).

The resemblance here between Rank's and Lacan's thinking is remarkable. But to see psychoanalysis as a mode of being seemed, to each of them, a liberation from the constraints of externally imposed technique which, they thought, made formulaic and rigid what should be spontaneous, flexible and creative. Because of this they sacrificed, to their perception of analysis as a vocation, other essential aspects of it. Lacan abandoned the framework of the session. Instead he determined its length according to his view of the patient's state at that particular moment, regarding each session as a unique manifestation of the unconscious. 'The laws of the unconscious don't reveal themselves in 45-minute intervals, and so neither do Lacan's sessions', said a follower (Turkle 1992: 115). Aside from any criticism of what this led to in practice, it is also wrong in theory. Because the unconscious works by primary process, that does not mean the analyst's investigation of it should mirror that primary process. If we do not wait time out when nothing appears to be happening we shall never learn what nothing happening means. As with the empty spaces in a Chinese painting, if the analyst does not provide the patient with space in

---

2 See Chapter 5 (pp. 72–3) for a discussion of Lacan's attempt to embody this in the procedure known as *la passe*.

which nothing *needs* to happen there is no space in which something *can* happen.

Rank did something different, but his abandonment of analytic technique had a similar basis. His theory led him to see resistance as an expression of the patient's will, a positive and constructive effort towards autonomy. Therefore it was to be fostered, strengthened and guided, rather than analysed either as an obstacle to be overcome or a communication to be understood. Alongside the will, the second key concept in Rank's therapy was relationship. For him this meant the relationship between the therapist's developed creativity and the neurotically hampered creativity of the patient. Rank would have the therapist use the dynamics of this relationship to guide the patient, so as to release the potential of the patient's will and help him resume his creative development. He compares the therapeutic relationship to the infant's libidinal bond to the mother, and sees therapy as aiming at a psychological equivalent of birth and separation, as he had described at a bodily level in *The Trauma of Birth* (Rank 1924). What is absent from this view of the therapeutic relationship, however, is transference. Rank thus rejected the analysis of both transference and resistance, Freud's (1914c: 16) two cornerstones of psychoanalysis. His statement of this in *Will Therapy* (Rank 1929–31) is explicit. He considered them, as Lacan did the framework of the session, to be part of a rule-bound procedure which deadened the individuality of the living therapeutic situation.

This is a reaction against technique seen as an automatic, repetitive procedure, a recipe for reproducing a standard, predictable result. That is indeed a deadening view of technique. A pianist does not practise scales because repeating them often enough will of itself make him replicate some great artist's performance. But to deny any need for technique at all would be just as mistaken. Pianists do practise technical exercises because this repetitive discipline is what can help them towards the point where creative playing becomes possible. The technique which they develop like this is what allows them to show an audience the human spirit at work.

Technique is not a matter of obeying rules but of following principles. Rules can only be kept or broken, while principles are for understanding and making use of. The point at issue with Rank and Lacan is not that they disobey rules, but that they depart from principles. Even the framework of the session and the need to work in the transference are not rules of psychoanalysis. They are still principles of technique, but so well grounded in theory and experience that they are usually taken for granted. Principles of technique are not to be followed blindly, of course. But it is by an awareness of what those principles reveal about the analyst's work that we can penetrate most deeply into its nature. The activity of analysis involves a fusion between the analyst's being and what he does. This does not free him, however, from paying detailed, routine attention to what the doing consists of, as though the analyst were a healer only, with nothing of the repairman about him. Unity of being and doing does not transcend technique. On the contrary, it is only to be achieved by the analyst's constantly grounding himself in the practice of that discipline.

As a fusion of who the analyst is and what he or she does, psychoanalysis calls for a particular quality of awareness, and explorations of this are not common in the analytic literature. The example of the karate class, on the other hand, showed clearly the mutual interdependence of spirit and technique, and the writings of the martial arts tradition have much to say about it. Chinese and Japanese martial arts grew up as functional fighting systems. In a violent culture they were ways of not getting killed and, if necessary, of killing an adversary. So they had to work. As society became less violent they evolved into disciplines for gaining insight into oneself and one's relationship to the world. Their goal is self-awareness and growth towards a new mode of being, akin to the self-determination of Rank and Lacan. But because of what these arts consist of, this goal can only be approached through painstaking, and often painful, practical study of the functional techniques.

T'ai Chi Ch'uan is an ancient Chinese method whose basic practice consists of a sequence of postures like a slow ritual dance. In practising this the mind is kept constantly attentive but without forced concentration, an attitude similar to the analyst's free-floating attention. Eventually one may arrive at a particular sensitivity to an opponent's intentions. This is called 'interpreting energy'. In a T'ai Chi text, several hundred years old, there is this statement:

> From the mastery of all the postures you will apprehend 'interpreting energy'; from apprehending interpreting energy, you will arrive at a complete mastery of your opponent . . . But without a long period of arduous practice, you cannot find yourself suddenly possessed of a wide and far-reaching insight.

> (Liang 1977: 35)

Compare this with statements by Miyamoto Musashi, the greatest figure in the history of Japanese swordsmanship, who wrote, in the mid-seventeenth century: 'If you practise day and night your spirit will naturally broaden' (Musashi 1645: 49). The practice he means consists of unremitting application to the basic techniques of swordsmanship: footwork, cuts, parries, counters, advancing, retreating and so on. He says of his book: 'Do not just read, memorise or imitate but so that you realise the principle from within your own heart study hard to absorb these things into your body' (Musashi 1645: 53). These passages are concerned with an inner development of the martial artist's being, but Musashi and the T'ai Chi text both insist unequivocally that this comes not through being released from basic technique but by being immersed in it.

The most ruthlessly simple example is the art of archery. The Japanese bowman devotes total commitment to one single act, drawing and releasing the bow, and will take years in learning it. The path to self-knowledge, which is the student's object, is through a gruelling and apparently monotonous study of technique. A well-known account is that of Eugen Herrigel (1953). Only after a year of learning to draw the bow did he move on to releasing the arrow. His teacher told him he must give up the idea that it was he who was doing it. When the bow was fully drawn, instead of releasing it Herrigel had to not release it – but not hold on to it either. Physically and psychologically this baffled him. When he asked his teacher how to do it the reply was 'You must learn to wait properly' (Herrigel 1953: 47). To be able, at the point of highest tension, to do nothing and wait, is just what is required of the psychoanalyst. Pearl King (1978), writing about how the analyst brings her own self into her work, says that the crucial thing is to be able to wait in a state of non-attachment – and she makes the link with Eastern philosophy – for whatever the patient may bring. It is important to see that this is not just waiting in a non-interfering way for the patient to bring his material so that the real business of listening and interpreting can then begin. The waiting is as central to the analysis as any voicing of insight which may come out of it. King recalls T.S. Eliot's (1940) lines:

> . . . the faith and the love and the hope are all in the waiting.
> Wait without thought, for you are not ready for thought:
> So the darkness shall be the light, and the stillness the dancing.

Finally, here is an excerpt from the account of a Canadian who went to Tokyo in the 1960s to study karate (Nicol 1975). This remarkable passage is worth quoting at some length. The practice C.W. Nicol is describing looks from the outside like just toughening the striking part of the hand, and might seem a primitive and stultifying aspect of karate training. His account shows, however, that the details of technique are exactly what make deep inward experience possible. The practice involves striking with the fist against what is called a *makiwara*. This is a wooden post set in the ground, just over waist high, with a pad of hard rubber at the top.

> I used the makiwara every day. It was (and still is) a deeply personal fight. Nobody could watch me, see my little victories and defeats . . . It was the mind that willed the leg to thrust, the hips to pivot, the punching arm to lance out and tense, twisting just on impact, while at the same time the opposite hand clenched and drew into the opposite side,

and at impact the air was forced out of the body as all the muscles of thorax and abdomen tensed. For a given portion of each day the makiwara target became the object of concentration, of focus . . . In facing the makiwara I had to become composed just as later I would have to learn composure before a human opponent . . . Each victory over my body, in delivering a good punch or a strike, was yet still a victory for the makiwara. It absorbed good and bad blows with impunity and took its toll from me in skin, blood and wrist sprains. I faced it and worked . . . It demanded a great deal of me, to stand thus alone, sometimes in the rain, sweating and striking, thinking and non-thinking, watching my form and trying to muster strength, speed and focus, hitting the pad so many times. Yet though demanding I found great peace in it. The target was simple, the conflict between nerve, bone, muscle, sinew, mind, rubber, wood and earth. Through my conflict with the makiwara I brought slow change to myself . . . This training was not a mere pounding of fists. It was an exercise of concentration and release. It had rhythm and the gradual building of awareness.

(Nicol 1975: 23–5)

After two years Nicol gained his black belt and he found the calluses on his hands beginning to disappear.

Perhaps I had learned to strike the board correctly . . . I believed that the continual pounding and tempering of my limbs had begun to be a tempering of mind-forces . . . The makiwara's nature as a target had changed. It was no longer an obstacle. In attacking it its hardness or its resistance were no longer noticeable. It merely occupied a space in which I sought to place my technique. I struck through it, and not at it.

(Nicol 1975: 148–9)

John Klauber (1981: 115) writes of 'interpretations that present themselves to the analyst spontaneously, and occasionally even interpose themselves to his surprise just when he was about to say something else'. The kind of waiting for which Herrigel, King and Eliot are all trying to find words, is the state which allows such interpretations to release themselves, and Nicol's account shows that it can be cultivated even in the midst of strenuous activity with crude and elemental material – a description of psychoanalysis as well as karate.

Analysts, though, do not have scales to practise or *makiwaras* to strike at. So what is the equivalent in psychoanalysis of this unremitting pursuit of the fundamentals of technique, through which to arrive at the being of an analyst? In an article quoted at the beginning of the next chapter, Paul Gray (1990) describes systematically the elements of his analytic technique.

He listens for various sorts of discontinuity in how the patient expresses himself. There may be a break in the flow of connections between topics, or a shift in the patient's tone of voice or manner of speaking. At such moments, according to Gray, the ego is being compelled by some anxiety to interfere with the emerging material. Having detected this interference, Gray tries to make the patient consciously aware of it, and thus also conscious of the anxiety which provoked it. Underlying this method is 'the principle of drawing more and more of the patient's ego into conscious participation in the analytic process' (Gray 1990: 1087). Klauber (1981: 77–90) likewise sets out, in a paper discussed in Chapter 5 (pp. 74–6), a programme for listening to and interpreting the patient's material. Gray's and Klauber's technical approaches are different, but this only highlights their similarity of purpose. Like the writers on martial arts, they are both specifying detailed, practical steps that can be consciously attended to, for the realisation of broad, long-term aims which cannot be defined in advance.

Otto Fenichel's (1941) and Ralph Greenson's (1967) primers of technique also set out principles to function as a constant backdrop for the analyst at work. Greenson (1967: 137ff.), for example, states the principle of interpreting from the surface, beginning with what is most available to the patient's conscious, reasonable ego. A specific application of this is to analyse resistance before content, and therefore ego, the agency of resistance, before id, where the repressed content resides. He instances a patient who brought a transparently Oedipal dream, with whom it was important to attend to the transference anxiety about revealing his sexual feelings, before taking up the nature of the sexual wishes themselves.

A session to be described in Chapter 4 (pp. 56–8) shows the analyst hanging on to basic forms of interpretation in an attempt to survive confusion. The following two examples date from early in my analytic experience, when maintaining basic technique was a continual, conscious concern. A patient recounted a dream. This was a woman with a way of telling me obviously important things but always moving on to the next just before I had found a way of responding to the last one. In one part of the dream *she could not speak; she prised her lips apart and then tried to prise them away from her teeth.* Having finished the dream she moved quickly on to a friend's pregnancy, a wish to spoil some work she was doing, a somatic symptom, a fantasy[3] of seeing me in the street, worry about her brother's illness and another dream. I felt swamped by the material. I saw that it might be a

3 I do not believe a clear distinction is possible between 'fantasy' as a product or activity of the imagination which may be conscious or unconscious, and 'phantasy' as an unconscious element of psychic structure. Having, therefore, to choose one spelling or the other, I have opted for 'fantasy' throughout, simply as being the more familiar contemporary usage. I think the only part of the book where, for some readers, this may jar, is the opening

way of spoiling the work but I did not know how to deal with it. Then I noticed a point in the dream where it seemed that incomplete secondary revision (Freud 1900: 488ff.) could be letting something show through. In order to speak you would prise your teeth apart, not prise your lips away from them. Furthermore she had quickly taken our attention away from this. So I pointed this out and asked for associations to prising the lips away. This led to her saying that when she masturbates she does not open her labia and in fact she had never really explored her genitals at all. It was the first time she had spoken so intimately about her body, and it is interesting that such an intervention, straight out of a beginner's handbook, as it were, had the power to release this material.

Another time the same patient was saying that she did not like being expected to succeed. She hated having to 'get on and do things'. I found myself thinking 'Get . . . on? Do . . . things?' It sounded like a child talking about its potty. I asked myself if she were referring to the analysis, but she had already moved on to something else. Later she said, about another woman, that the whole female part of her was so rigid that she could not move at all. I wondered aloud whether she might be alerting me, with this remark, to some sexual confusion in her. Normally it would be the male 'part' that was rigid and needing to move. I was able to say this because my previous thoughts had already attuned me to listening in body-ego terms.

The point of these examples is that they are not sophisticated. They are instances of a novice using such basic elements of analysis as secondary revision in dreams and the ego as a body-ego, to try and listen to the unconscious. The less experienced analyst, like Nicol in the early stages of his *makiwara* training, needs to remind himself consciously of the various elements which contribute to good technique. As that technique becomes more internalised, the healing function of the analyst's inner attitude towards the patient, and to the analysis, can find its own voice.

---

discussion in Chapter 7 where some of Melanie Klein's ideas are considered, for which the spelling 'phantasy' is commonly used. 'Fantasy', however, like many psychoanalytic terms, can carry multiple connotations and have different shades of meaning according to its context. A variant spelling does not seem necessary. In quotations and references I have, of course, retained the original spelling.

22

2

The other in the self

If the soul [*psychē*] is to come to know itself, must it not look into a soul?

Plato Alcibiades I: 133B

Psychoanalysis tries to approach, as rationally as may be, something which can never be known completely. The emphasis in analytic writings is sometimes on the rationality, sometimes on the sense of the unknown. Compare, for example, these two statements.

> One specific advantage of this method is its greater dependence on confirmable observation, rather than on data depending considerably on the analyst's use, at least initially, of references to his own unconscious.
>
> (Gray 1990: 1095)

> It is of the essence of our impossible profession that in a very singular way we do not know what we are doing. Do not be distracted by random associations to this idea. I am not undermining our deep, exacting training; nor discounting the ways in which – unlike many people who master a subject and then just 'do' it, or teach it – we have to keep 'at' ourselves, our literature and our clinical crosstalk with colleagues. All these daily operations are the efficient, skilful and thinkable tools with which we constantly approach the heart of our work, which is a mystery.
>
> (Coltart 1992: 2)

Both of these attitudes are plain in Freud's own work and in his character.[1] He thought his single greatest achievement was his understanding of dreams

---

1 See Chapter 5 (pp. 77–80).

– 'insight such as this falls to one's lot but once in a lifetime' (Strachey 1953: xx) – yet even in *The Interpretation of Dreams*, amid all its rational elucidation, he writes: 'There is at least one spot in every dream at which it is unplumbable – a navel, as it were, that is its point of contact with the unknown' (Freud 1900: 111).

A good night's sleep needs its dreaming. Not just its dreams, but its dreaming. Towards the end of his analysis a man said that he had got 'real dreaming' back again. He had been out of touch with his inner world, with little capacity for fantasy, and for much of his analysis he hardly remembered dreams at all. As the analysis helped him make more contact with his inner world he began to dream more and the quality of his dreaming changed. His dreams, when they came, had tended to be well-ordered narratives, or rather obvious representations of some real-life situation. Now they became more complicated and less rational but felt, despite the new obscurity, richer in meaning. This was not a new experience; he recognised it. He said it was what dreaming had been like for him as a child. The content of these dreams, of course, provided the analysis with material, but what mattered more to this patient was the experience of recovering an activity he had lost, which enabled him to value the unknown within himself.

The same unplumbable quality is present in creativity. An idea, a perception, the expression of feeling in a turn of phrase – all sorts of everyday things may suddenly, apparently out of the blue, show us ourselves and the world in a new light. These moments of illumination may be slight or epiphanic. Seeming to come from nowhere, they come from nowhere but within ourselves and, like dreaming, give us the sense of a deep internal process, part of ourselves and strange to us at the same time.

Psychoanalysis aims to help people be more open to what is unconscious within themselves. But Freud discovered, as his work progressed, how strongly people resist awareness of their inward natures. This resistance appears both individually, in the clinical situation, and in society, in the hostility aroused by psychoanalysis. Jonathan Lear has argued that behind attacks on psychoanalytic theory, and on Freud's personal and scientific integrity, lies a wish to deny the whole idea of unconscious mental life.

> The real object of attack – for which Freud is only a stalking horse – is the very idea that humans have unconscious motivation. A battle may be fought over Freud, but the war is over our culture's image of the human soul. Are we to see humans as having depth – as complex psychological organisms who generate layers of meaning which lie beneath the surface of their own understanding? Or are we to take ourselves as transparent to ourselves?
>
> (Lear 1998: 27)

There is a wish, Lear says, 'to ignore the complexity, depth and darkness of human life' (1998: 27). That wish exists in everyone, and having an analysis involves confronting it. The unconscious can only be a source of nourishment if one's own complexity, depth and darkness are faced and investigated. That calls for a particular sort of courageous curiosity about oneself. I heard it said, at a colleague's funeral, that he had had a way of getting his patients interested in themselves, of arousing their curiosity about what went on inside them. Analysts too have to overcome their wishes not to know, and this colleague seemed to have had an unthreatening curiosity about himself as well as other people, which could arouse the same in his patients. It is a fine gift in a psychoanalyst.

Psychoanalysis involves a stillness, an apparently passive attentiveness in the analyst, which depends on a framework set up expressly to make things possible that cannot happen in an ordinary social relationship. Responsiveness at the level of ordinary reality is subordinated to an intensity of response at the level of psychic reality. The work of the analyst, the day-to-day doing of psychoanalysis, requires a sustained commitment to that level of response. This offers patients a steady, unthreatening receptivity that can help them risk being curious about themselves. But the analyst's curiosity needs also to be active enough to stimulate the patient's self-questioning. The passage by Nina Coltart, quoted above, is from an article (Coltart 1992: 1–14) written around W.B. Yeats' 1921 poem 'The second coming'. Yeats laments that

> The best lack all conviction, while the worst
> Are full of passionate intensity.

Yeats is wanting to reclaim passionate intensity. To speak of the analyst's being 'curious' about the patient might sound too eager or intrusive, but an intense and passionate 'willingness to know'[2] should permeate the stillness and silent receptivity.

Rationality and the sense of mystery, passion and passivity: these are further elements in the complex balance of the analytic equilibrium which the previous chapter began to explore. Certain analysts are exceptional for the way the quality of their subjective experiencing finds objective expression in their analytic work. Freud is the prime example. His working through of his own life experience became a foundation for the development of psychoanalysis. Freud, however, concealed much of his work on himself and it has needed such scholars as Anzieu (1986) to uncover it. An analyst who lets us watch her at it, in detail and over many years, is Marion Milner.

---

2 See the discussion of Bion's 'K link' in Chapter 3 (pp. 47–9).

Milner's writing belongs to two traditions and in each one it is out of the ordinary. There is a strand in European letters which begins with St Augustine and runs through Rousseau's *Confessions* and Wordsworth's *The Prelude* up to, for example, Kazantzakis' (1965) *Report to Greco*. These autobiographies of the interior life find something universal reflected in the experience of an individual. Milner uses her own intellectual and emotional life as the material for her writing in a way which places her clearly in this tradition. Her three autobiographical books, *A Life of One's Own*, *An Experiment in Leisure* and *Eternity's Sunrise* (Milner 1934, 1937, 1987a), are outstanding examples of the objective use of intense subjective experience.

In the middle, however, of what has seemed this kind of existential self-exploration, we suddenly hear the voice of a scientist. 'Thus it was that I began a task which has absorbed my efforts for many years: trying to manage my life, not according to tradition, or authority, or rational theory, but by experiment' (Milner 1934: 30). Milner's other books, *The Hands of the Living God* and *The Suppressed Madness of Sane Men* (Milner 1969, 1987b) position her also in the second tradition, that of psychoanalysis, which from Freud onwards has considered itself, in one way or another, as scientific. This scientist, however, is making unusual use of her own subjectivity.

> While trying to link up these statements of Winnicott's with my own enquiries I even remembered an example of how I had, long before becoming an analyst, observed the effects of simple non-purposive looking. For example, I had noticed how, through staring at an outside object . . . in a contemplative way, without any ideas about making use of it, there had gradually emerged a feeling of change in one's whole body perception as well as a move towards a feeling of intense interest in the sheer 'thusness', the separate and unique identity of the thing I was staring at . . . Further, it seemed that this kind of direct body awareness must be, developmentally, a capacity intimately bound up with the mother's . . . loving care of the infant's body and so can be an important aspect of what Winnicott calls 'the facilitating environment' that is necessary for the infant if fullest maturation is to occur.
>
> (Milner 1987b: 281–2)

Such interpenetration of the two modes of thought is characteristic of Milner's writing. Her personal curiosity about her inner world and her psychoanalytic curiosity about her work and her patients are interdependent and inseparable. Another striking feature is the continuity of her effort. *A Life of One's Own* is based on a diary begun in December 1926, and was published in 1934. *An Experiment in Leisure* followed in 1937. Fifty years later we get *Eternity's Sunrise*. All this time she has been at it, with the same critical curiosity about her thought processes, her hidden motives, what it is in life that really matters to her. *The Hands of the Living God* is the detailed description of a 16-year-long psychoanalytic treatment, an account unique in the analytic literature. The papers collected in *The Suppressed Madness of Sane Men* date from 1942 to 1977, with a chapter of 'After-thoughts' from 1986. The book thus traces the consistent themes and preoccupations underlying 44 years of work. The rest of this chapter will be largely concerned with a detailed consideration of Milner's three auto-biographical books. They reveal her passionate and courageous curiosity and confirm the sense of a remarkable attempt to understand, steadily main-tained over decades.

When, aged 34, Milner published *A Life of One's Own* (Milner 1934), she had had only a brief and relatively superficial experience of psycho-analytic therapy, and she did not yet find much use in analytic theory. Nevertheless the book contains descriptions in vivid, ordinary language of, for example, repression, infantile omnipotence and splitting: not as theo-retical concepts but simply as observations about herself. The book is a classic of self-analysis and it is fascinating to see in it the traces of the psychoanalyst that Milner was in due course to become. It opens with her in her mid-twenties, feeling that her life is not properly her own and that she has no sense of direction. When she tries to put into words what her goals are she finds she does not know, and she has the idea of letting herself write down freely whatever presents itself without bothering about what it means: in effect, free association on paper. What appears is very different from how she usually thinks, and she decides not to be so concerned with what she *ought* to do, but to observe what actually goes on in her mind. She says, wryly: 'I little knew what this comparatively simple act of trying to be aware of my own experience would involve me in' (Milner 1934: 25).

She caught certain distinct moments of happiness to see what made them special. They were associated with a change in her state of conscious-ness to something clearer and more passionate than her usual frame of mind. The happiness was more to do with the act of seeing in this way than with any particular thing that she saw. This kind of awareness looked at the world 'with a wide focus, wanting nothing and prepared for any-thing' (1934: 199), as opposed to her usual narrow, purposive focus based on judgements and intentions. The connection with the analyst's free-floating attention is evident. For Milner this is not just a means to an end, some-thing to help her perceive things which she would otherwise have missed. She is already pointing, beyond the content of awareness, to a particular quality of it, whose creative value to her she gradually elaborates.

She discovered internal gestures which helped her move into this 'wide looking' and feel the change of mood that it brought. But now that she could do this, she noticed something in her that avoided it. Giving up her usual relation to the world aroused a mysterious panic, which she came to realise was a fear of losing her identity and even the sense of her own existence. Here she puts her finger on something that the analyst at work may defend against. With borderline or psychotic patients it is not uncommon for analysts to feel that their sense of who they are is under attack. It is less easy to recognise that the quality of awareness required of psychoanalysts calls their identity into question all the time. It is not due to particular patients but intrinsic to the work.

Examining what her thoughts did when she 'forgot' to move herself towards the wide sort of looking, Milner discovered a whole vein of 'blind' thinking which went on outside her usual awareness. It was totally self-centred and made no distinction between wish and reality. It had, in effect, the features of infantile narcissism and omnipotence. Her description of this discovery, and of eventually finding how to escape from blind thinking by putting into words what she had not known was in her mind, dates from before she embarked on her analysis. With hindsight, *A Life of One's Own* reads as the unfolding of a vocation.

A drawing she made of a dragon symbolised fears she had not been able to articulate in words. She discovered many such 'outcasts of thought' seeking expression as the dragon had done. Being prepared to entertain these outcast thoughts allowed her wide-seeing to become more consistent, and she discovered that 'an idea could be both itself and several other things at the same time' (1934: 160).

> I saw that to see only the ridiculousness of humanity was just as misleading as to see only its dignity, that what one said or thought about anything must always be a distortion, that the mistake was to believe that any one expression could be the last word, for experience was always bigger than the formula.
>
> (Milner 1934: 157)

Milner also came upon the importance of physical relaxation, finding that full awareness, of oneself, the world, or a patient, depends on experiencing with one's body and not just the mind. One of Milner's distinctive contributions to psychoanalysis has been to help analysts listen with their whole bodies and not their ears alone (Milner 1987b: ch. 14; 1969: xxix–xxx (this book, pp. 41–2)).

A Life of One's Own ends with Milner's discovery that the hidden areas of her self were not just to be understood, dealt with and, so to speak, conquered, but could be trusted and relied on. In them she 'made contact with her own source of life' (1934: 186). To trust in this way, however, was difficult.

It was then that the idea occurred to me that until you have, once at least, faced everything you know – the whole universe – with utter giving in, and let all that is 'not you'[3] flow over and engulf you there can be no lasting sense of security. Only by being prepared to accept annihilation can one escape from that spiritual 'abiding alone' which is in fact the truly death-like state.

(Milner 1934: 193)

Milner's description recalls what psychoanalysts know as 'annihilation anxiety'. But she values the experience. Her willingness to give up the sense of her own self, and her discovery of purpose fulfilled by giving up purpose, mark this as being also a spiritual exploration. Milner is one of the few psychoanalysts to take spiritual experience seriously. She bridges realms of discourse, and an interest in the relation between psychoanalytic and mystical experience recurs throughout her work (cf. Milner 1987b: ch. 18).[4]

Three years later there followed *An Experiment in Leisure* (Milner 1937). Here Milner asks herself what she enjoys doing in her spare time and, as with *A Life of One's Own*, the unremarkable question becomes a starting point for surprising journeys. Her interest in the wilder aspects of nature led to a preoccupation with volcanic eruptions and a fascination with witchcraft, the devil and archaic religion. To her surprise she discovered a profound wish to submit herself, not just to an ideal good but to something overwhelmingly powerful regardless of whether it were good or evil: a desire to have her will broken and her sense of self destroyed, even if only momentarily, by something alien. This seemed a masochistic, self-abasing impulse. She remembered, however, the gesture of internal poverty she had discovered in *A Life of One's Own*, the deliberate abandonment of her hopes, her strivings and even her sense of herself as a person. This had involved a similar submission and a willingness, by an act of conscious acceptance, to be nothing. When she could make this internal act of sacrifice her anxieties and feelings of inadequacy gave way to serenity, and creative solutions appeared to problems that had seemed hopeless. When she did sometimes treat herself masochistically she came to see it not simply as a bit of pathology but as the distortion of an impulse which, when properly understood and used, could be a key to well-being.

Physical relaxation and the body's awareness were again important in arriving at this inner state. Milner found that certain images, which she called 'organic', carried particular significance for her. 'They seemed to be

---

3 The phrase 'all that is "not you"' is a pre-echo of what will appear later in Milner's work as the 'not-self' (see note 5).

4 See p. 47 for references to writings by other analysts on this topic. Bion's view of faith as a scientific concept (p. 197) also links with Milner's decision to manage her life 'by experiment'.

deeply rooted in the whole of my body, whereas the casual images that flitted in and out of what Yeats calls the "daily mood" always seemed to belong to the head only' (Milner 1937: 153). As she developed this awareness she found a sense of something 'other' within herself, and she discovered in Groddeck and Freud the idea that we are 'lived by' something other than our conscious selves. This encountering of the other within oneself is also recognised in spiritual experience, and she found herself looking at religion with fresh eyes. Elements in the Gospel story, for example, which appear as moralistic instructions about what is required by an externalised parental figure called God, might really be something quite different. Statements about being ready to lose one's life in order to save it, and sacrificing all that one has for the pearl of great price, were so close to her empirical psychological experience that she thought they might not be moral instructions at all, but practical statements about the conditions necessary for creative thinking and awareness. Despite the cruelty of the bullfight she found exaltation there, in the ceremonial acceptance of the inevitability of death. Similarly the Crucifixion, instead of an act of supernatural redeeming magic, might more profoundly be 'the culminating poetic dramatisation of an inner process of immense importance to humanity, a process which was not an escape from reality but the only condition under which the inner reality could be fully perceived' (Milner 1937: 139). She writes of an 'expectant stillness', a kind of meditative state of awareness in the whole of her body, which allowed these organic images to convey unlooked-for meaning to her. They were instruments of reflection which brought her closer to the truth of her experience than abstract reasoning did. The imagery of alchemy, for example, offered a powerful metaphor of intrapsychic growth and evolution, and in *The Hands of the Living God* (Milner 1969: xxii) she calls the consulting-room a crucible.

An essential characteristic of these images was a kind of ambiguity. Not only did they carry multiple meanings but they operated simultaneously at different levels in Milner herself. Several could be interpreted psychoanalytically in terms of sexual desire or the wish for a baby, but they also touched a level of desire and creativity which involved her whole sense of being. This capacity for 'striding the gulf between the inner and the outer' was what gave these images the sense of being 'truly real' (Milner 1937: 171). Looking back at her early interests and enthusiasms, like natural history and geography, she now perceived in them the same quality. They had been fuelled both by instinctual impulse and by the sense of something 'other', something greater than but also within herself, to which she needed to surrender.

Such images as these certainly gave form to feelings of compelling power that had grown during the course of this experiment. Just in so far as I held myself still and watched the flickering movements of the mind, trying to give them expression in words or drawings, just so far would I become aware of some answering activity, an activity that I can only describe as a knowing, yet a knowing that was nothing to do with me; it was a knowing that could see forwards and backwards and in a flash give form to the confusions of everyday living and to the chaos of sensation. I still felt that I was being lived by something not myself, but now it seemed like something I could trust, something that knew better than I did where I was going. Once I had bothered over whether you should have a purpose in life or just drift along; now I was sure that I must do neither but, patiently and watchfully, let purposes have me, watch myself being lived by something that is 'other'.

(Milner 1937: 184–5)

This discovery of an 'answering activity', which she also describes as the 'not-self'[5] (1937: 177, 179), is the culmination of *An Experiment in Leisure*.

Milner introduces *Eternity's Sunrise* (Milner 1987a), the third volume in what amounts to a trilogy, as a repeat, 50 years on, of what she had done in *An Experiment in Leisure*. She wants to see what effect her years of analytic work may have had on her. It turns out to be just as personal a book, not overtly psychoanalytic but actually full of psychoanalysis, and the same themes declare themselves with notable continuity. It is written around a set of organic images which she calls 'beads'. These might be visual images, memories, moments of experience, objects made or found or bought on holiday, paintings, dreams – whatever demanded her attention by the way it spoke to the deeper reaches of her being. Some came from visits to Greece: passing through the Corinth canal, the image of an asphodel plant, a girl dancing, a reliquary, eagles at Delphi. Their impact was related to the state, one of relaxation and awareness of her breathing, in which she experienced them. They gave her a profound sense of aliveness and of who she was, but also led into a darkness where it seemed her life might be extinguished at any moment. This was the same fear of ceasing to exist that she had already encountered, and she links it again to her analytic work. Helping patients to confront the fear of being abandoned, the 'agonies of disillusionment', and the dread of annihilation was 'the very bread and butter of my daily psychoanalytic task' (Milner 1987a: 36). But Milner was certain there was more to be said. Awareness was something with the potential to be more than a solution to conflict and anxiety. A certain kind of internal

5 This looks ahead to an important paper which Milner published under the title 'Aspects of symbolism in comprehension of the not-self' (Milner 1952b: 83–113). It is quoted and discussed in Chapters 9 and 10 (pp. 152–3, 175).

awareness of her body, with a deep sense of tranquillity, a passive consciousness of 'being breathed' rather than of breathing, and the giving up of any sense of striving or assertion, became especially important to her. It was her key to making contact with something that was part of her but also other than herself. This is the 'answering activity' of *An Experiment in Leisure*, and the central theme of *Eternity's Sunrise* is an investigation of its nature.

She finds it difficult to know what words to use for it. It seems nothing to do with her, not her self 'in the ordinary sense of the word "self"' (1987a: 47). She implies, though, that there might be deeper meanings to that word. Is it the 'good internalised object'? Well, yes, but that does not convey how independent of her it feels and how naturally she is drawn to talk to it, as though it were another person. She finds herself using religious language and wonders if it is God. Certainly it demands respect. Sometimes it is the Answering Activity, with capital letters. She entrusts problems to it, saying 'I leave it to you.' It feels wrong, though, to identify it with the God that is usually talked about in church, a separate, outside source of commands and judgement. What did become clear was that contact with it came by experiencing her thoughts and feelings as things happening in her body.

> So – incarnation, finding in one's own body the Answering Activity or whatever one wants to call it. Surely this is all a way of redeeming the body, not feeling it an enemy, not splitting it off and calling it the 'flesh' and lumping it with the devil. Nor yet giving in to its unredeemed state, its laziness, its hatred of pain or its terrible slowness, resistance in learning anything new.

> So it still seems as if one has to create one's own body in some way by attending to it from inside. As if by this meeting of 'soul' and 'body' something new is created, something quite different from the body as used just for satisfying one's instincts. This deep source of something, all its cells taking part both as being fed by one's awareness of them and as themselves feeding, being sources of food, of psychic nourishment.
>
> (Milner 1987a: 67, 68)

At moments when she was able to turn the same gaze outwards, and connect with the world around her as she did with her own body from the inside, she encountered an awareness that opened more and more deeply into the very meaning of love and creativity.

It was somewhat unexpectedly that she found herself impelled to visit Israel, being, as she says, 'by now nearer eighty than seventy'. To her surprise it was images of violence and impoverishment which declared themselves as beads, not those of beauty and historical grandeur. Can one love the Answering Activity, she wonders, when it is like an empty breast and gives no answer; or even when it is murderous like Abraham about to sacrifice Isaac or the heathen sacrificing their children at Gehenna? Her inward awareness had all along led her not only to a beneficent source of creativity but also to something destructive and annihilating. She quotes the phrase 'Our opponents are our co-creators' (Follet 1924: 174). The most powerful of these experiences, which provoked 'a kind of silent explosion from within' (1987a: 136), arose from a visit to the Holocaust Museum. The next day she made a painting, with no conscious thought of the visit in mind. It turned out, however, to contain images of horror, of the destruction of the feeding breast which is turned into faeces and becomes a destructive, sucking whirlpool. Other images, though, connoted the Eucharist, a cannibalism which allows one to become what one loves by taking it inside oneself as divine nourishment.

The theme which gradually emerges as central in these three books is awareness of a deep internal process that is part of, and, at the same time, strange to, oneself – the theme touched on at the beginning of this chapter in relation to dreaming and creativity. Milner learnt to cultivate the Answering Activity by directing her wide vision inwards, with a breadth that could encompass creation and destruction, knowing them both in the experience of her own body. She closes *Eternity's Sunrise* with two chapters called 'The Source of Transformation' and 'The Place of Transformation'. The nature of the Answering Activity remains enigmatic, but she leaves no doubt that searching out an inner relationship to something which is both oneself and other than oneself can produce a transformation of being.

The sense of mystery is evident in Milner's writing, but it was her intellectual and practical discipline that made her pursuit of the mysterious so fruitful. Moving herself towards the wide looking, attentiveness to her bodily experience, awareness of her breathing – none of these techniques were automatic or accidental. Throughout, Milner is consistently and rigorously articulating a search for her true self, and we see how interrelated this self-inquiry was with her analytic work. A constant cross-referencing between profound personal experience and psychoanalytic conceptualising pervades all her writing. There is nobody who keeps the need to integrate the two so unceasingly in the foreground. In this sense, Milner's is a life lived as a vocation: not just in discovering psychoanalysis as a profession, but in the steady pursuit of what mattered most profoundly to her as a person. What she did as a psychoanalyst was unmistakably an expression of who she was.

To use a term introduced by Christopher Bollas, Milner's life was a search for, and an expression of, her personal 'idiom'. Bollas (1989: chs 1, 2) has expanded Winnicott's (1960) notion of the 'true self' with the idea of 'idiom', and with a distinction between 'destiny' and 'fate'. He posits an innate impulse to find and make use of objects so as to live according to the potential of the true self. The form that this impulse takes is the expression of one's individual idiom, and to live according to that idiom is to make life a continuing act of self-discovery and self-creation. People who manage to do this, 'creative' characters in Rank's vocabulary, are working out a destiny for themselves. If one is preoccupied, instead, with the concerns of the false self, the sense is less of living one's life than of being at the mercy of fate. Psychoanalysis is a vocation in so far as the analyst finds in it the way of being which most profoundly articulates his sense of who he is. This takes time.

> The day that one qualifies as an analyst, the analyst that one is *going to be* is a mystery. Ten years later, we may just about be able to look back and discern the shape of the rough beast – ourselves as analysts in embryo – as it slouches along under the months and years until, its hour come round at last, there is some clearer sense of ourselves as analysts. The process of doing analysis has slowly given birth to an identity.
>
> (Coltart 1992: 2)

Each individual analysis also needs to discover its own idiom. In an analysis that works well, patient and analyst share the experience, over time, of developing a language, unique to them as a couple, for expressing just those things that need to be talked about in that particular partnership. This is their idiom, the gradually discovered expression of what, in that analysis, really matters. The next chapter pursues this further, showing how both analyst and patient need to be open to this process. If an analyst can constantly rediscover psychoanalysis as an idiom to articulate who he is and what really matters to him, the better chance there is for him and his patient together to find an idiom for what really matters to them. The patient may then move towards articulating, in the larger frame of his life, his own sense of who he is.

3

Suddenly finding it really matters

> He thought he saw a Rattlesnake
> That questioned him in Greek:
> He looked again, and found it was
> The Middle of Next Week.
> 'The one thing I regret', he said,
> 'Is that it cannot Speak!'
> Lewis Carroll (1904: ch. 4)
> *The Story of Sylvie and Bruno*

Throughout her books Milner shows a willingness to take herself by surprise. She has a capacity for questioning herself and, like the man faced with the rattlesnake, for 'looking again'. Patient and analyst need to find that same capacity in their relation towards each other. If patients are to make new discoveries about themselves in analysis, they need a willingness to be taken, or to take themselves, by surprise. Fostering and facilitating such an openness requires the same thing in the analyst. 'Looking again' is what, for both analyst and patient, can allow the other to stop being a dangerous creature making demands in an unknown language and become, instead, the future; which they must then somehow try and help, after all, into speech.

A patient came back from a visit to a country in Eastern Europe. This was before the fall of the Soviet Union in 1991. He talked about a woman he had met there and become fond of. She was warm and sensitive but she had learned to live under her country's regime by knowing her way around with a particular kind of lucid pragmatism. She knew what there was a way of doing and what there was not. If scarce lemons could be procured, or 'unavailable' seats for a concert made available, she would know how. If there was no way, she would know that too, and then she refused to waste time trying. She said she could not stand people who could not distinguish fantasy from reality. When this man floated the idea of coming to visit her

35

again she was not interested in it as a fantasy to play with. She just said 'When?' Her statement about reality and fantasy was not theoretical. Her life in her society throws it into relief that distinguishing fantasy from reality is not something you do for fun; it is how you survive. We are used to the idea of reality-testing. We are doing it all the time and we take it for granted that we know how important it is. This woman, however, brought my patient, and myself also, rather sharply up against the realisation that distinguishing fantasy from reality really matters.

In the political regime in Czechoslovakia that followed the Soviet invasion of 1968, a philosopher called Julius Tomin was deprived of his job. He refused to stop teaching philosophy and held informal seminars, known as the 'Patocka University'. Deprived of all facilities, he and his students had nothing to work with but original texts, which were themselves scarce. He invited philosophers from Western Europe to visit his group, and some went from Oxford. On their return they reported a remarkable atmosphere in his seminar. His group had a passionate sense of the importance of what they were doing. This was not just in resisting persecution. It was the philosophy that mattered. The visitors were struck by the intense involvement in the work and its high quality. Philosophers obviously work at philosophy because they think it is important. But Tomin's circumstances forced him and his group to read their texts of Plato and Aristotle afresh and, because they were all they had, to take them seriously in a new way. Being forced back on themselves they had to find out what it was about philosophy that really mattered to them. This was what gave their efforts such aliveness and conviction (Tomin 1980; Hitchens 1980; Kenny 1997: 115–26).

Analysts may presume that they know they should not be judgemental towards their patients nor impose a viewpoint, but let them arrive at their own truth. How well, though, do they really know this? A hierarchical attitude which assumes the analyst's reality as the norm, by which the patient's reality has to be modified, may be more deeply embedded in analysts' thinking than they realise. Among much writing about this, an article by Evelyne Schwaber (1983) demonstrates cogently that analysts cannot afford to take it too comfortably for granted that they do respect the patient's reality without passing judgement on it. Genuinely to enter into the patient's viewpoint can involve an unexpectedly profound shift of position.

These are all examples of a certain kind of shock. We know that something matters. Then something happens which jolts us into seeing it afresh and throws into relief just how much it really does matter. It cannot not be taken seriously. Its importance has a sharper edge of necessity than we had appreciated. We did realise it was important and we knew why, but from where we stand now, seeing how acute its significance truly is, our previous attitude cannot help seeming a bit bland and superficial.

Certain turning points in the history of psychoanalysis depended upon Freud's openness to this experience. One is his revision of the seduction theory. For some ten years he had been making revolutionary discoveries and developing an entire new field of knowledge on the basis of respecting what his patients told him, and taking seriously what went on in their minds. Then he was forced to realise that a major element in what they were saying, which he had made fundamental to his theories, was not necessarily true. This was a shock to him (Freud 1954: 215ff. letter 69). The result, however, was unexpected. Freud saw that, even if an event had not taken place in reality, what counted was indeed what his patients were *telling* him, what was happening in their *minds*. He thought he had known this all along and of course he had done, but now he could only overcome the apparent setback by taking this idea more seriously than before. He either had to abandon his work or realise that what he had been doing was only a beginning. Respecting what his patients said, whether it was objectively true or not, really did matter in a way he had not seen until then. Only by being open to this was he able to discover the importance of fantasy and continue the development of psychoanalysis.

Three years later Dora staged her abrupt departure. The impact this had on Freud's understanding of transference is another example of his capacity to look again. He had already described the phenomenon in *Studies on Hysteria*, and he knew it was a necessary element in every analysis (Breuer and Freud 1893–5: 266). When Dora developed a father-transference which made her suspect Freud of secrecy and deviousness he saw what was going on. When she showed transference related to Herr K as well, however, and warned herself in her dream to leave Freud's treatment as she had formerly left Herr K's house, he says: 'I was deaf to this first note of warning, thinking I had ample time before me, since no further stages of transference developed and the material for the analysis had not yet run dry. In this way the transference took me unawares . . .' (Freud 1905a: 119). She did leave, and in doing so showed him that although he had taken the idea of transference seriously, he had not taken it seriously enough. As with the seduction theory and fantasy, we can see Freud's preparedness to be shocked into a new understanding of something which had grown familiar. In the postscript to the case history come these two statements:

Transference, which seems ordained to be the greatest obstacle to psychoanalysis, becomes its most powerful ally, if its presence can be detected each time and explained to the patient.

She . . . deserted me as she believed herself to have been deceived and deserted by him. Thus she *acted out* an essential part of her recollections and phantasies instead of reproducing it in the treatment.

(Freud 1905a: 117, 119)

Such an account of acting out did not come into its own until 'Remember-ing, repeating and working through' (Freud 1914a), and awareness of the positive aspects of transference not fully until 'The dynamics of trans-ference' (Freud 1912). Yet here they both are, clear as crystal in January 1901 (Strachey 1953), waiting for Freud to look yet again and see how they really mattered.

Looking again at what really matters has not only been important his-torically in the development of psychoanalysis. It plays its part in the unfolding of an individual analysis too. The clinical material to be given in the next chapter illustrates this, but another analysis failed to unfold because such looking again was not possible, as the patient herself said in so many words. She had gained a certain amount from her analysis, perhaps quite a lot, because there were indications that she secretly made more use of it than she let me know. But overall it remained unsatisfactory. More than once she was on the point of really letting herself into the process but went back to withholding herself from it. In her next to last session she said the trouble was that she had come into analysis 'more from curiosity than desire' and this had never really changed. The phrase put it in a nutshell. Analysis was important enough for her to get into and stay in for three and a half years, but we did not find a way for her to have the shock of its turning out to be more important than she had reckoned on.

Patients do not have to know what they need their analyses for when they start. They discover as they go along. But they would not embark on them at all unless they felt some sort of necessity. The initial sense of need has to deepen, maybe quite suddenly and sharply, as the discoveries made in the analysis show up the true significance of the patient's situation. This is the point at which a patient may say she did not realise what she was letting herself in for, or how little she understood what was really the matter when she started. It is a transition from the beginning state into a deeper level of analysis, just as Freud's revising of the seduction theory was a point of transition from his early, perfectly genuine and indeed essential, discoveries into psychoanalysis proper.

What really matters about an analysis is a double question. There is 'What really matters to the patient?' and 'What really matters to the ana-lyst?' The two answers must not be too far apart if the analysis is to work, but for some time both may remain unknown. Just as the patient does not know his answer to begin with, neither does the analyst. An initial assess-ment must have allowed him to make a beginning, as the patient has his starting point. But for the analyst too, what really matters is something which has to declare itself and the analyst must be open to this experience. There are in fact four questions and answers and not just two. There are the patient's answers to 'What matters to me?' and 'What matters to him?'; and the analyst's answers to 'What matters to him?' and 'What matters to me?'

The analyst's answer to what matters to the patient needs time to discover and we are used to thinking of analysis as, in part, the business of the analyst's finding this out. The patient's answer to what matters to the analyst probably remains the most uncertain, but if the patient has no sense that there is an answer at all, then the outlook for the analysis is not good. It is the pair of 'What matters to me?' questions, that this chapter is chiefly concerned with. They are parallel questions, to be answered by parallel experiences. Like the patient, the analyst needs to be open to a shock of discovery. If there is no 'What really matters to me?' question around for the analyst, and if he is not open to being ambushed by the answer, the analysis will probably not be a very creative one. The two parallel experiences may even be linked, to mix a geometrical metaphor, in the sense of being dependent on each other. It may be difficult for either patient or analyst to find an answer to the question of what really matters to him unless the other, for his part, is opening himself to what really matters to him also. The patient whose analysis did not unfold was, in fact, my first training case, and I have wondered how far her remaining stuck at the level of curiosity was connected with what really mattered to me in that analysis.

Whether or not this was a case of mutual 'stuckness', there is certainly an example of mutual unsticking in a paper by Roger Kennedy (1984). He tried to express something to his patient in terms of the transference having a 'dual aspect'. Kennedy writes:

> When I put forward the dual aspect idea to her, to my intense surprise she felt at once that I had understood something for the first time in years! There was some truth in this . . . and it might well have saved considerable effort if I had thought of this concept earlier. I was, on the other hand, thinking that in this session she had understood me for the first time. Perhaps I had finally hit upon words that made sense to her. Or perhaps I myself was finally convinced, as a trainee, that the transference existed and was not merely something one experienced in one's own analysis or that one learned in books, but was something that happened to patients.
>
> (Kennedy 1984: 481)

The interrelation between the analyst's and patient's experiences of suddenly understanding each other is striking. The analyst's appreciation of the real meaning of transference makes January 1901 seem close at hand, and underlines the need constantly to rediscover psychoanalysis itself within the particular analysis.[1] When such looking again does manage to happen, as in this case, new meanings may emerge on both sides of the partnership.

1 One has to tread Freud's path after him, start as he started not where he left off (Sharpe 1943: 645).

This need not be on any grand scale, as the following examples show. Indeed its effect may be the greater for the ordinariness of the interchange that acts as a vehicle for it.

A patient had been offered work and asked if I could change a session time to fit in with this. It was a new, more substantial, job in an institution where she was already working. I told her I would probably be able to make the change but could not confirm it for a few days. She wondered what she would do if I could not. Would she pass up the job or drop a session? She did not want to lose a session but this job would be a definite rise in status, the extra money was important and she knew she would come under pressure from her husband to accept it. She said it was a difficult decision to contemplate, then apparently stopped contemplating it and talked about other things. Later in the session she was describing a recent visit to her parents. She had wanted to go and see a certain aunt who, as she had found in the analysis, was more important to her than she had thought. Her mother did not like this aunt and wanted her to spend the time with herself instead. At this point I asked if she thought whether the conflict over visiting her aunt or giving in to her mother might be like the potential clash between her session and the job. I linked this to her familiar difficulty in knowing what she really wanted to do for herself. She thought they did feel similar and went on to say that what she would really want for herself might be to take the job and drop the session. This brought me up short. I realised it was not at all what I had in mind. I was meant to be the aunt and the demands pulling her into the job were meant to be the mother impeding the analysis which she really wanted. I had to realise rather briskly that 'what she wanted for herself' meant exactly what it said, regardless of what I might wish she wanted. Since I had said it, I had better have intended it. There was indeed a risk of my being more like the mother than the aunt!

The point is that I was not being hypocritical. I had not just been pretending to respect her autonomy. I really was trying to help her towards a true sense of what she wanted. But when she responded to my intervention, I had to take my own words more seriously than I had bargained for. She went on to tell me how much getting established in this work really mattered to her. When she had tried before, the jobs always went to people already on the inside. Now that she was on the inside herself and the chance had come, she hoped not to have to pass it up. We were both needing to be freshly aware of what mattered most, and it seemed that through that shared process she was finding a way to let me know how much both sorts of work, her job and the analysis, meant to her.

A man in the first three weeks of his analysis went systematically through his biography, session after session. It was carefully arranged in exact chronological detail. The story was a horrifying one of drug abuse, perverse and destructive sexual relationships and a generally disintegrated life, but it was unfolded in a very measured way. He would start sessions with remarks like 'Today I think I will go back to the story of Helen' or 'I was telling you about being in Rome with Janet. Now where had I got to?', and out would come the next grisly episode. He spoke without emotion and his narrative technique obviously served to keep him affectively out of touch with what he was describing. Near the end of one session I commented on his organised way of presenting himself: perhaps it might be to try and ward off inner feelings of chaos. The next day he was talking about a time when he lived with a girlfriend who used to pick up other men and bring them back home while he was there. He and she alternated between taking drugs together, passionate sado-masochistic sex and furious rows. She had been badly hurt in a car accident one day, round about the time they had argued over her share of an electricity bill. He was describing in detail getting the news of the accident and also the row about the bill. It sounded as though they had happened on the same day and I found myself wanting to know if this was the case. The chronology might be important if he had the fantasy that because of the row he was responsible for her injuries. As I was thinking this, I heard him say in a grim voice: 'This is getting a bit less organised, isn't it?' I realised that in the last few minutes he had lost his fluency and was talking in a heavy, bewildered fashion that was new. His words shook me because they came just as I had been wanting to organise his narrative in my own mind. I thought back to my remark of the day before. The important thing was not grasping the events but getting nearer the chaos. I was operating his own defence just as he was beginning to give it up in response to my intervention. Suddenly I had to find a fresh awareness of what really mattered. I said nothing but tried to stop bothering about chronology. In the rest of the session he did allow himself to get considerably upset. At the end he looked at the clock in surprise and said, sounding exhausted, that he felt he had been in the room for hours.

These commonplace bits of clinical experience are a far cry from Freud's having to rethink the seduction theory or the new understanding of transference forced on him by Dora. But they show that what we observe in those landmarks of psychoanalytic history can also be seen, happening or failing to happen, on a different scale in day-to-day clinical practice.

Analyst and patient share the necessity of seeing that what they always knew is more importantly and deeply true than they had appreciated. There are many descriptions of experience that is mutual to patient and analyst, with the same process at work in each of them. In her introduction to *The Hands of the Living God*, Milner writes:

> Certainly one of the main practical things I learnt from her was to do
> with the variations and fluctuations in the depths of the way I attended

41

to what she said; that is, how deeply the emergence of some of the most primitive levels of psychic and body-ego experience in the patient can depend on the body-ego perceptions in the analyst . . .

(Milner 1969: xxix–xxx)

Harold Searles (1975) suggests that human beings have an innate therapeutic impulse towards their fellows, and that psychological illness is related to a disturbance of this therapeutic striving. This implies that if the analyst is really going to help his patient, he must be able to experience the patient as really, and not just in fantasy, doing something therapeutic for him, the analyst. Irma Brenman Pick (1985) has written that countertransference is not a question of either a restimulation of the analyst's own pathology, or the fruitful use of her subjectivity. The analyst should poise herself between these two. If she is to use the countertransference therapeutically, it will be by opening herself to having a real emotional disturbance provoked in her, to be worked through as the patient needs to work through his own disturbance. Neville Symington (1985) describes certain fantasies as not existing just in the person who 'has' them. The fantasy which inhibits a patient's development may also occupy a susceptible 'host' area in the analyst's mind. Then patient and analyst are subject to the same mental process which blocks progress, and interpretations emanating from that area, however true they may be, will in fact operate against development. This is an example of a shared process which the analyst needs to disengage from.

These are all instances of the need to 'look again', and if we ourselves look again at the earlier examples, we may notice a common element: suddenly finding that something really matters involves an experience of loss. A gain in understanding means giving something up. Freud had to give up believing in the information on which he had founded his theories. Later he had to give up his confidence that he knew how to handle transference. My patient who went to Eastern Europe and I were deprived of the easy assurance that we knew all about reality testing. The Oxford philosophers who visited Tomin had the value they themselves had really given to philosophy called into question. Schwaber's article asks us to give up automatic assumptions about our open-mindedness. It might have been possible for my patient to move from curiosity to desire, if only I could have given up my anxiety about how I performed with my first training case. I had to realise, with the woman who was offered the job and the inwardly chaotic man, that I had not meant what I said to them as wholeheartedly as I liked to think. When I saw how their truth really mattered, the interpretations as I had made them seemed rather stereotyped.

It is not a question of giving up something false, however, but something true. That is what provokes the sense of shock. Even if my interpretations were stereotyped, they were still good ones and they had an effect.

It would be unrealistic not to mind how well I did with my training case. Analysts do take care not to impose their own views on patients. Neither myself nor my patient who visited Eastern Europe are psychotic. Freud's early findings were genuine discoveries. Of course the Oxford philosophers valued philosophy; they would not have gone to Czechoslovakia otherwise. The point is that to achieve a new depth of understanding and penetrate further into what something means, we have to sacrifice the way we have understood it up to now. That understanding does not become false, but its truth is no longer large enough. It is not disproved, but in order to advance beyond it we have to let it go.

This puts us in exactly the same position as a patient who is called on to give up his pathology. Every analyst knows only too well how hard it is for people to change. Freud was continually exercised by it. Early on he was disappointed to find that telling people what their unconscious conflicts were did not necessarily make them better (Freud 1913a: 141), and near the end of his life he was still writing pessimistically about the therapeutic effects of analysis (Freud 1937). Patients come to analysis hoping to lose their symptoms or resolve their character problems. Once embarked on the process, however, they do not treat it as a welcome opportunity to get rid of unwanted burdens, but as though they are being called upon, much against their will, to give up something they do not want to be deprived of. They behave like this because it is true. Letting go of their pathology is so difficult because it means abandoning something which, up to the point when the price became too high, has served them well. It has been the best adaptation they could make. The point is not that this is how ill they are, but that this is how healthy they have managed to be. So it makes good sense to try to hang on to it. The analyst thinks he is offering a better possibility; the patient has no reason in his experience to believe any such thing. All analysts have examples of this in their work. One which comes to mind is of a young man who said I kept talking as though he might form some kind of relationship with me, but it was no good; he knew the world was not like that. He was quite right. His world had not been like that. Why believe me?

All this is well recognised. It is no truism, however, when we link it to what was said earlier. The patient is called on to give up what is the best approach he has been able to make to living his life and being who he is. This has the same configuration as the demands made on Freud during the development of psychoanalysis, and the demand to which the analyst must endeavour to keep himself or herself open. The patient is there to see further into the things that really matter about himself and his life. But for this to happen he has to sacrifice the arrangement which, until now, it has mattered very much to preserve. The analyst needs to see further into what really matters about the analysis. But to do that he must be prepared to let go of the way he has seen things so far. The two situations reflect each other, and the analyst's being open to his version helps the patient to experience his.

The earlier clinical illustrations were in the nature of cautionary tales and highlighted the necessity of giving something up. Here is a session where the analyst was more able to open himself to unexpected perceptions which took both him and the patient by surprise. The patient was a young man, a creative artist with a promising career but who did not really know, within his field, what sort of work he wanted to do. He was subject to his family's expectations of social and intellectual success and he had tried to fit in with this from early on. He had held fashionably left-wing political views about which he was now uncertain. At the time of this session he had been in five times weekly analysis for almost four years.

He began by telling me a dream, associating as he went along. *He was in a church high up on some horseshoe-shaped cliffs above Liverpool.* The cliffs made him think of Wolfe capturing Quebec by scaling the Heights of Abraham. *There was a priest in the church who announced a new hymn to be sung in praise of Che Guevara. The music had a strange quality which was difficult to describe. The notes were broken and interrupted. He was contemptuous of the people singing just because it was trendy.* This led him to a recent conversation with a homosexual colleague. This man had told my patient about a male friend of his who picked up an adolescent boy and was doing no more than kissing him when he was arrested and then beaten up by the police. My patient said the police should not have beaten him up but he could not completely sympathise with the man. Later in their conversation he had said that although he was well disposed towards homosexuals in general, he did not like the idea of cruising in public lavatories. It seemed a loveless kind of promiscuity. At this his colleague got angry and abused him for his stereotyped, reactionary views. This made my patient worry that perhaps he was after all conservative and unsympathetic. Then he went back to the music in the dream. As a child he did something he called 'being romantic'. This meant escaping from the real world when he was miserable by letting himself be carried away on a tide of emotion. Yesterday, in an unhappy mood, he had listened to a tape of Russian folk music which sent him into a reverie. He found himself visualising the pictures in a book of Russian icons. They had passed before him in a marvellous procession to the music, like something he might create in his own art form. Then he thought this was perhaps just the kind of sentimental, romantic escapism he had gone in for when he was a child. He went back to the dream. *Three unemployed Liverpudlian youths appeared and asked him if he knew what it was really like being out of work. He spoke to them reasonably but realistically. His girlfriend was there and said to him critically: 'You're so unambiguous.' He threatened her with a cleaver which he was using to slice up the bottom half of a frozen Egyptian mummy, but he turned the threatening gesture into a joke. The dream ended.*

It was not difficult to guess at some of the latent content. He was asking if I knew what it was really like to be him; he was expressing contempt for his own 'radical chic'; the youths and the reference to ambiguity might join up with his association about homosexuality; there was a question about what kinds of feeling might appear between him and me; the bottom half of a mummy sounded Oedipal, especially with a father like Abraham in the offing; something aggressive was being avoided by the dream ending as it did; and so on. It was the images I could not understand, however, that made the greater impact on me, because they opened in so many directions at once. I was thinking 'Why Liverpool? Why Wolfe? Something frozen? A cleaver? What does it mean to be criticised as unambiguous? Broken up hymn tunes? Horseshoes?' The profusion did not feel either defensive or seductive, and stirred me with a sense of meaning. I might have tried to pin down the images by asking for further associations, but that did not feel right. (I realised later that he was giving me the same experience that he had had with the Russian music. It was probably important that I was prepared to let the procession pass before me, and be moved by it but not interfere.) I said to him that there was something I thought I saw pretty clearly, but that it felt less important than what I had not seen. What I did see was a similarity about the conversation with his homosexual colleague and what had happened with the Russian music. In fact he had neither been stereotyped nor sentimental. In each case he was working towards a view-point, or a vision, which could be his own, but something interfered and made him doubt his own honesty. He said it was not that simple. He just did not seem able to hang on to his own way of seeing things. I said that was exactly the difficulty I was pointing to. He then said he was sometimes able to use me, so as to do this hanging on to his own ideas or feelings. I was an internal reference point that he checked things against to see if they felt true or alien. It was like his friend Paul who had once talked about loveless relationships. This let him realise that he too thought there were such things and that it was all right to say so.

At this point I felt something eerie happen. Shapes I was already looking at seemed to declare themselves, and what was in my field of vision became visible. I said: 'You have me and Paul as internal reference points who help you to know what belongs to yourself. I think in the dream we can see other internal reference points, but ones which destroy your ability to know and to have what belongs to you. I mean the frozen mummy that you want to cut up, and Abraham, who was ready to kill his own son.' He said he did not think he had ever told me how terribly shocked he had been as a child by that story. When Abraham was taking Isaac up the mountain to kill him he used to think it must be a mistake. That could not really be what was happening. (It was true that he had not told me this before.) Then he said: 'Yes, I suppose I have a fantasy of my parents being like that.' I said: 'Calling it a fantasy misses the point. When you use Paul or me as you described we are not fantasies.' (Theoretically speaking we may be, but I was not talking that language with my patient.) He said in a stunned voice: 'My God! You mean they are really there.'

There was a long silence and we were near the end of the session. I broke the silence, saying: 'And yet I notice that the dream is also talking about a "new him".' (It was the clergyman who announced the new hymn: perhaps a Parson, but I did not say so.) He said: 'It frightens me for you to say that'. After another pause he said that this session had felt like hard work, and was silent again. Then he said that most people complained that psychoanalysis was too slow; it went at a snail's pace. But he felt the opposite. Sometimes things happened so fast you could hardly believe it. In the next session he used an image which again had the quality of being unforeseeable but absolutely right. He said he felt like a snake that was shedding a skin; but the skin was on the inside of him, not the outside.

Not every session makes the impact on patient and analyst that this one did. But for all its intensity, it is also worth noticing how ordinary it is. The patient tells a dream and the analyst comments on some of the patient's associations. The patient responds by talking about what the analyst means to him. The analyst then makes an interpretation about the latent content of the dream itself. Although it turns out to be powerful, it is a standard sort of interpretation about bad internal objects. Such material is an example of what happens in analysis all the time. This 'looking again' at what goes into routine, everyday analytic work, is an attempt to approach the unconscious without being limited only to ways of seeing with which we are already familiar.

What emerges from this is, once more, a tension between opposites. The analyst must be deeply concerned to understand the things that matter. He must also be ready to be taken by surprise in seeing that what he thought he already understood matters in fresh and unexpected ways. This can only happen if he is ready to let go of his previous forms of understanding, so he must not be too deeply concerned with how he understands things at the moment after all. The understanding is able to deepen if, and only if, there is no particular concern with whatever the present form of it is.

This has a familiar ring. One of the martial arts mentioned in Chapter 1 was T'ai Chi Ch'uan, a form whose quality is of softness, yielding, not insisting on holding your position, allowing yourself to be moved but never losing contact with the force that is moving you. It is also more than a martial art. It is an instrument of self-development based on Taoist ideas, and a principal tenet of Taoist writings is similarly to avoid rigidity or fixedness, so that one's contact with the world may continue in an unbroken movement. The opening chapter of the *Tao Te Ching* (Lao Tsu 1972) says: 'The name that can be named is not the eternal name.' Compare this with Milner's remark, already quoted (p. 28), that 'the mistake was to believe that any one expression could be the last word, for experience was always bigger than the formula'. The chapter continues:

> The nameless is the beginning of heaven and earth.
> The named is the mother of ten thousand things.
> Ever desireless, one can see the mystery.
> Ever desiring, one can see the manifestations.

That expresses very well the paradox of the analyst's simultaneous attachment and non-attachment. This is not, however, a link with Taoism alone. Other martial arts which show parallels to psychoanalysis are disciplines within Zen Buddhism. This tradition aims for insight that is free from the limitations of any particular forms of understanding. The goal is ultimately to see with direct vision into the nature of reality, so that particular insights, hard won though they may be, can be left behind. Different forms of the same teaching are present in other traditions. In the *Bhagavad Gita* (1962: 52 bk.2 v.47) Krishna says to Arjuna: 'Set thy heart upon thy work, but never on its reward. Work not for a reward, but never cease to do thy work.' Judaism, Christianity and Islam all teach that man must strive to know and do the will of God, but also that whatever he does is not his own but the action of God working within him. So he can have no personal attachment to the results of his work, even though it remains central to his life.

It seems, then, that something common to all these spiritual traditions turns out to be an essential element in psychoanalysis as well. There are analysts who have been interested in such parallels (Arden 1998; Franco 1998; Eigen 1993, 1998; Coltart 1992, 1996; Black 1993; Meissner 1984; Menninger 1963: 365–80), and references to spiritual experience in Milner's work have been noted in Chapter 2. In general, though, analysts are understandably wary of being drawn down interesting pathways only to find that what they are talking about has ceased to be psychoanalysis. Two writers, however, who do help to locate these sorts of experience explicitly within the framework of psychoanalytic theory, are Wilfred Bion and Ignacio Matte Blanco.

In 'Attention and Interpretation' Bion (1970) describes the relations between his concepts O and K and what he calls 'memory' and 'desire'. By O he means ultimate reality. For individual objects and events this is the thing in itself, its essence over and above any particular perception of it. O cannot be known directly. The only form of direct relationship with O is to become it. O does evolve into the domain of K, however, and there it can be known indirectly through the things which are its evolved manifestations. The various spiritual traditions are examples of such manifestations.

The objects and events of the everyday world are also 'evolutions' of the essence of these things in themselves. This brings them within the domain of K and they become knowable. Everything knowable, according to Bion, represents an evolution of O into K. This includes the analyst, the patient and everything that either of them says or does in the session. So although the analyst is always seeking to approach O more closely, that can only be done by operating in the domain of K. K is a function of all human beings, perhaps best described as a readiness to know. It is not simply the state of knowing, because there is also minus K (−K) and this is not just ignorance but the active avoidance of knowledge, or even the wish to destroy the capacity for it. Knowing things by K is dependent on sense experience, and with regard to the complex totality of experience which constitutes an analytic session, the analyst should hold himself as far as possible in a +K state and try to help the patient do the same.

Helping the patient overcome his resistance to knowing is a familiar enough idea, but helping him move from −K to +K is more than this. −K is a compulsive state. It is an insistence on not knowing. +K is its opposite, not just as a state of wanting to know as against wanting not to know, but also as a state of freedom as against one of compulsion. If −K is insisting on not knowing, +K is being willing to know but not insisting on knowledge. Bion (1958) regarded the central crime of Oedipus as his insistence on knowing the truth at all costs.

This sheds light on his warnings against memory and desire. Memory, in Bion's terms, is an attachment to past experience and desire is a wish for it in the future. K belongs to the sensory realm, and its effectiveness depends on an ease of movement there. For the exploratory quality of K to do its work, a person needs to be able to shift freely from one experience to another within the immediacy of the present moment. Attachment to any particular sensory experience, through memory or desire, is a compulsion which restricts the freedom of K, working against the unexpected discovery of fresh meanings that could move the analyst closer to O. Bion (1970: chs 3, 4) advises analysts to take deliberate steps about their own mental states to see that they do not inhibit themselves in this way, and his practical recommendations are notably similar to the *Tao Te Ching* and the *Bhagavad Gita*.

Memory and desire are human attributes, which analysts have in common with their patients. Divesting oneself of them might look, on the face of it, like a retreat from personal relationship to a psychological crow's-nest, allowing exact observation but little in the way of shared experience. So it is important to bear in mind that Bion (1970: 41) also said that what is ordinarily called forgetting is as bad as remembering. Moreover, the clinical examples given earlier do not indicate a disengagement between analyst and patient. The woman who was contemplating a new job showed me my desire to mean more to her than her work or her mother and I had to divest myself of that. But that led to my realising more clearly what I did mean to her as her analyst. With the man who was warding off feelings of disorganisation, I found myself wanting memory, his memory of the course of events, and I needed to give that up. But this was in order to get closer to, not further from, what he was really bringing. In the session described at length I was more able to be free of desire for the meaning of the patient's material. And the result? He told me about the personal meaning I held for him. It was emphasised in Chapter 1 that psychoanalysis, as a vocation which expresses the analyst's being, can only be arrived at by the analyst's immersing himself or herself in basic technique. The processes Bion describes, which might appear so transcendent as to become impersonal, are similarly to be found in the ordinary details of the everyday analytic interaction.

In 'Attention and Interpretation' Bion instances a patient who produced an association with many possible meanings. He considers how to respond and says of the patient's statement: 'I can represent it to myself by the visual image of a geometric solid with an infinite number of surfaces' (Bion 1970: 7–8). Bion's image is of a solid whose surfaces form an infinite set. This calls to mind the work of Matte Blanco, and there is a close relation between their ways of thinking. Matte Blanco's basic frame of reference is the link between the nature of the unconscious and the logical and mathematical characteristics of infinite sets. From this abstruse starting point he generates a way of thinking about psychoanalysis which is both intellectually precise and evocative at many levels.[2]

The concepts of symmetrical and asymmetrical thinking are central to Matte Blanco's work. Asymmetrical thinking distinguishes individuals from one another by the relationships between them. It discriminates and perceives differences. This is the normal everyday logic of reality-testing. Symmetrical thinking, by contrast, sees relations as holding indiscriminately across a field of individuals, so that distinctions disappear. This does not favour accurate reality-testing, and is the kind of 'logic' associated with unconscious thought processes. Eric Rayner gives the example of a child at play.

> For instance, a child may lie on the beach lapped by the waves and declaim 'I am a stone'. As he is playing he knows he is not a stone, but the point of the game is that he *is* a stone. Without symmetry there is no

---

2 Matte Blanco's (1975, 1988) writings appear forbidding, and many analysts fight shy of them. Among others his ideas command an increasing interest (Rey 1976; Arden 1984; *International Review of Psycho-Analysis* 1990). Eric Rayner's (1981, 1995) expositions of Matte Blanco's work provide a detailed but accessible introduction.

play, but without asymmetrical logic, play breaks down into delusion, he *believes* he is a stone.[3]

(Rayner 1981: 406)

Conscious thought is not always asymmetrical, nor unconscious thought always symmetrical. Symmetry and asymmetry are intertwined in both conscious and unconscious thinking. The constantly varying relation between them is what matters, and much of the work of analysis involves disentangling the interplay between symmetrical and asymmetrical elements in the analytic relationship.

Matte Blanco lays particular emphasis on the concept of the unrepressed unconscious. The repressed unconscious contains material which could in principle be conscious. There is asymmetrical thinking in it which is only kept out of consciousness by the active forces of repression. The unrepressed unconscious, on the other hand, contains predominantly symmetrical material which is not actively kept from becoming conscious at all. It is in principle incapable of entering consciousness because the conscious mind does not accommodate thinking which is too exclusively symmetrical. Just as there are feelings that will not go into words, there are contents of the mind that will not go into thoughts. These are, perhaps, the mind's 'unplumbable navel'. Matte Blanco writes of an 'unfolding' or 'translating' function in the mind, which tries to represent such literally unthinkable material in ways that the conscious mind does find possible to accommodate. Such representations, though, are bound to be imperfect approximations, just as any representation of O can only be an imperfect approach to it. Matte Blanco (1975: 110) says that 'the translating function is, by definition, a failure'. The name that can be named is not the eternal name.

To feel at home in an infinite set demands the same paradoxical non-attachment as it does to be free from memory and desire. Consider the set of all prime numbers. Euclid proved, around 300 BC, that there can be no largest prime. They are infinite in number. As a series this infinite set has an interesting quality: no rule has been discovered governing the distribution of primes within the sequence of whole numbers. In the prime series 1, 2, 3, 5, 7, 11, 13, 17, 19, . . . , 5 is the fourth prime, for example, 13 is the seventh and 19 the ninth. But no relation is known between the value of a prime number and the place it occupies in the series, so the value of the next prime can never be calculated and their occurrence in the general number sequence remains unpredictable. What about the mental stance of

---

3 It is striking, given this example, to find Winnicott choosing, as epigraph to one of the chapters in *Playing and Reality*, a quotation from Tagore: 'On the seashore of endless worlds, children play' (Winnicott 1971: 95). The relation of play to symmetrical and asymmetrical thinking is considered further in Chapter 8.

the mathematician who embarks on enumerating the set of primes? There will always be a number which is the largest prime he knows so far. That is the culmination of his knowledge to date and it will justifiably matter a lot to him. But he knows it is only a way-station on the road to knowledge of greater prime numbers that he has not yet found. It means a lot, but at the same time he cannot attach himself to it. Moreover, however many more primes he does discover, because they are infinite in number the proportion of the whole set that he knows is not increased one jot. He will never get any nearer to the end of his task. So he had better not suffer from desire nor be attached to the fruits of his labour because, like the Red Queen, however fast he runs he stays in the same place. One could say that all there is to know about the infinite number of primes is contained in any single one of them, as the fragments of a hologram each contain the whole image. So memory of any smaller ones, or desire for larger ones, is irrelevant. Another version might be to say that you can never know what is coming next, but once you do find out, you realise it has been there right from the beginning. But the only way of understanding is still to go on waiting to see what does come next. I think any practising psychoanalyst would recognise this description.

4

Refinding theory in clinical practice

'Silly old bear', he said, 'what *were* you doing? First you went round the spinney twice by yourself, and then Piglet ran after you and you went round again together, and then you were just going round a fourth time –'

'Wait a moment', said Winnie-the-Pooh, holding up his paw.

He sat down and thought, in the most thoughtful way he could think. Then he fitted his paw into one of the Tracks . . . and then he scratched his nose twice, and stood up.

'Yes', said Winnie-the-Pooh.

'I see now', said Winnie-the-Pooh.

A.A. Milne (1926: ch. 3) *Winnie-the-Pooh*

The relation between lived experience and psychoanalytic conceptualising sometimes appears in a broad sweep on a large canvas, as with Milner, and sometimes in single, particular examples. André Green (1994: 23) says that his '*vocation psychiatrique*' (his use of the word '*vocation*' is worth noting) was connected to the depression his mother went through after her younger sister died in a fire, when Green himself was two years old. His well-known paper, 'The Dead Mother' (Green 1983), deals with the infant's experience of a mother who is absorbed in a bereavement and cannot properly be there for him because of her depression.[1] Green has commented that one of the roots of this paper must have been his own experience of his mother's state when he was so little. He discovered during his analysis 'how many elements I had put into my work which, although not part of my biography, did belong to my own structural development' (Green 1994: 24).

---

1 'The dead mother' (Green [1983] 1986) is discussed in Chapter 10 (pp. 184–5).

Kenneth Wright (1991: 304) also considers that 'a therapist's theory in many ways mirrors the structure of his own self'. He sees theory as having two faces, a public and a personal one.

> On the one hand it mediates his relation to a group – a group of practitioners who all believe a similar theory. In this sense it exists 'out there' as something that is independent of the therapist's self. On the other hand it can be thought of as lying between the therapist and his patient, mediating that relationship, and forming and being formed (or re-formed) at that interface. Between these two, it occupies an essentially intimate relationship to the therapist's own self – it is 'in there', part of him, inside him.
>
> (Wright 1991: 303)

Joseph Sandler (1983: 38) similarly distinguished between 'official, or public theory' and the hardly articulated, even unconscious, elements of theory which are what analysts at work actually use.

Understanding grows by integrating what is learned from outside with what acquires meaning from within, and the theory that has a real effect in the consulting-room is that to which analysts have themselves given meaning through their own experience. Pursuing this theme, Wright draws attention to Bennett Simon's (1988) paper on the relationship between Bion and Samuel Beckett, about which Didier Anzieu (1989) has written in similar terms. Beckett had analysis with Bion early in both their careers. From a reading of their work Anzieu and Simon find it to have been a formative experience for each of them. They both consider that Beckett's difficulties resonated with problems Bion himself was struggling with, in a way that had a lasting impact on the development of Bion's psychoanalytic thinking.[2] Simon writes:

> I believe this is, in fact, not a rare event in the lives of analysts, particularly with patients they have encountered early in their careers. Something unfinished, unsatisfying, unresolved, but intriguing and attractive, gets into 'the system' of the analyst, and does not let him alone. In the happier instance, the analyst is not merely puzzled or traumatised, but creatively works out some of the implications of the only partially successful therapeutic encounter.
>
> (Simon 1988: 331)

An analyst cannot separate his theory from his own self. It might seem that clinical practice in psychoanalysis should be derived by using theory to

2 For the influence of psychoanalysis on Beckett's work see Baker (1997).

understand a patient's pathology, and then seeing, from that theoretical understanding, how to proceed in clinical terms. Experience, however, seems to belie this. When they are with their patients analysts seldom work things out so deliberately. They are immediately involved in the interaction with an individual and they do not generally find their interpretations by deducing them from theory. As with a transitional object (Winnicott 1971: 1–25), it is indeterminate whether theory arises from within or is received from without. It does have to be learned, of course, but if theory is to be made living use of, and not simply be put into application, this will spring from the freshness of immediate experience.

Approaches to this topic all emphasise the importance of the preconscious. One view is exemplified by Freud and Fenichel in their responses to a paper by Ferenczi first published in 1928. Freud, responding critically to Ferenczi's notions of the analyst's 'elasticity' and 'tact', said, as quoted by Ferenczi himself:

> What in reality we undertake is a weighing up – generally at the preconscious level – of the various reactions that we may expect from our intervention, and the most important aspect in this is quantitative assessment of the dynamic factors in the situation. Rules for making such an assessment can naturally not be given. The decisive factors are the analyst's experience and normality. But tact should be robbed of its mystical character.
>
> (Ferenczi 1928: 99)

Fenichel clearly had Ferenczi's paper in mind when he wrote:

> The so-called 'tact', which determines when and how a given matter is to be revealed to the patient, seems to me . . . quite determinable in a systematic way and therefore teachable in a proper degree through comprehension of the definite dynamic changes which take place in the patient during the analysis.[3]
>
> (Fenichel 1941: 5)

These statements imply that analysts do hold their metapsychological theory in mind, and refer the patient's material to it so as to derive, by a complex set of implications, a correct way of proceeding clinically. The theory is usually held in the preconscious and the tracing of its clinical implications is descriptively speaking unconscious, which accounts for the subjective

---

3 This passage, and Freud's response to Ferenczi as translated by Ernest Jones, are quoted at greater length in Chapter 9 (pp. 148–9).

experience of spontaneity and intuition. This account is related to Freud's view of metapsychology as a set of factual hypotheses concerning the human mind, just as natural scientists have factual hypotheses about the material world. The need for metapsychology has been challenged (Klein 1976; Schafer 1976) and defended (Ellman and Moskowitz 1980; Modell 1981). Even a purely clinical theory, however, could be taken as having the same relation, in formal terms, to clinical practice. That is to say, the analyst knows what the clinical theory is, holds it preconsciously in mind and derives from it, also preconsciously for the most part, how to proceed with the patient. Greenson's (1967) book on clinical technique offers many lucid illustrations of such a process.

Sandler (1983) offers a radically different view. He agrees that the preconscious is where most of the analyst's theoretical work in the session goes on, outside conscious awareness but available for scrutiny if need be. But where Freud and Fenichel would say that analysts know so well what their theory is that they can use it preconsciously, Sandler maintains that they use many theoretical concepts without ever defining them, because they are implicit in their practice without being consciously articulated. For Sandler it is the less formulated concepts which may, in fact, be the most serviceable, precisely because the analyst is unconscious of them, and so can use them without querying their relation to other concepts. This implies that analysts would have to examine their preconscious in order to find out what their theory is, which is very different from saying that they can make use of their theory preconsciously because of how thoroughly they know it. Theoretical pluralism has become familiar within the analytic community (Wallerstein 1988), but on the part of the individual analyst it may seem more startling. Central to Sandler's viewpoint is the idea that concepts can be elastic:

> Such an approach to psychoanalytic concepts regards each as having a set of dimensions of meaning, as existing in a meaning-space, in which it moves as its context and sense changes. The examination of the different dimensions of our major psychoanalytic concepts may then prove to be as profitable as the search for precise definitions – possibly even more profitable, for some of our most useful concepts are incapable of being pinned down by being defined, and today's precision may be tomorrow's rigidity.
>
> (Sandler 1983: 36)

This is the theoretical counterpart of Ferenczi's (1928) technical elasticity.

The following clinical material shows the analyst's need for an active, personal engagement with theory and not the mere application of it as a received body of knowledge. Wright speaks, in the passage quoted above, of theory being 're-formed' at the interface between therapist and patient, and I had a sense of refinding, even of recreating, theory in the course of this analysis. I refound concepts with which I was familiar, but they gained a new power from their refinding out of the particular need of the moment. This patient produced an unusually strong and persistent sense of confusion in me. His own life history had been extremely confusing and he certainly conveyed to me in this way something of what it was like to be him. But this is not a case study, and the material is not intended as a narrative of the analysis. Sessions from different stages of the analysis are presented to illustrate how my attempts to deal with the confusion set me thinking about the place of theory in clinical practice. I discovered that an analyst, as he listens and responds to his patient, is listening and responding to his theories as well.

He was in his mid-twenties when he came for analysis following a bout of depression. By the time he saw me he felt better, but he was also aware of a long-standing difficulty in contact with people. He could manage an appearance of sociability but said he had not really made any friends since leaving school. He was also at risk of drug abuse. He had taken drugs to disguise his social anxieties and it seemed to be a resolution to avoid this in future that had provoked the depression. In the early stages of his five times weekly analysis there was little sense of direction. He often talked about his penis, about masturbation and impulsive sexual thoughts concerning me. He might start a session, for example, by saying that he thought he hated me; he had a picture of masturbating and deliberately leaving drops of semen on the couch; coming upstairs behind me he was thinking 'Bugger him! Bugger him!' Then he would say 'I shouldn't tell you all this. It might make you angry if you thought I meant it.' He seemed to be recognising that these were disturbing sexual thoughts about me and trying to dismiss them. Shortly before the first holiday break he became acutely hypomanic. He was sleepless and hyperactive, and his behaviour was disinhibited. He had frank delusions of a grandiose nature. Psychiatrically the diagnosis was clear and hospital admission would certainly have been justified, but in the event it was possible to avoid it. The episode passed and did not recur, although sometimes before subsequent breaks he felt his thoughts speeding up and feared they might get out of control again.

The following session took place when he had been coming for 20 months. It conveys the confusing flow of his material and shows the sort of basic, rather obvious, interpretations with which I tried somehow to keep things anchored. He came in and saw the bill by the couch. He felt reassured by this: things did go on as usual. He had been abroad to visit his mother and felt lonely on the journey. He had asked his mother how she felt about his not having lent some money to one of his sisters, as he had been asked to do. She wished the problem could have been dealt with more comfortably. He thought his sister should realise that he was too occupied with difficulties of his own to be able to help. He had looked at his hand while practising on his violin, and thought how amazing it was that it could carry out such detailed movements. It was a relief to know his brain controlled it so well. He felt more confidence in things, and was more able to trust doctors about his sinus trouble. He had had a dream about a girl he knows: her bush stopped and she had a vagina like a little girl's. Then he said the vagina was what was inside so he could not have seen it. He had got it wrong again. But I hadn't run away screaming or laughing.

All this was without a word from me. I now said the question in his mind was whether he could trust this doctor to go on not screaming or laughing. He said that was right. He had a feeling of the end of the world. I said that he showed me, in needing to reassure himself about normal routine with the bill, how strong and how fearful that feeling was. In fact I felt lost in the stream of material and did not at this stage find theoretical signposts to help me discover meaning in it. No doubt I could have devised interpretations or pulled the material into the transference, but it would have felt artificial. Instead I stuck to these simple comments that I was sure were true, partly to keep my own bearings and partly to show him that I understood his fear about communicating with me.

He moved on to going out with girls. He had never invited a girl out on his own initiative. He would like to fuck the girl in his dream. But how could he tell her that he might prefer someone else? He thinks that sometime he is bound to ask a girl out; he is just waiting until it happens. Tomorrow a tricky situation needs dealing with at work. He thinks he will somehow upset everyone involved and produce complete disaster. He implied that this would be entirely his fault. If he broaches something with me it might make me run away. He had a sudden thought of a condom. He sometimes masturbated with one. That seemed disgusting. Then he switched to something about his father and said he was 'steering away from that'. I said he might fear that if he broached masturbation here, that would make me run away. He said he never thought he could talk about it without its being found disgusting. He remembered someone at school and wondered what would happen if he now said to him 'Do you remember how I sucked you off?' He would seem very screwed up. He had the thought that men never really want him in their games, like not being picked for teams at school, although in fact this was not true. His father had said he would come on holiday with him after all. His father said his objections would always be there (I did not know what this meant) so he might as well go now. Then he said he wanted to learn all he could about a particular artist so as to outdo his father who knew a lot about him. The session ended.

I was working to grasp whatever moments of clarity I could. There was a question of whether I wanted him in my game. There was also the competitiveness with the father, the interest in genital sexuality which had to regress to picture the girl's vagina as infantile, the preoccupation with money and control, the sucking at the penis and the sense of isolation as he travels towards his mother. Some of these things I registered, but I did not fully appreciate at the time what a disordered jumble of references to different stages of development I was listening to.

His sense of identity was precarious and the anxiety about a sudden catastrophe, or the end of the world, was recurrent. We began to put into words how unsure he was of his own existence or, if he did exist, of who he was. Analysts often relate the sense of identity to primitive aspects of mental functioning and very early experiences. I reflected that a secure identity also depends on passing in more or less orderly fashion through a series of developmental experiences which evolve one out of the other. One can only be someone that one has arrived at being. The pattern of this man's material, together with his history, began to suggest that his childhood had not been like that. He was trying to be someone 'out of the blue', so to speak, without a process of internal evolution to give him the experience of arriving at who he was. His material was confusing because I did not know, from one moment to the next, at what developmental level I was working. To be aware of how he was constantly slipping between levels might help me not only to orientate myself but also to speak to his own confusion. In the following example I am beginning to make use of this idea.

He had a thought about his penis as he was getting out of the car. Why should he want to talk about that? He felt chaotic today. He had just scraped together some clothes to wear. He was giving old clothes to a local housing association. Did I think he was interested in it? No, it was just closer than Oxfam, that was all. His cleaner could have some, but then she might start stealing from him. She was angry at a friend's having slept in his bed while he was away. I felt a familiar sense of bewilderment and said we had never heard his thought, so we had lost contact with why he should want to talk about whatever it was. He said it was the bit that was missing. Then he spun off into an agitated state, wondering what he was doing here, telling me to fuck off and saying he was whirling around in cosmic dust, not making sense like he should. I said that if a bit of him was missing he might well feel he didn't make sense. He agreed and wondered if he would ever really want a girlfriend. He didn't feel he was ready; he was too isolated. Maybe there has to be someone to contain you, he said, but he didn't want to seem to be trying to be back in the womb. During the previous day's session he had wanted to feel he was part of me and I referred to this now, wondering if that might be the containing he desired. He said that yesterday's feeling was like a small child wanting to know he is the only one. This was different; it was wanting help not to lose control of his mind. Disagreeing with me like that felt good. He could let something out. Maybe he has a hole in his chest. A penis might come out of it, or else vomit. He doesn't know where babies are born from and he has no idea about female anatomy. Putting his trousers on today he noticed his penis and thought it was withered. How could it be any good for a girl-friend? He had talked before about its being withered and rotting and I said that perhaps his penis was the bit he felt was missing. He said, very startled, that this was the thought he had had while getting out of the car: his penis was not there.

This material is again confusing but by now I was orientating myself better. He was swinging between a wish for fusion and the hope of genital sexuality, the latter producing extreme castration anxiety. This uncertain oscillation was linked to his anatomical confusions between the vomiting mouth, the ejaculating penis and wherever babies might come out of. Underlying it all was his fear, which was occupying us a lot at this time, of another psychotic breakdown.

Ten weeks later he heard paper rustle during a session and thought I must be looking at my diary to say I could not see him on such-and-such a day. He adjusted his head on the pillow and hoped I would not think he was trying to get close to me. He said he thought I was trying to get him to suck me off. He was mentally calling me 'fucking cunt' and 'cocksucker'. I said he might be afraid that he really did want to get close to me because of his own wish to suck me. He answered by remembering a dream. *He was having a session in which I gave him vegetable rissoles to eat. There were two unknown women in the room. As he took his plate out of the room I poured milk over it. It splashed off the plate on to the carpet. He hoped I would not notice the mess.* His immediate association was to semen. I interpreted that behind a fantasy of sucking my penis and getting semen in his mouth, he was wanting to relate to me as a woman who could feed him with her breast. Near the end of the session he was aware of losing me until the next day and I could link this to the loss of his father when his parents divorced, which had spoiled his chances of finding out what a penis was really for.

I could make these interpretations, about the feeding woman whose breast was supplanted by the penis, and about his missing the discovery of true genitality, because the idea of dissecting out the confusion in terms of developmental levels was becoming clearer to me. I was beginning to refind theory which I already knew, through my personal struggle to understand this patient. It is this personal struggle which enables a move from precon-scious conceptual awareness to a rediscovery of theory which can then be consciously put to use. The following two sessions illustrate this further.

He began with a typical stream of chaotic sounding associations. He thought he was angry with me. He sneered at my short-sleeved shirt: 'Ah!

Getting down to work!' Then he imagined me naked and thought 'Bugger you!' He was angry with me for going away over the weekend. He switched to a party where he was disappointed at finding an attractive girl was going out with a glamorous man. Nevertheless he had an intimate talk with her and was pleased to find he could talk openly and directly with a woman. He had a sudden feeling of being like a small boy, effeminate, not a real man, but quickly went back to his sense of progress. What is he really talking about, though? He wants to say 'Piss off!' to me. There was a phone call from work: the computer had gone down. He had a doom-laden sense of everything falling apart. There had been no break in these transitions but now he paused and said 'Please, you say something.'

I said it seemed he could not keep it going all on his own any longer. He said Yes, he had a feeling of being shot away from this planet out into space with blues and greens of the atmosphere all round him. I pointed out that he had twice mentioned hostile feelings towards me, but then abandoned them. Perhaps the sense of things falling apart was between us, and being shot into space on his own was what he felt when I left him at the weekend. He was struck, as he listened, by the thought of me as a real person, separate from him, who was trying to think about him. I said I understood that seeing me as a separate person gave him a sense of new possibilities. Sometimes that was what he wanted, but at other times he wanted to feel there was no difference between us, that he was a part of me so I could never leave him.

This conscious attempt to speak to his sense of chaos by pointing out the way he swung between different phases of development, seemed validated by what followed. He said that that morning he had looked at his penis in the bath and realised that he had not looked at his balls for ages. He was worried that they were not there. I asked what he was afraid had happened to them. He said obscurely that they would be lost in a dream from long ago at school. After getting out of his bath he had a sudden pain in his jaw and thought he had mumps. I noticed the switch from castration anxiety to an anxiety about his mouth which still implied fear of sterility. Next he spoke about a time at school when a boy known for his big penis masturbated into a saucer while he and others watched in admiration. He had a picture of himself licking up the semen and tasting it. He was not sure if he had actually done this or not. The oscillation between genital and oral was now very striking and I said that he might have feelings about me that appeared sexual, with a wish to see my big penis; but behind that was another wish to take something of mine into his mouth and feed from it.

In the final example, seven months after the first session described here, the early part of the session consisted of talk about masturbating, with fantasies of ejaculating in the consulting-room and thoughts that I had been masturbating, alongside telling me about a real sense of change and progress in his life. He talked about his stepmother, saying that in a kind of way he loved her but also could not stand her. I said I thought he had the same mixture of feelings about me, both appreciating my help and wanting to mess up my room with his semen. He told me, in response, about masturbating and then playing the violin with a drop of semen still on his hand. He went back to talking about some positive developments at work, but felt his thoughts running away with him and became anxious. He said he hated me. He felt 'so fucking uncontained'. He wanted to hit out at something. He had a fantasy of bashing my head so that it crumbled to a pulp. I talked of his wanting to have me to hit against, to bash at me and have me not crumble: then he might feel contained. He became panicky, saying he had a 'Help! What's happening?' feeling. He thought he might be going to cry, something that had never happened in his analysis. I said I understood he was longing to be able to cry but was also terrified to, and that I thought he had no idea whether he would cry tears, shit or semen. He said I should add piss or mouth-dribble. It might be either of them too. After this he relaxed a bit and said 'Yes, but how do I get out of this?' and moved straight on to tell me how hopeless his violin teacher was. He had played some Mozart and his teacher had said it was very good, although he thought the piece was feeble and he had been playing it as destructively as he could. How stupid his teacher must be! I said another way of looking at it was that Mozart's music seemed to be strong enough to survive his efforts to destroy it. 'Bach, maybe!', he retorted. A certain violinist put real venom into his playing of the D minor Chaconne and you could hear how the music stood up to it. But he had never thought Mozart was capable of that. He had Mozart down as a wimp. Then he realised 'wimp' was how he sometimes labelled me too. Thoughtfully he said that if he had been wrong about the Mozart piece then perhaps I could contain him after all.

In these sessions my preconscious awareness of the absence of ordering, and of the need for it, was helping me find interventions out of which gradually emerged the conscious reformulation of a developmental sequence. My interpretation about his tears was derived from this refinding of theory. With it, I voiced a confusion that I had sensed in him, between tears and anal or phallic body products. His joining in the discovery, by adding the urethral and oral elements, confirmed the process of refinding and led on to an experience in the transference which helped to modify the anxieties arising from his developmental confusion.[4]

Refinding is what lets theory shift from being something that we know about to something that we know. Two central aspects of psychoanalysis are the recovery, by recollection and reconstruction, of a patient's early

---

4 This session is discussed further, in relation to clinical technique, in Chapter 9 (p. 151).

history and, secondly, the replication of the patient's predicament in the transference, which thus becomes a focus of the analysis. Both are essential to analytic work, but analysts tend to group themselves according to which receives the greater emphasis. This patient forced me to straddle any such divide. He remembered little about his childhood, and told me still less. I needed his history, but to begin with I could find it only in the transference. Later on he began to investigate his past. From the beginning he had spoken of his mother as a woman conscious of her beauty. When he started asking her about her own childhood, he found that her parents had often left her in the care of others and she was uncertain whether they really loved her. She tried to please them by being sweet, pretty and good at performing. It seemed that a kind of narcissistic glamour had become her way of sustaining a precarious self-esteem and that this might have been threatened by the practical, unglamorous routine of looking after a baby. The space he was shot into, where there were bright colours but no containment, acquired a historical context. He learnt that a lot of caring for him as an infant was done by a competent, down-to-earth woman of whom he had a few memories: someone, it seemed, who would not crumble and who did help him to feel contained. The question of whether I was just a wimp like Mozart, or whether I had some Bach-like solidity after all, was connected in the transference to this relationship. So although I found his history in the transference it was important to move from the transference into his history, and back and forth between them. This living relation between history and transference is another bit of theory, elementary and already familiar, which I refound and made my own with this patient.

If rediscovering what we already know seems paradoxical, the need to let theory *happen* to us may be clearer when it concerns something which has not been understood before. Problems in the longitudinal, evolutionary aspects of development tend to be seen by analysts as more relevant to the psychogenesis of neurotic disorder, while primitive processes are usually thought more significant in the development of borderline or psychotic conditions. My experience with this man, however, suggests that the former kind of difficulty may have an important part to play in psychotic disturbance. The theoretical insight that occurred, that *happened*, to me with this patient has to do with the essentially organic growth of the psyche. He showed me how significant it is that we have to evolve into being who we are, through a process of becoming. What breaks down in a psychotic breakdown may be the attempt to be someone who has not been properly arrived at.

The analysis of someone so disturbed could never be described as easy or elementary. But am I making too much of what is basic common currency? The central notion that I 'refound' in this case was of evolution through an orderly developmental sequence. This is something analytic students learn about in their first year of training. It might seem that all I did was what a good supervisor could have helped me do more quickly: to apply correctly the theory I already knew. Viewed in that way, theory is a set of propositions, or hypotheses, impersonally available in the same way to anyone who informs himself or herself, which can be applied from the general to the particular in a given instance. This view, which Freud and Fenichel implicitly took in their critique of Ferenczi, is what Wright calls theory's public face. The power of theory to inform clinical practice, however, depends on linking this external aspect to the internal, less articulate aspect of it emphasised by Wright and Sandler, that finds its personal meaning through lived experience.

The external aspect of theory was heavily favoured by Karl Popper's introduction in 1934 of the criterion of falsifiability, which was to define scientific methodology for several decades. Knowledge became that which could be objectively defined, and publicly articulated, with a specificity that allowed for it to be disproved. In the clinical situation, this implies that analysts would be trying to see clearly what was *not* true of their patients, so as to know how they could, provisionally, go on thinking about them. Analysts do consider possibilities about their patients, and discard them if they turn out to be wrong. But observing myself at work with this man revealed that, more than ruling out what was not true, I was finding theory that I did need for understanding him. What I found was not unfamiliar. Discovering it afresh, however, in connection with a particular person, let me make living use of it in ways not available to me before.

In my refinding, I was not stumbling across concepts – developmental sequences, the relation between history and transference – as isolated nuggets of theory. They were preconsciously available for me to refind because they were part of a coherent network of ideas that I was already drawing on. Theory tends to be seen, in its external aspect, as a matter of discrete hypotheses to be supported or refuted. The personal aspect, on the other hand, and Sandler's notion of elasticity, are linked rather to a view of meaning as belonging, not to single statements in isolation (Quine 1961) but to a network of language. Meaning then resides in the network as a whole, and individual propositions cannot be true or false without affecting the rest of the network. This has powerful implications. If empirical evidence is found which runs counter to a certain hypothesis, the simple Popperian falsificationist view would be that this disproves the hypothesis and it must be discarded. If the hypothesis is seen, however, not as a free-standing idea but as an integral part of a network of theory, then a wider range of responses becomes available. The apparent disconfirmation will create perturbations throughout the network, like a fly landing on a spider's web. Rather than just cut out the affected bit and leave a hole in the network, we might readjust the significance we give to certain concepts, or realign the logical relations between theoretical statements, so as to preserve the overall network intact in a new configuration which accommodates the fresh understanding. Sandler (1983: 39–41) illustrates this very process with regard to the concept of transference. However, the freedom which the elasticity of concepts allows the analyst is not indiscriminate. Not any and every proposition or theoretical idea can belong to the same network, or the coherent interrelation of concepts would disappear and there would no longer be a network at all. Analysts do have to discover the theory they are preconsciously using, but this does not mean just spotting individual bits of theory as they appear. It means gradually getting to know one's preconscious theoretical network as a whole. Such a network of ideas is too complex to encompass all at one time, and if it is flexible rather than rigid, no single, once-and-for-all description of it could suffice in any case. Gradually coming to delineate it, through the experience of finding and refinding its various elements, is a task that has no end-point.

Thirty years on from Popper's (1934) *The Logic of Scientific Discovery*, Thomas Kuhn's (1962) *The Structure of Scientific Revolutions* was a new landmark in the philosophy of science. Here the central concept is of a scientific 'paradigm'. This refers to a framework of ideas, which scientists agree on as the background to their work. It is the implicit context within which scientific research proceeds. The acceptance of the paradigm is what makes scientific activity possible, and it is not to be questioned, therefore, by those who work within it. If observations appear to conflict with the paradigm, supplementary explanations have to be found, or the meaning of concepts has to be adjusted, and these explanations and adjustments become part of the paradigm. This is exactly the sort of activity that Sandler and Quine were drawing attention to. When this process can no longer be sustained, 'normal science', as Kuhn called it, undergoes a revolution which leads to a new paradigm being accepted. For Kuhn, then, knowledge exists as a framework of ideas that an intellectual community has, albeit tacitly, chosen to accept.

The picture of psychoanalytic theory as consisting of a network of ideas, within which individual propositions have meaning by virtue of their relation to the network as a whole, clearly has more affinity with the notion of a paradigm than with Popper's view of science. But Kuhn's ideas provoked much controversy. An important claim of his was that, when one paradigm displaces another because the scientific community judges that the first can no longer be sustained, there are no reference criteria, external to the paradigms themselves, against which they can both be measured to determine which one is really nearer the truth. Any such independent criterion would simply amount to another view of scientific truth; that is to say, a new alternative paradigm. There was opposition to this claim on the grounds that it reduced science to a matter of subjective preference between theories rather than the rationally based discovery of objective truths. Imre

Lakatos, a leading opponent of Kuhn's views, charged him with 'irrational-ism', saying: 'For Kuhn scientific change – from one "paradigm" to another – is a mystical conversion which is not and cannot be governed by rules of reason' (Lakatos 1974: 93).

Lakatos, while still seeing theory as organised into intellectual structures rather than isolated hypotheses, developed an account aimed at rescuing the rationality of science. He conceived of science as operating according to 'research programmes'. The double function of these organising frame-works was to indicate which avenues were likely to yield advances in know-ledge (the 'positive heuristic'), and to stipulate the 'negative heuristic', which was the set of background assumptions and beliefs implicitly agreed to by the participants in a research programme, which formed a basis for their work. This 'hard core' could not be challenged without abandoning the research programme. Lakatos' own description of it, however, is revealing: 'This "core" is "irrefutable" by the methodological decision of its prot-agonists: anomalies must lead to changes only in the "protective" belt of auxiliary, "observational" hypotheses and initial conditions' (Lakatos 1974: 133). The operative phrase here is 'methodological decision'. The hard core turns out to be privileged against falsification in just the same way as a Kuhnian paradigm during the period of 'normal science'.

Even if we go back to Popper, the arch-rationalist of the philosophy of science, we find him aware of the same difficulty. It is well recognised that theory is not derived purely from observation, because observations them-selves are already dependent on the theory used in making and describing them. As Einstein said to the young Heisenberg: 'It is quite wrong to try founding a theory on observable magnitudes alone. In reality the very opposite happens. It is the theory which decides what we can observe' (Heisenberg 1971: 63). Freud too was aware of the issue.

> Even at the stage of description it is not possible to avoid applying certain abstract ideas to the material in hand, ideas derived from some-where or other but certainly not from the new observations alone. Such ideas – which will later become the basic concepts of the science – are still more indispensable as the material is worked over. . . . we come to an understanding about their meaning by making repeated reference to the material of observation from which they appear to have been derived, but upon which, in fact, they have been imposed.
>
> (Freud 1915a: 117)

Observation statements which go to falsify a hypothesis are just as theory-bound as the supposedly confirmatory observation statements Popper was criticising. All observation statements depend on the theory they carry with them; and since, for Popper, theories are hypotheses which must remain fallible, observation statements also remain fallible. Even for a hypothesis to be falsified, scientists must agree to accept as valid the observations which refute it. Popper (1934: 104) himself wrote: 'Every test of a theory, whether resulting in its corroboration or falsification, must stop at some basic statement or other which we decide to accept'.[5]

Some psychoanalysts emphasise the external, objectively available, aspects of theory that form common, or disputed, ground with colleagues. Others attend more to the private, internal aspects that draw their meaning from personal experience. What this excursion into the philosophy of science demonstrates, though, is that, wherever we locate ourselves in that regard, we cannot view knowledge, even from the most rationalist standpoint, separately from a personal engagement with it.

Such reasoning is sometimes rejected as though it condemns us to an arbitrary subjectivism. For example:

> Pattern-making by the analyst is not required so long as resistances and defences are interpreted in such a way as to allow the intrinsic forces at work in the psychic life of the patient to make themselves known. These forces will determine the pattern as they will determine the transference. The forces in question are the drives, their vicissitudes and their derivatives. The ideas of pattern-making, of theory-bound observation and the like, are rationalisations for counter-transferential resistance to the threats posed by the drives, that is, by the instinctual unconscious.
>
> (Hanly 1990: 379)

But that itself is a very theory-bound observation. It is true, as Charles Hanly goes on to say, that a theory about black holes does not itself necessarily influence the astronomical observations required to test it. But the point is that the observations, whatever their outcome, cannot be made without accepting the particular antecedent theories on which they depend. Of course there are constraints on what theories may legitimately be held, but the notion that truth is properly approached by detached objective evaluation that is independent of personal involvement, is a mistake.

Amongst philosophers of science, Michael Polanyi has recognised this explicitly. In the preface to his book *Personal Knowledge* (Polanyi 1962) he writes as follows:

> I start by rejecting the ideal of scientific detachment. In the exact sciences, this false ideal is perhaps harmless, for it is in fact disregarded there

---

5 It is noteworthy to find Popper implying in this statement that a test of a theory might corroborate it.

by scientists. But we shall see that it exercises a destructive influence in biology, psychology and sociology, and falsifies our whole outlook far beyond the domain of science. I want to establish an alternative ideal of knowledge . . .

I have shown that into every act of knowing there enters a passionate contribution of the person knowing what is being known, and that this coefficient is no mere imperfection but a vital component of his knowledge.

Such is the personal participation of the knower in all acts of understanding. But this does not make our understanding subjective. Comprehension is neither an arbitrary act nor a passive experience, but a responsible act claiming universal validity . . . It seems reasonable to describe this fusion of the personal and the objective as Personal Knowledge.

(Polanyi 1962: vii–viii)

Amongst psychoanalysts, Bion is notable for the connection he makes between psychoanalysis and the philosophy of science.

The failure of patients suffering from disorders of thought is patently within the personality. Psychoanalysis of that failure is impossible without understanding the problem of the philosopher of science and conversely his problem is incompletely stated without the aid of psychoanalytic experience of disorders of thought.

(Bion 1962: 66)

It is significant that Bion described his concept of K[6] as the 'K link'. He was emphasising that knowledge is not a thing that we have, but a link between ourselves and what we know. The parallel he draws with love and hatred, the 'L' and 'H' links, shows knowledge as an activity which develops between the knower and the known, not something to be obtained by a once-and-for-all exercise in fact-finding.

In the sessions I have described I was doing something all analysts do all the time: using theory to try to understand a patient. What the clinical situation demanded of me was to refind the theory I needed with this patient; and that meant, in broader terms, to refind psychoanalysis in this analysis. Analysts need an evolving, interactive relationship with their theories so that, as they discover their patients by listening to and responding to them, they discover their analytic knowledge by listening to and responding to it as well. Psychoanalysis is about both knowing and being. An analyst serves truth not only by trying to see it and point it out to his

6 See Chapter 3, pp. 47–8.

patient, but by embodying it in his relationship to his patient and to his theory. That is what links the analyst to the object of his understanding, which is at once the individual patient and psychoanalysis itself. In this way he may help the patient become the embodiment of his own truth. Psychoanalysis uniquely combines the scientific and the personal. This does not just mean that it is both scientific and personal. Its scientific nature is embedded in its personal nature: it is scientific *only in so far as* it is personal as well.

5

Psychoanalytic and personal identity: the garden of forking paths

We are doomed to choose, and every choice may entail an irreparable loss.
Isaiah Berlin (1990: 13) 'The pursuit of the ideal'

Since the beginning of psychoanalysis there have been attempts to define its uniqueness, either in terms of its difference from psychotherapy, or by claiming some clinical or theoretical criterion, typically the transference neurosis, as specific to it. Neither approach has been very fruitful. Psychoanalytic psychotherapy has evolved over the years, becoming harder to differentiate from analysis. Having once been 'the copper of direct suggestion' as opposed to 'the pure gold of analysis' (Freud 1919a: 168), it is now a non-directive process, generally open-ended, aiming to resolve unconscious conflicts by work in the transference and by analysing resistance: a process which can reasonably lay claim to the essential characteristics of psychoanalysis (Freud 1914c: 16). The transference neurosis, as a criterion of psychoanalysis, has likewise been overtaken by history. In 1954 Merton Gill wrote: 'Psychoanalysis is that treatment which, employed by a neutral analyst, results in the development of a regressive transference neurosis and the ultimate resolution of this neurosis by techniques of interpretation alone' (Gill 1954: 775). The understanding of transference, however, has developed so that what is transferred into the analytic relationship is usually considered nowadays to be not a circumscribed neurosis, but a more global representation of the patient's predicament. Gill himself revised his view (Gill 1984; Wallerstein 1997), and although the regressive transference neurosis remains an important concept, it no longer serves as a touchstone of psychoanalysis (Wallerstein 1995: 245–63).

Attempts to characterise psychoanalysis by its difference from something else, or to claim this or that as a criterion of it, fail to recognise that the identity of a psychoanalyst has a double meaning. What it means to be a psychoanalyst cannot be isolated from how an individual analyst's identity is achieved, through a process of becoming that is unique to that analyst. Milner's exploration and pursuit of her personal and analytic identity, described in Chapter 2, reveal the work that may go into this. Her account also suggests that what most distinguishes the identity of a psychoanalyst is the relationship that the analyst develops with his or her own unconscious.

A patient starts a session by saying he feels cow-like, with nothing to talk about. He just wants to lie there and be comfortable. He feels he can unwind. He knows he does not have to entertain me or produce material for my benefit. His sense of pleasure and relaxation as he says this is unmistakable. I have the thought that a historical transference interpretation might be helpful, about how the chance of enjoying such an atmosphere with his parents was blocked because he felt he always had to consider their needs. But the interpretation might itself feel like my needing something from him – insight or understanding – and break the atmosphere, replicating the situation with his parents. (This would itself be part of the transference, of course, but I do not want to interpret myself as a demanding parent just when he is exploring a different experience.) It is early in the session and I simply wait. He says, out of silence: 'Two active minds . . . in companionable silence . . . with no upsets.' I like the phrase and find myself thinking of an almost blank canvas, with an ambiguous but satisfying design placed somewhere off centre in it. Should I say anything about that? Probably not. It is very much my association and may be irrelevant, or self-indulgent on my part. But it doesn't go away. I let it stay around and somehow it goes on seeming true. Eventually I say: 'That sounds like the title of an abstract painting.' He laughs a bit and so do I. The silence goes on. Suddenly I realise I can say: 'But I don't suppose abstract art would have had much place in your family.' 'My God, no!', he replies. More silence. Then he says: 'Each single element in what I said was impossible. Our minds weren't active, silence was never companionable, there were never no upsets.' More silence, intensely aware. The interpretation was making itself without breaking the experience of the session.

What seems to make such a piece of work possible is the analyst's ability to rely on his unconscious. This permits him to entrust himself and the patient to unconscious elements in the analytic process between them. But this vignette could be differently perceived. I am presenting it as showing how, without a transference interpretation having to be spelt out, the analyst's preparedness to trust in the unconscious processes between him and his patient, helped the patient discover that his feeling in the session contained an awareness of something that had been lacking between him and his parents. Some colleagues have thought that my account of this episode sounds rather too comfortable, and that it might be the collusive setting up of patient and analyst as a couple who can admire themselves in contrast to the bad parents. How to respond to this? It is not a matter of evidence.

No further evidence, for either view, is available. There is only what happened, described as truly as I can. Even if this were part of an extended clinical description, it would still be only that, a description, and the reader would be left to accept it or not. It comes down to this. In presenting the vignette, I can do no more than invite the reader to trust my sense of what was happening; that is, to trust the processes of my unconscious. Any clinical presentation, however brief or elaborate, poses the same question. If the reader or listener has the sense of being in contact with a mind whose unconscious processes can be trusted, he may be willing to accept the account. If not, he will not. What is at issue, therefore, between author and reader in such a description, is just what is at issue in the clinical moment itself. Accepting the work as having a truly analytic quality depends on trusting the author-analyst's unconscious.

The relation to one's own unconscious is so profound and inward that making it central, as I am suggesting, to the analyst's analytic identity, puts a sharper edge on some familiar themes. With regard to countertransference, for example, it underlines how important it is not to lose touch, alongside more recent views of it, with the classical concept. If 'who we are' expresses itself in the 'how we work' of analysis, it becomes all the more crucially important that the analyst's individuality should be subject to a well-analysed awareness, so that whatever influence it has on his clinical practice is as open as possible to his monitoring and control. On the other hand psychoanalysis, above all things, declares that whatever we do is shaped out of the depths of our personalities which, however well analysed, remain unconscious, never fully predictable or controllable. This is as true for analysis itself as for anything else. The unplumbable navel of the unconscious, that which is both ourselves and strange to us, is not to be analysed away. This view of analytic identity, at the same time as emphasising the necessity for self-knowledge in the analyst, gives central place to exactly the thing which makes that most problematic. The patient needs an implicit sense that the analyst's subjectivity does not contaminate his therapeutic method and, at the same time, that he is working personally and authentically out of his own true nature.

If only the analyst could *know* that what emerges from him or her will be therapeutic, benign, good for the patient! If only the reader could be sure, when he hears that the patient and I both laughed, that I was not being drawn into some collusive identification! Because the unconscious is truly unplumbable, however, neither analyst nor reader can ever be certain. Psychoanalysis can never stop being an act of trust in the unconscious. And that means, however well-analysed the unconscious, however experienced the analyst, a constant willingness to mistrust ourselves.

The judgements that this calls for, over and over again, are very difficult. But, more than that, it entails complex and knotty questions about what *kinds* of judgement are at issue. In 1952–3 there was disagreement in the Paris Psychoanalytical Society about the function of its newly formed training institute. Some thought training should be loosely structured to facilitate the development of those who had committed themselves to a certain way of listening to people. That self-commitment, it was believed, was the essence of what made someone an analyst. Others thought training should be organised towards certification of trainees as having achieved suffi-cient knowledge of, and practical ability in, psychoanalysis, and having progressed sufficiently in their own personal analyses. What makes someone an analyst, according to this view, is that evaluation, carried out by others. These different attitudes to training continue, as Anne-Marie Sandler (1982) has illustrated by comparing 'open' institutes, such as the French, Paris and Swiss, with 'closed' ones like the British, Finnish, Spanish and Australian.

For Lacan, at that time a member of the Paris Society, to be a psycho-analyst was a matter of self-determination and not something that could be externally conferred by a committee or training organisation.[1] In his under-standing, becoming a psychoanalyst involved an inner change in how one perceived oneself, by which one moved from the position of analysand to that of analyst. Being at odds over this with the institutional structures of the Paris Society, Lacan resigned from it and started his own organisation: first the French Psychoanalytical Society, then the Freudian School of Paris. This did not, however, solve the problem. Lacan took a most serious view of this internal act of choosing a vocation, and was determined to hold to the position that being an analyst was a self-authenticating expression of the analyst's being. But if the organisation were to have any boundaries or structure at all, there had to be some way of monitoring when a claim to be a psychoanalyst was indeed authentic and when the choice was superficial or self-deceiving. Even raising that question might seem to undermine the principle of self-determination but, short of institutional anarchy, it could not be avoided.

Lacan never resolved this issue and in the end it was instrumental in the break-up of the Freudian School; but his attempt was heroic. It is also very instructive. Two grades of analyst were recognised in the organisation: *Analystes Membres de l'Ecole* who were simply practitioners, and *Analystes de l'Ecole* who were recognised as capable, in addition, of making a theoretical contribution. The problem crystallised around how one moved from the first of these grades to the second. Being determined to avoid institutional ranks and certification, Lacan replaced the idea of hierarchy with that of *gradus* which referred to the analyst's inward awareness of his psychoanalytic

---

1 This view of Lacan's, and its connection with Rank's view of the creative artist, is also mentioned in Chapter 1 (p. 16).

level. The move from *Analyste Membre de l'Ecole* to *Analyste de l'Ecole* was intended as a change in *gradus*, not in institutional status. It was to be confirmed by a procedure known as the 'pass', *la passe* (Roudinesco 1986: 443–61). Someone aspiring to the grade of *Analyste de l'Ecole* would present a testimony about their experience in analysis to two colleagues who were recognised as *passeurs*. They would transmit that testimony to a panel of existing *Analystes de l'Ecole*, who would in turn decide for or against the analyst's being recognised as an *Analyste de l'Ecole*. This procedure was an attempt to insist that, rather than promotion in an institutional hierarchy, the move was a shift of internal analytic identity which had nevertheless to be validated by colleagues. The validation was to avoid the risk of introducing dubious people into central positions of influence. That in itself, however, put a question-mark against the idea of self-authentication, and there was no getting round the fact that external validation was the very thing which Lacan had been trying to avoid. It was pointed out that the *passe* which changed the analyst was a passage from one inner state to another, while the *passe* which recognised the new status was a formalised external procedure. This shift in meaning undermined the principle at stake. There was also the question of who should be able to act as *passeur*. The proposed procedure did not seem to take into account that to be a *passeur* was a powerful position in an institutional hierarchy! The proposal turned out, in all these ways, to be self-defeating.

The problems with it arose, however, and this is why it is both heroic and instructive, because Lacan had a vision on which he would not compromise, of what it means to be a psychoanalyst. He also saw that the question of the authenticity of psychoanalytic experience, and the implications of that for analytic training, had to be addressed. I do not think the failure to incorporate his view of the identity of an analyst into the procedures of the Freudian School was because his scheme was poorly designed or not properly implemented. It may be impossible to incorporate this aspect of psychoanalysis into institutional categories or formal training procedures. If the heart of an analyst's identity is a certain kind of inwardness, what matters for a training institution is to set up the conditions which foster its development, to work as hard as possible at maintaining those conditions, and then to trust the results, knowing that they will be imperfect.

To think this makes formal training procedures less important, however, would be to sacrifice one aspect of psychoanalysis to another. A training needs to teach a level of theoretical knowledge and clinical skill such that the analyst who has completed it will be competent and safe. It is exceedingly important that an analyst should not qualify without that being the case and it can, within reasonable limits, be examined and certified. A training organisation should also seek, however, to keep itself open to what is mysterious in psychoanalysis, generating an atmosphere that will nourish the individuality and creativity of its students. Otto Kernberg's (1996) satire on the ways in which organisations can do exactly the opposite makes painfully ironic reading. An institute can be as demanding in its requirements of students, and as cautious about the accreditation of supervisors and training analysts, as it sees fit. But the purpose of any such conservatism should be to protect a space in which students may begin, unpredictably, to discover the analysts they are going to become. The framework of a session does not of itself make psychoanalysis happen. It creates a space in which analytic exploration is possible. In the same way the framework of a training is there, not because it automatically turns a student into an analyst, but to maintain a safe and reliable space for the possible development of analytic identities.

Qualifying as an analyst is only the start of becoming one, as Milner's 50-year odyssey illustrates. Klauber had something similar to say about the patient's experience.

> I try to base my own technique on one cardinal assumption. That is that psychoanalysis is a long process in which what happens after the patient has left the psychoanalyst's consulting room for the last time is more important than what happens during the analysis.

> We have long- and short-term aims in psychoanalysis. The short-term aim is to relieve the anxieties and conflicts which the patient keeps in the forefront of the analysis. The long-term aim is to foster his development by means of a process, started in the consulting room, which will help him in the much longer period of his life after he has left the consulting room for the last time.

> (Klauber 1981: xvi, 110)

For patients and analysts alike, the analysis and the training, which may appear to be formative experiences, exist in the context of a longer process of development.

Klauber, like Milner, allows us to observe in his writing the evolution of an analytic identity (Klauber 1981; all subsequent page references to Klauber refer to this book). He wrote two papers on interpretation: 'The structure of the session as a guide to interpretation' in 1961 and, in 1979, 'Formulating interpretations in clinical psychoanalysis' (77–90, 109–120). When he wrote the first, he says, 'I had been a full-time psychoanalyst for more than eight years, and all I had achieved was a certain mastery of basic technique' (xix). Eighteen years later his second paper describes 'the mode of operation of the analyst who has achieved a secure identity' (109). As a pair, they show clearly how Klauber's development as an analyst was connected to his increasing ability to trust his unconscious processes.

The first paper advocates disciplined understanding as an antidote to 'subjectivism' (xviii). Klauber offers a scheme for structuring the material of a session. First he scans it for transference references. Next he asks himself what is the predominant anxiety being expressed, and then what defences that anxiety is stimulating. Finally, at the point of maximal defensiveness, he looks for the underlying wish. This formal scheme is intended to protect the analyst against 'contamination with his patient's emotion' (90). To this end he encourages 'the operation of the analyst's ego as a means of ordering the mass of free association' (77), and the sense of material being ordered is indeed what permeates the paper. The second paper is in a different register. Here Klauber writes, as quoted above, of the analyst's concern that the process begun in the analysis should continue during the rest of the patient's life (110). That process 'is mediated by the person of the analyst' (111). The change from 'the analyst's ego' to 'the person of the analyst' is significant, and the emphasis on ordering has disappeared. Klauber has become more like the analyst described by Enid Balint (1993: 166) 'who can tolerate the absence of a consistent story for a time, and use the muddle'.

Throughout both papers Klauber is concerned to balance rigour and freedom, emphasising now one, now the other. While he begins the first paper by offering 'a typical structure for the psychoanalytic session' (78), he immediately notes that analysts also rely on intuition. He says he does not want to work like a computer, but then comments that Freud's advice about free-floating attention is not 'a veto against the exercise of the intellectual functions' (78). In the second paper he affirms the analyst's spontaneous creativity and individuality, but only if it is underpinned by theoretical understanding and craftsmanlike 'matching' of the material to its meaning. The passage quoted in Chapter 1 (p. 20) about 'interpretations that present themselves to the analyst spontaneously' is followed by a caution that the analyst should 'wait until he has carried the careful process of matching to a stage at which he finds that he can interpret spontaneously, free of any feeling that he is carrying out a wild analysis' (116–17).

None the less, the overall difference between the ordering of the first paper and the spontaneity of the second remains striking. In the second paper, the person of the analyst has

> strengths and weaknesses, which may facilitate or disrupt the patient's ability to internalise the [analytic] function, just as the mothering function is mediated by the personality of the mothering person. What this paper is concerned with is the way in which the formulation of interpretations can foster such an internalisation of the analytic function and the way in which it can set up barriers against it.
>
> (Klauber 1981: 111)

This is a more open, more vulnerable conception of interpretation than the controlled, protective view of it in the first paper, and the dialectic between the two expresses the polarity inherent in psychoanalysis. The first paper is about the craft of analysis, about how the analyst works. The second is about who the analyst is. Klauber repeatedly asserts in the second paper that the human quality of the analyst's spontaneity, which detraumatises the analytic process and allows it to work, rests on a recognition of the patient's values. Impulses are amalgamated, he says, with fantasies, feelings and values,[2] and value systems are degraded if they are interpreted simply as defensive structures. 'It is in the interpretation of the values of the ego that the wisdom, humanity and freedom of thought of psychoanalysis are largely experienced' (119). The analyst's art, and not just his craft, resides, for Klauber, in this recognition of, and respect for, the patient's values. It calls for a particular kind of openness in the analyst, to which, with hindsight, one can see a clue in the first paper. Klauber states there that symptoms are 'a condensed and exacerbated version of the conflicts latent in the character', so that 'each patient repeats in every session something of his own life history' (88). What Klauber says of the patient may be applied to the analyst as well. We have already encountered Wright's idea of psychoanalytic theory as autobiography, and Green's related comment on himself (p. 52). Every session, for both patient and analyst, is, in this respect, a fragment of a hologram. In every session the analyst expresses, in the theory he makes use of, the person that he has become. If the analyst is open to this awareness, that how he works is who he is, then his interpretations will not be just the application of certain theories to certain sorts of material, but will express the interaction of two life-paradigms with their impulses, fantasies, feelings and values on both sides.

Bion is another analyst who lets us see his younger and older analytic selves side by side. *Second Thoughts* (Bion 1967) contains papers dating from 1950 to 1962, followed by a commentary giving Bion's current thoughts about his earlier work. 'The imaginary twin' is the most extended, detailed clinical account in Bion's writings. It is also the earliest paper, separated from its commentary by about the same distance in time as Klauber's two papers on interpretation. In 1950 Bion is applying theory to the patient's material in order to arrive at interpretations, while by 1967 he too is questioning the assumptions about the nature of interpretation which lay behind his earlier way of working. At one point in the commentary he says: 'in my opinion the interpretation was a good one – "correct" as I would then have said' (Bion 1967: 128). More explicitly he writes of 'the futility of comparing association with interpretation. Associations are infinite in number and so are interpretations; it is therefore idle to discuss matching the one to

2 The passage in question is quoted in Chapter 11 (pp. 189–90).

the other' (1967: 133). Bion and Klauber came to different views of matching. Bion seems keen, at least in this passage, to leave it behind altogether, while Klauber kept an important place for it. Both of them, however, having found in the process of matching an initial basis for interpretation, needed to move beyond it towards something more rooted in their unconscious perceptions.

For Bion, the important shift was away from systematic interpretation to the intuitive perception of what he called an 'evolution'. In discussing two paragraphs, 15 and 16, of the original paper, he says:

> The description in 16 cannot 'evolve' anything now as the description in 15 can. I do not attribute this to the inferior quality of 16 but to a difference in kind in the nature of the two formulations. I find myself unable to be impressed either with the truth or falsity of the interpretation. With 15 I experience an 'evolution' of emotional experience now; with 16 I experience nothing but a sense of manipulation of theories.
>
> (Bion 1967: 128–9)

He describes 'evolution' as

> the coming together, by a sudden precipitating intuition, of a mass of apparently unrelated incoherent phenomena which are thereby given coherence and meaning not previously possessed . . . From the material the patient produces there emerges, like the pattern from a kaleidoscope, a configuration which seems to belong not only to the situation unfolding, but to a number of others not previously seen to be connected and which it has not been designed to connect.
>
> (Bion 1967: 127)

The moment in the clinical material of Chapter 3, when 'shapes which I was already looking at seemed to declare themselves . . .' (p. 45), fits this description. The important thing for Bion was that such experiences should not be obstructed by the manipulation of theories.

Guntrip's comment (p. 12) on how naturally Winnicott's personality expressed itself in his clinical work, and Milner's cross-referencing between personal experience and psychoanalytic ideas, have already been noted. The relationship between Freud's personal and analytic identities was complicated. He had a strong natural bent for abstract speculation which was at odds both with his empirical stance as a scientist and, to an extent, with his therapeutic role of caring for individuals. Luciana Nissim Momigliano (1992: 1–32) and Beate Lohser and Peter Newton (1996) have surveyed the accounts of those who were analysed by him. These show that he was undoubtedly at ease in the consulting room, and his clinical work was clearly, in many respects, a natural expression of his personality.[3] Nissim Momigliano quotes Abraham Kardiner's (1977) statement that 'One could not tell from his behaviour in the office what a real giant he was, because he was unassuming and quite natural.' She also refers, however, to Kardiner's questioning Freud about what he thought of himself as an analyst. Freud replied:

> I'm glad you ask, because, frankly, I have no great interest in therapeutic problems. I am much too impatient now. I have several handicaps that disqualify me as a great analyst. One of them is that I am too much the father. Second, I am much too much occupied with theoretical problems all the time, so that whenever I get occasion, I am working on my own theoretical problems, rather than paying attention to the therapeutic problems. Third, I have no patience in keeping people for a long time. I tire of them and I want to spread my influence.
>
> (Nissim Momigliano 1992: 8, quoting Kardiner 1977)

Freud said elsewhere that his inclination was more for discovering things than for relieving suffering. 'Neither at that time [at school], nor indeed in my later life, did I feel any particular predilection for the career of a doctor' (Freud 1925d: 8). 'I have no knowledge of having had in my early years any craving to help suffering humanity' (Freud 1927: 253).

He wrote to Fliess in 1896: 'As a young man I knew no longing other than for philosophical knowledge, and now I am about to fulfil it as I move from medicine to psychology' (Masson 1985: 180). Peter Gay (1988: 119) explains that '*his* [Freud's] philosophy was scientific empiricism, as embodied in a scientific theory of the mind'. But it was not scientific empiricism that made him, as a medical student, go to lectures on Aristotle by Brentano, with whom there was enough of a connection for Brentano to recommend him as a translator (Jones 1954: 41–2, 61). There is also Jones' statement:

> Wittels has made the shrewd suggestion that Freud was perhaps one of those whose bent towards speculative abstractions is so powerful that he is afraid of being mastered by it and feels it necessary to counter it by studying concrete scientific data. This is confirmed by a reply Freud once made to my question of how much philosophy he had read. The

3 Questions of Freud's clinical technique, and of how it reflected his personality, are much debated. Their complexity is revealed in the exchange of letters between Lohser and Newton, and George Makari who reviewed their book in the *International Journal of Psycho-Analysis* (Newton and Lohser 1998; Makari 1998). See also Chapter 9 (pp. 146ff.).

answer was: 'Very little. As a young man I felt a strong attraction towards speculation and ruthlessly checked it'.

(Jones 1954: 32)

And not just as a young man, for Freud (1925d: 57) also wrote: 'In the works of my later years . . . I have given free rein to the inclination, which I have kept down for so long, to speculation.' Not long before his death he was writing to Marie Bonaparte of 'a certain aversion to my subjective tendency of granting the imagination too free a rein' (Freud 1961: 451). Phrases like 'ruthlessly checked' and 'which I have kept down for so long' show that this speculative aspect of his nature was not easily set aside, and the references to philosophy throughout his writings demonstrate his conflict. He has no shortage of jibes against it (Freud 1916–17: 97–8, 1918: 105–6, 1933: 165–6), but in other passages his engagement with it is evident (Freud 1913b: 178–9, 1925a: 216–17, 1940: 158–9). While never conceding that philosophy has any useful contribution to make, Freud none the less enters into serious dialogue with it.

Just how variously the analyst's identity can function as an expression of his being is shown by comparing Freud with Rank and Ferenczi. The book written by the latter two (Ferenczi and Rank 1925) has, as one of its themes, the relation between theory and practice. But although Chapter 4, for example, is called 'The reciprocal effect of theory and practice', the constant tendency in that chapter, and throughout the book, is to see them as being in conflict.

In a young science, in a state of development such as psychoanalysis was, one could find it justifiable that the analytic practitioner was able to combine the two tasks of healing and research, as Freud himself did in such an exemplary way. One can readily understand, however, that the attempt to follow this example frequently led more to a mixing up of these tasks than to their combination. The theoretic analyst always runs the danger of looking, for example, for arguments to prove the correctness of a new statement, while he thinks that he is promoting the process of curing a neurosis.

(Ferenczi and Rank 1925: 51–2)

Freud's remarks to Kardiner show that he was aware of this conflict in his own work. There is no doubt where Ferenczi and Rank's priorities lie. They comment on 'a state of increasing confusion . . . among psychoanalysts' because 'the technical and therapeutic factor, which was originally the heart of the matter and the actual stimulus to every important advance in the theory, has been strikingly neglected' (1925: 2). Later they write of 'the disastrous mistake of neglecting the actual task for the sake of the psychological interest' (1925: 24–5). For Freud the therapeutic factor, although of course important, was not the heart of the matter. The psychological interest *was* the actual task.

The last words quoted are from a paragraph which anticipates by decades what has come to be an important element in present-day analytic technique. Ferenczi and Rank counsel against over-interpreting the detailed content of the material, saying that 'the associations are often only brought forward by the patient for some purpose and this must then be made conscious to the patient instead of losing oneself in the details of interpreting single associations' (1925: 24). Similarly with dreams, one must take out of them 'what corresponds in importance to the analytic situation' (1925: 24). They emphasise that the patient uses associations not only to communicate with the analyst, but also to do something to him, and that this may be what needs to be interpreted. While stressing the importance of understanding the analytic situation as a whole, they also warn against 'interpreting every expression of the patient above all as a reaction to the present analytical situation' (1925: 25). They are not generally given the credit they deserve for emphasising these aspects of technique as early as they did.

Such clinical understanding belonged to people whose psychoanalytic vocation was by nature a therapeutic one. Ferenczi's clinical experiments, mistaken as he himself discovered them to be, grew out of his wish to widen the therapeutic potential of psychoanalysis. This therapeutic impulse, and the way that he did not 'ruthlessly check' his own gift for speculation, show how differently from Freud he perceived his identity as a psychoanalyst. For both Ferenczi and Freud, to be an analyst was an expression of their being; but different expressions of different beings.

In Chapter 1 psychoanalysis was described as 'the uniquely appropriate choice by which the analyst expresses who he is' (p. 15). A crucial word here is 'choice'. This does not, of course, only mean conscious decision-making. When Freud speaks of checking his attraction for philosophy, and keeping down his inclination towards speculation, he may appear to present these as matters of conscious choice. It is true that his scientific training gave him a specific, anti-speculative commitment to empiricism. But his criticisms of philosophy are not just statements of intellectual ideology. They are one side of a lifelong struggle between fundamental aspects of his personality. The particular psychoanalyst that any one analyst arrives at being is the result of a multitude of conscious, preconscious and unconscious choices. In every analyst's development there are nodal points, and how a person chooses to negotiate them forms the unique, individual path leading to the analyst that, years down the road from qualifying, he or she may have become.

This is no more than the reflection in a particular situation of the process by which all human beings arrive at their identities. The clinical material described in Chapter 4 brought home that we arrive at being the people we are by 'passing in more or less orderly fashion through a series of developmental experiences which evolve one out of the other' (p. 58). To think of the infant making developmental choices would seem strange if choosing did only mean conscious decision-making. But the infant's choices, like Freud's against lending himself to philosophical speculation, express an internal process. The people we know as ourselves are the outcome of our unique responses to experience that our adult imaginations can no longer properly encompass. The processes of maturation are always facing an infant with fresh conflicts and fresh options. Psychoanalytic conceptualisations of development are cumulative accounts of how individual infants find their own particular solutions to this sequence of challenges.

All of us are confronted with the fact of not being, and not being able to be, the people we might wish. Fully to accept who we are not, involves psychic work in two directions, which both require a capacity for bearing loss, for mourning and for separation.

It was noted in Chapter 3 (p. 43) how hard it is for patients to face giving up aspects of themselves which are the best ways of being they have known so far. Freud said of the Wolf-Man:

> Any position of the libido which he had once taken up was obstinately defended by him from fear of what he would lose by giving it up and from distrust of the probability of a complete substitute being offered by the new position that was in view.
>
> (Freud 1918: 115)

All development, not just in the work of analysis, poses that same challenge of leaving known and familiar satisfactions behind, for something perhaps more evolved, but unknown and uncertain. This relinquishing would be impossible without a trust in whatever process is carrying us towards the people, at that stage unknown, that we shall one day become. Trust need not be conscious. The infant is not thinking to itself: 'I don't know who I'm becoming but there's a process here I have confidence in.' Successful progress through the pathways of development does nevertheless call for the infant to have a kind of trust in its own processes. Janine Chasseguet-Smirgel comments, on the passage about the Wolf-Man just quoted:

> Perhaps one can understand this difficulty in giving up one phase of development for a new one, this libidinal inertia, at least in part, as being linked to early deficiencies which prevented the child (the future

Wolf-Man) from cathecting his *development* as such, in which the projection 'before him' of his ego-ideal plays an important role. Each new acquisition is always accompanied by the (at least partial) loss of the object and 'way of being' of the preceding phase and hence implies some mourning.

(Chasseguet-Smirgel 1985: 30–1)

Freud (1923: 29) wrote that it was 'possible to suppose that the character of the ego is a precipitate of abandoned object-cathexes and that it contains the history of those object choices'. What he did not bring out, though, in that famous passage, is the psychic work that has to go into the abandoning of the previous object-choices.

A mother's trust in her unconscious processes, out of which she cares for the baby, is probably what most helps the infant cathect its development, and find a similar unconscious reliance on its own processes. This is what Winnicott was talking about to Guntrip when he said 'You know about "being active", but not about "just growing, just breathing" ' (Guntrip 1975: 152). This trust is central to personal identity of any sort, including an analyst's analytic identity. As with the infant's mother, the analyst's confidence in his unconscious helps the patient towards a trust in his own, that can allow him to re-cathect his development. The journey is never concluded. There is no terminus to arrive at. Becoming who one is, as with arriving at a psychoanalytic identity, is a lifelong process. Accepting who we are not is an important kind of stability to attain, but the only finality is in who we shall have been.

What, though, about the paths that we did not follow? The particular way an infant chooses of managing a stage of development is an implicit renunciation of other potential ways forward. The depressive position, for example, is not single and homogeneous, as though all infants who move into it from the paranoid–schizoid position are taking the same step, leading to the same outcome. Individual infants experience concern for the object in all sorts of different ways, and will handle their wish not to damage it and their guilt when they do, in certain ways and not in others. Alongside the mourning for what is left behind, potential ways forward that we do not take are lost to us as well. Arriving at who we are means that there are also all those people we might have arrived at being but did not. There is a genre of science fiction story where the hero encounters another version of himself, and it turns out that there is a parallel world, or maybe several parallel worlds, where slight but crucial changes in events are amplified to produce major differences in how a character's life develops. John Wyndham's (1956) 'Opposite Number' is a classic example, and the film *Sliding Doors* (1998) a more recent one. The developmental universe consists of parallel worlds, and the growing infant inhabits the one amongst them that the pathways he chose have led him into.

82

How do we relate to the inhabitants of our parallel worlds? There are people who, whether or not we are conscious of it, represent to us what we might have become if, at certain points in our development, we had made different choices. Those people are, in a particular way, who we are not. The second aspect of the psychic work of accepting who we are not, means discovering how not to fear or envy these alternate selves, but to be grateful for their existence.

Euripides' *Bacchae*, one of the plays to be considered in the next chapter, shows in the character of Pentheus a person dominated by prejudice which ultimately breaks down into madness. The view of development put forward here may help to understand such a situation. It emphasises that prejudice arises on the basis of developmental experience that is universal. Each one of us has arrived at being who we are by the route we have taken through a garden of forking paths, to borrow an image from a remarkable 'parallel worlds' story by Borges (1962), and for all of us there are the people that we did not arrive at being. Our identities are formed around the relation between the people that we are and those that we are not. If we have not been sufficiently able to trust our own developmental processes we may be left with an unconscious sense of doubt about who we are, haunted by ghosts of the selves we did not become. Amongst our various anti-identities, many do not matter that much. But there are some that, for whatever reason, keep an intense unconscious cathexis. Perhaps the potential they represent was especially painful to give up; or it may have been particularly important *not* to arrive at being them. If one of those turns out to exist, that will test how securely we have succeeded in being ourselves.

The science fiction reference suggests a break in the order of reality, and that is indeed what underlies prejudice. The defence mechanisms most importantly at work in it are splitting and projection. They deal with intrapsychic conflict not by addressing it, but by sidestepping it. Splitting works by separating aspects of oneself so absolutely that one side of the split is obliterated, and the question of conflict does not arise, while projection simply expels the internal antagonist from the field. Certain people respond, to the tension between who they are and who they are not, predominantly in these ways. Winnicott (1956) likened the mother's absolute preoccupation with her baby to a 'normal illness' in its detachment from external reality. Freud (1917) pointed out that the same thing is happening in bereavement, at an unconscious level, as in depression. In this sense mourning is a 'normal' depressive illness. Prejudice can be seen as another example of a 'normal illness', provoked by an intolerable exposure to variety and difference. What characterises prejudice is not that a prejudiced belief is necessarily false, but the way that the belief is held. Even if it happens to be true, that is incidental to the prejudiced state of mind. If the belief is false, rationally demonstrating its falsity does not change the prejudice. The crucial element is a break in the perception of reality, which suggests that prejudice can be understood as a 'normal psychosis'. If, in characters whose prejudice is extreme, the splitting and projection fail, and 'who they are not' refuses to be expelled or obliterated, there is a risk of the normal psychosis developing into a psychotic breakdown.

Inability to bear variety and difference may be acted out in society, as minorities know only too well. The next chapter will show, for example, how Pentheus' need to suppress diversity within himself is reflected in his oppression of a religious minority. Bion's (1961) analysis of collective states of mind in groups reveals how social attacks on diversity may develop. The 'work group' accepts differences between its members and explores them in a way that leads to psychological development for its individual members and for the group as a whole. But the group may fall into a different condition, operating by one or other of what Bion called 'basic assumptions'. He described three versions of this: the 'dependency', 'pairing' and 'fight–flight' groups. Under these conditions groups show hatred for new ideas, a corresponding avoidance of developmental process, and a tendency to obstruct any expression of difference between group members. Individuality is undermined and the only acceptable thoughts or behaviour become those that conform to the prevailing basic assumption (Caper 1975).

At the extreme, a totalitarian regime cannot tolerate any kind of self-determination, and sets out to destroy the very concept of individual identity. Systematic assaults of this kind on individuality are described in Robert Jay Lifton's (1961) study of the 'thought reform' programme in the People's Republic of China, and in Bruno Bettelheim's (1961) account of Nazi concentration camps. The Chinese thought reform camps had the specific purpose of altering the patterns of thinking of political opponents of the regime. They also shared with the concentration camps the general aims of disintegrating the personalities of their inmates, and of destroying the concept of individuality, not only in external, social terms but within the minds of the inmates. In both instances, that is to say, the aim was to undo the developmental choices which those people had made their own.[4]

The suppression of difference between individuals is linked with suppression of difference within the person. Developmental processes depend on the interaction of different areas of the mind. Lifton describes how in all sorts of ways the external environment in the thought reform camps was manipulated so as to subvert the individual's mental structures, always pushing the internal world towards de-differentiation.

---

4 In his account Bettelheim is not dealing primarily with the use of the camps for genocide, but with their function of destroying political opposition to the Nazi regime.

A prime element in this process was the subordination of experience to the claims of doctrine. The varieties of individual human experience were devalued in favour of a simplistic, homogeneous view of human nature, making developmental choice a meaningless idea. Communication with the world outside the prison camp was cut off. Any opportunity to debate, to consider, to make one's own judgements, was removed. Internally, this reduces communication between different parts of the mind. The ego receives input from the id, the superego and the outside world, and has to judge how to balance their conflicting demands (Freud 1923: 56). But in an environment where debate and judgement have no meaning, internal debate and judgement lose their meaning too.

Subjects were manipulated in bizarre ways to provoke self-punitive patterns of thought and feeling, which were then made to appear normal. A Dutch priest who had been kept continuously in a cell for 18 months was surprised, when he returned to Holland, to find that people found this cruel. He had thought it was ordinary. Analysts know the internal equivalent only too well, when people take for granted something that constricts and damages them, not recognising that it represents a cruel internalised figure which they have come to accept as part of themselves.

The environment of the thought reform camps was deliberately polarised. All thoughts, feelings and actions were treated as either absolutely good, if they conformed to ideology, or else absolutely bad. Any deviation from perfect conformity was enough to categorise something as totally bad. Such an external environment reduces the internal world also to a primitive level of functioning, similarly organised around idealisation and persecution, and dominated by paranoid–schizoid mechanisms. Linked to this was the cult of confession. In the totalist world there is a horror of inwardness; everything must be revealed. Since the implication of confession is guilt, this means that everything, by virtue of being revealed, denounces itself as bad. The individual is polarised into a totally bad object, set against the ideal perfection of the regime.

Bettelheim also emphasises how the concentration camp environment forced prisoners, in the crudest possible ways, into situations of regression, abolishing the meaning for them of individual existence. His version of the methodology for inducing personalities to disintegrate corresponds closely to Lifton's, despite the differences in the two situations. Bettelheim's description is remarkable for being written from personal experience.[5] He was himself imprisoned in Dachau and Buchenwald, where he made use of his psychoanalytic awareness consciously to resist the disintegration of his

5 For a firsthand report of life in a Chinese thought reform camp, which agrees closely with Lifton's account, see Bao Ruo-Wang and Rudolph Chelminski (1976).

own personality. The ways he found for doing this can be seen as counter-acting just those sorts of manipulation described by Lifton. Bettelheim would, for example, deliberately look for things in his surroundings that could interest him. He made himself curious about his fellow-inmates' reactions. He tried to maintain his external environment, however night-marish it might be, as something that could be thought about. It was specially important for him that he found two other prisoners who wanted to do the same, and the three would discuss their observations together (Bettelheim 1961: 117–18). This was a strategy for keeping the outside world differentiated, in order to go on being able to debate with himself and form judgements, and thus to maintain the differentiation of his inter-nal world. One thing, which Bettelheim calls 'the last human freedom', had an absolute significance for psychic survival.

> But to survive as a man not a walking corpse, as a debased and degraded but still human being, one had first and foremost to remain informed and aware of what made up one's personal point of no return, the point beyond which one would never, under any circumstance, give in to the oppressor, even if it meant risking and losing one's life.
>
> (Bettelheim 1961: 157)

A person who can hold on to that is maintaining an essential truth – the truth of having made choices about what kind of person he or she should become.

The totalist milieu is a social enactment of the psychosis underlying prejudiced states of mind. Externally and internally, basic assumptions have to be maintained at all costs. To question them is not an act of scientific curiosity or an exploration to be valued, but an attack on received truth. Assumptions are defended not by the reality-testing and comparisons that belong to secondary process, but by absolute authority and the inability of primary process to comprehend difference. Parallel worlds are not conceiv-able. Instead of identity being formed by conscious and unconscious choices which progressively differentiate the individual, it is obliterated by a re-versal of that process, a forced retreat through the garden of forking paths.

Part II
Loss, acceptance, creativity

Above all, do not deceive yourself, do not say
it was a dream, your hearing was mistaken:
do not condescend to such vain hopes as these.
Like one for long prepared, like a courageous man,
as it becomes you who have had the honour of such a city,
go firmly to the window
and listen, with feeling but not
with a coward's supplication and complaint –
listen as the final enjoyment to the music,
to the exquisite instruments of the mysterious company,
and say good-bye to her, to the Alexandria you are losing.

C.P. Cavafy (1911)
from 'The god abandons Antony'

I have come into the hour of a white healing.
Grief's surgery is over and I wear
The scar of my remorse and of my feeling.

I have come into a sudden sunlit hour
When ghosts are scared to corners. I have come
Into the time when grief begins to flower

Into a new love. It had filled my room
Long before I recognised it. Now
I speak its name. Grief finds its good way home.

Elizabeth Jennings (1980)
from 'Into the hour'

6

Self-knowledge refused and accepted: Euripides' *Bacchae* and Sophocles' *Oedipus at Colonus*[1]

Ere Babylon was dust,
The Magus Zoroaster, my dead child,
Met his own image walking in the garden.
Shelley *Prometheus Unbound*, Act I: 191–3

Bacchae and *Oedipus at Colonus* are among the masterpieces of Greek tragedy. *Oedipus at Colonus* dates from 408/7 BC, near the end of Sophocles' life, while *Bacchae* was found among Euripides' effects when he died in 406. They are the last works of two great tragedians, written close together in time. There are intriguing similarities of detail between them,[2] and both have provoked differing and controversial interpretations. Dramatic though their action is, they both reflect, in their external, political tensions, an intrapsychic conflict that revolves around the theme of the previous chapter.

What happens when a parallel world breaks through, and we are brought face to face with those who represent the selves we did not become? Pentheus, in *Bacchae*, epitomises the relation between prejudice and psychosis. He has arrived only very insecurely at who he is. Faced with an alternate self that embodies too much that is still conflicted in his own self, he finds the confrontation unbearable and is driven to attack this Other, denying any connection between them. When his attempts to obliterate the Other collapse, the normal psychosis of his prejudice turns to overt madness.

---

1 This chapter derives from a lecture and seminar given at the Institute of Classical Studies at London University. Its exposition of psychoanalytic theory was written with a non-analytic audience in mind.

2 In each play, for example, the messenger's speech has an unearthly silence broken by the voice of a god (*Bacch.* 1078ff., *O.C.* 1621ff.).

Theseus, by contrast, in *Oedipus at Colonus*, is secure in who he has become. He can acknowledge the parallel self that he avoided being, and allow a relationship that will enrich both of them.

In *Bacchae* Cadmus, King of Thebes, has turned the government of the city over to Pentheus, the son of Agave, one of Cadmus' four daughters. Cadmus was the founder of Thebes, populating it with men who grew from the earth where he sowed dragon's teeth. The father of Pentheus was Echion, one of these 'earth-born' men. Pentheus has to decide how to deal with the cult of the god Dionysos, newly arrived from Asia Minor and sweeping through the community. Dionysos is the son by Zeus of Semele, another daughter of Cadmus, who perished when she insisted Zeus show himself to her in his full majesty. The cult of Dionysos appeals particularly to women. Leaving their families and everyday occupations they roam the mountains, celebrating the god in an ecstatic state where normal inhibitions are overturned. What they do remains a mystery, but it is known that in their trance they tear live animals to pieces and eat the raw flesh. The Chorus of the play is a group of these Bacchants from Asia Minor who proclaim their religion as offering recognition and release for a part of human nature that needs to be acknowledged. Pentheus, however, can see it only as licentious and degenerate, a depraved threat to the established social order. His own mother, Agave, and Cadmus' other daughters, are on Mount Cithaeron leading bands of the god's worshippers. He decides to stamp out the cult.

A beautiful and enigmatic young stranger is the play's second main character. He is Dionysos himself in disguise. The audience knows this but Pentheus and the others on stage do not. The play revolves around the confrontation between the two. The stranger tries to persuade Pentheus not to be so repressive, but Pentheus refuses to give up his relentless hostility. He imprisons Dionysos and some of his followers, but the power of the god causes an earthquake, destroying Pentheus' palace and freeing the prisoners. Eventually the stranger, coming closer all the time to revealing who he is, makes Pentheus mad, disguises him as a Bacchant and leads him out on to Cithaeron, where his mother mistakes him for a wild beast and tears him limb from limb. The play ends with Agave's horrified recognition of what she has done, and the appearance of Dionysos in his divinity without disguise.

In *Oedipus at Colonus* Theseus, King of Athens, is faced with a wandering blind beggar who has arrived in Colonus, just outside Athens. This is Oedipus. In the years since his self-blinding and exile from Thebes he has lived as a homeless outcast, cared for by his daughter Antigone. Nearing his death, he now seeks sanctuary from Theseus. An oracle has foretold that if he dies on Athenian soil he will bring great rewards to the city. At first the villagers of Colonus are horrified at his presence and insist that the accursed monster leave. His noble bearing, however, and Antigone's devotion, win their sympathy and they call on Theseus to decide what to do. Theseus accepts Oedipus and agrees that Colonus should be his final resting-place. When Oedipus feels his end approaching he bids farewell to his daughters and leaves the stage. A messenger tells how he was summoned by a god and, in the presence of Theseus alone, vanished from the face of the earth.

In each play the ruler of a city is confronted with a stranger, a disturbing figure imbued with sacred meaning who demands recognition. The relationships between Pentheus and Dionysos, and between Theseus and Oedipus, show the same issues being worked out, with opposite conclusions.

Bacchae opens with Dionysos emphasising his strangeness. His first word means 'I am come': he has arrived from somewhere else. The description of his journey which follows is full of barbarian place-names. Clearly he is very foreign indeed. When his chorus of maenads arrive their first words reinforce the exotic impression (64ff.):

> From the land of Asia
> Leaving sacred Tmolus . . .

Dionysos speaks later of his mysteries as barbarian (482–4) and Pentheus uses this to reject them as alien and inferior to whatever is Greek. At the same time, though, Dionysos' arrival in Thebes is a homecoming. It is his mother's city, as he reminds the audience, and Pentheus is his first cousin. This tension pervades the play, as Pentheus, and Semele's sisters too, are so insistent on rejecting Dionysos as alien that they cannot see he also represents something native to them.

Euripides, however, gives us clues from the start to the close connection between Dionysos and Pentheus. He introduces them in parallel. The first mention of Pentheus is when Dionysos says that Cadmus has handed over the government to him as 'his daughter's offspring' (44). In the first reference to Dionysos, apart from the prologue which he speaks himself, Cadmus says he is 'my daughter's child' (181). Then Pentheus enters and speaks for 32 lines as though he is alone on stage. The effect is to give Pentheus a prologue of his own, in counterpoint to Dionysos, in which he introduces the action from his perspective. Like Dionysos, Pentheus begins his speech by explaining that he has just arrived in the city. Parallels of this sort between the two run throughout the play, but already we can see that Euripides is showing us conflict between characters who are at odds but also identified with each other.

The theme is emerging of how to manage the impact of threatening forces which present themselves as alien, but which may be closer to home than we like to think. Freud's fundamental discoveries were to do with the denial and repression of forces in ourselves that we are afraid of and do not want to acknowledge. He found that unconscious ideas do not just happen to be so. Some of them, at least, are actively prevented from reaching consciousness, and when Freud tried to bring back into consciousness the forgotten memories that were related to his patients' symptoms, instead of being grateful for his help, they fought him all the way. Try as we may, though, to repudiate what we find intolerable, it keeps looking for ways to make itself felt. Dionysos likewise demands recognition. He has come to Thebes 'so that I may be visible as a god to men' (22), and E.R. Dodds (1960: 238), in his edition of the play, quotes R.P. Winnington-Ingram as referring to 'a world structure in which the forces Dionysos represents are an inescapable element'. Pentheus' response, however, is to allow no expression of any kind to what Dionysos represents. Semele's sisters have also refused to acknowledge him, saying that the story of her affair with Zeus was just a figment to protect the pregnant Semele's reputation. Euripides stresses the futility of rejecting Dionysos with the word *theomachein*, meaning 'to fight against the gods', which occurs three times in the play (45, 325, 1255). Freud similarly found that however hard his patients tried to repress something it would return in some form or other. If no expression of it was accepted, it would return unacceptably in symptomatic form.

Semele's sisters have been stricken with Dionysiac frenzy, which has driven them out of their minds and turned them into maenads against their will: maenads, moreover, who will prove capable of the most ghastly horror. This pathological maenadism is to be distinguished from the true maenadism of the Chorus. Moral categories do not apply to Dionysos. It is not him, but a person's response to him that makes things turn to good or ill (Dodds 1960: xlv, 159). The Chorus accept the power of Dionysos and find that, once acknowledged, it brings fulfilment. The daughters of Cadmus deny it, and find it returns upon them in an overwhelming and destructive form.

Pentheus' similar efforts at repression are enacted in his imprisonment of Dionysos and the maenads. Sure enough, it does not work. What is meant to be confined breaks out. His unconscious vulnerability to the return of the repressed (Freud 1915b: 154) is also exposed when Cadmus, having himself decided to worship Dionysos, invites Pentheus to join him. Pentheus replies: 'Get your hands off me! Go to your revels then, but don't wipe your idiocy off on to me!' (343–4). Analysts are familiar with just this rush of mixed fear and anger when something comes dangerously near the surface. 'Wipe off' powerfully highlights the bodily contact which Pentheus fears and evokes his horror that something belonging to Cadmus might get smeared off on to him. Cadmus' invitation has aroused primitive anxiety and Pentheus speaks from a level of his mind where body-products and stuff which can be smeared may be the vehicle of dangerous attacks. Freud was recognising such early infantile states of mind when he famously said: 'The ego is first and foremost a bodily ego . . . i.e. [it] is ultimately derived from bodily sensations, chiefly from those springing from the surface of the body' (Freud 1923: 26). If no way is found to deal with such anxieties he says that what is repressed

> proliferates in the dark, as it were, and takes on extreme forms of expression, which when they are translated and presented to the neurotic are not only bound to seem alien to him, but to frighten him by giving him the picture of an extraordinary and dangerous strength of instinct.
> (Freud 1915b: 149)

This captures very well Pentheus' attitude towards Dionysos. Because his attempt at repression is so absolute, when the power of Dionysos does break through we find that it has indeed proliferated in an extraordinary, dangerous and extreme way.

We have seen Euripides introduce Pentheus and Dionysos in close parallel. Suppose we tell someone unfamiliar with the play that there is a character in it who speaks a prologue, which he starts by announcing his arrival in the city. He is introduced as the son of Cadmus' daughter, but his father was not an ordinary human being. His reaction to someone who opposes him is to turn his house, literally, 'upside down'. Our listener will think he must know who we are talking about. It would be far too confusing if such a specific, detailed description applied to more than one character. In fact, however, he has no idea yet whether we are talking about Pentheus or Dionysos. These common features have been mentioned already, except the last. Pentheus gives instructions, at one point, to destroy the seat of the prophet Teiresias 'tumbling everything upside down together' (349); while when Dionysos destroys Pentheus' palace the Chorus say (601ff):

> The Lord, the son of Zeus,
> Attacks this house and turns it upside down.

The phrase *anō katō* is emphatically placed at the beginning of the line in both passages.

Pentheus and Dionysos are revealed, by this view of the play, as sharing an identity. This is what Winnington-Ingram (1948: 103) also implies when he says of Pentheus that 'his vivid imagination and the persuasive Stranger (ultimately are they not the same force?) have control of him'. The detailed, specific description does apply to one person after all; but a person who exists in parallel, conflicting versions of himself. Euripides' Pentheus is a man unconsciously riven with internal conflict. One aspect of himself he can tolerate, the other not. By a process of splitting which, like the conflict, is unconscious, he tries to keep them as far apart as possible. This is why Pentheus keeps insisting that he and the Stranger have nothing in common, while all the time the fascination the Stranger holds for him is plain to see.

Throughout the text Euripides keeps pointing to their sameness and their difference.

The story that Semele was killed for claiming *falsely* that Zeus was the father of her baby is mentioned by each, and in identical fashion. Dionysos at line 31 and Pentheus at line 245 say 'for lying about her union', and each time the identical phrase occupies the final three and a half feet of the line. The repetition cannot be missed. Not surprisingly, however, they take opposite views. Pentheus accepts that Semele was lying, while Dionysos condemns it as slander.

Pentheus sends servants to hunt for 'the female-seeming stranger, who is bringing in a new sickness for women' (353–4). A few lines later, Teiresias says to Cadmus 'May Pentheus not bring new sorrow into your house' (367). In the Greek the same verb, 'bring into', occupies the same position in the line. Euripides is emphasising an activity that Pentheus and Dionysos are both engaged in.

A servant announces that the 'beast' has been hunted down, and Dionysos is brought in. Pentheus abuses him for his pale skin and says he has obviously been in the shadows 'hunting Aphrodite with his beauty' (459). He accuses Dionysos of hunting, just as he himself has been hunting Dionysos. Their mirroring of each other may reflect even more. For all Pentheus' abuse he is fascinated by Dionysos' physical appearance (453ff.) and his accusation may be an unconscious acknowledgement of the sexual quality of his own hunting, a parallel hunting of Aphrodite.[3]

Details in the text make it clear that Pentheus is continually defending himself against awareness of his own sexuality (cf. 233–41, 344–5, 353, 487, 455 and 493 and 928 taken together, 796; lines 810ff. are not just the temptation but the seduction of Pentheus by Dionysos). Especially noteworthy is Pentheus' own description of his involvement with Dionysos: 'I am hopelessly entangled with this stranger' (800). Euripides' verb 'entangled' is drawn from the technical language of wrestling. But beyond the image of bodily contact, there is a specifically sexual *double entendre*, which does

---

3 Whenever hunting appears in the play the figure of Actaeon is in the background. He was the son of Cadmus' daughter Autonoë, and thus first cousin to both Pentheus and Dionysos. He claimed to be a better huntsman than Artemis (337–40), and for this contempt to a divinity he, the hunter, was hunted to death. When Pentheus, in a further identification with Dionysos, himself becomes the hunted beast, the same thing will happen to him in the very same place (1291; cf. 337ff.). Dionysos is both Artemis and Aphrodite to Pentheus.

not seem to have been noted by other commentators (cf. Plato *Symp.*191A; Sophocles *Fr.*618).

There is a fine piece of dramatic irony when Pentheus says he will have Dionysos stoned, the ritual execution for sacrilege (356). In fact it is Pentheus who will be attacked with missiles for his sacrilege. The irony lies not just in Pentheus' ignorance of what awaits him. It is because he refuses to own something in himself, and splits it off into Dionysos instead, that finally he must suffer death from it in his own person.

In the third chorus (519–75) Dionysos' sacred name, Dithyrambos, is announced, highlighting the idea of identity, and there follow two juxtaposed revelations of the births of Dionysos and of Pentheus. The pairing is stressed by introducing each with the verb 'I show forth' (528, 538). The revelations emphasise their abnormal parentage: Dionysos' father divine, Pentheus' father born out of the soil; again the polarisation between opposite versions of the same thing.

Towards the end of the play Agave, still mad, cradles the head of Pentheus, her son whom she has dismembered. She calls it 'the young bull' (1185, see Dodds 1960 ad loc.). Elsewhere in the play the bull always represents Dionysos. There is even a parallel hallucination. Here Agave mistakes Pentheus for a bull. Earlier in the play (618ff.) Pentheus mistakes a bull for Dionysos.

Euripides indicates, in all these passages, the parallel identities of Dionysos and Pentheus, and the simultaneous identification and opposition between them.

This tension between splitting and unity is related to the developmental journey referred to in the previous chapter. A baby is constantly faced with powerful new experiences. Some are good and pleasurable, and the person who produces them is, for the baby, a good and pleasurable figure. Some of them are bad, and the person who produces these is a bad and fearsome figure. As adults we know that both figures are the same. Sometimes a mother feeds her hungry baby right away; sometimes it has to wait. Sometimes she picks it up and plays with it; sometimes she has to leave it on its own. For the baby, however, the power of these experiences can make them so good on the one hand, and so bad on the other, that it cannot join them up and relate them to one and the same person. Instead it experiences a good and a bad mother who are separate from each other. Moreover the infant has to keep them separated in its mind because the bad figure is a danger to the other. If they come too close the good figure and the good experiences might get wiped out. Naturally enough, the baby has loving feelings towards one figure and, towards the other, feelings that may be unbearable. The immature psyche maintains a split in itself, corresponding to these two sets of feelings. By splitting the internal representation of the mother, and so also splitting its perception of its own self, the infant attempts

95

to manage the terror of being left with nothing good outside and nothing good inside itself either.

These splits are no longer necessary once an infant is able to recognise that it is the same person who sometimes gives pleasure but sometimes frustrates it, and that its own loving and hateful feelings are responses to the same single figure. Reaching this stage involves accepting that one may oneself cause damage. Hating the mother we love, we hurt her, and we have to bear the pain of knowing that. We also have to bear the responses we may provoke. Recognising that we can hurt who we love is an essential part of being human, made possible by a developing confidence that we can also repair damage. In parallel, we discover that those we love and hurt, though injured, will not want to destroy us in return. Some people grow up, however, in a way that does not enable the original split to unify, and so does not help them develop this trust in their own, and other people's, generosity of spirit. They are left with the fear that love may be annihilated. This means anything bad, in themselves or in the world outside, can threaten absolute destruction. Then everything becomes either all good or all bad, ambivalence is not possible, and anything that poses a threat has to be eradicated. The previous chapter emphasised the relation between this way of being and the totalist state of mind. It is a fragile basis for relating to a world that is, by its nature, full of ambivalence and ambiguity.

The stability of characters whose mental life is dominated by such absolute desires and terrors is precarious. Personalities in such a predicament may try to defend against what they are afraid of in themselves, by locating it in another person instead. Since what is attributed like that is something unacceptable, this process of projection can turn the other into a threatening figure. When Pentheus, for example, projects on to Dionysos the sexuality he cannot tolerate in himself, Dionysos becomes at once fascinating and dangerous. On learning that the Dionysiac mysteries are celebrated by night, Pentheus makes a sexual accusation against Dionysos. Dionysos invites him to take back this projection, saying that if you are looking for something hard enough you can always find it. Pentheus, evidently stung by the truth of this, loses his temper (489–90).

Pen. You will pay the price for your wicked sophistries.
Dion. No, you will, for your ignorance and disrespect to the god.

With the emphatic 'No, you will' at the beginning of the line, Dionysos is saying 'Think. What you are talking about does not belong to me. It belongs to you.' Later Dionysos offers Pentheus a final chance to undo the splitting and projection. Describing his escape from prison he twice speaks of himself, rather emphatically, as 'tranquil' (622, 636). Pentheus is furious at finding Dionysos free and Dionysos tells him (647):

96

Stop! Place a tranquil foot upon your anger.

He is doing more than using an idiomatic turn of phrase (cf. Eur. *Medea* 216) to calm Pentheus. Because Euripides has attached the word so carefully to Dionysos in the preceding lines, the advice to Pentheus that he himself should be tranquil becomes an invitation to accept an identification with Dionysos instead of fighting against it. Pentheus, however, replies (655):

You are clever-clever, but not how you ought to be clever.

Phrases of the same distinctive kind have already been twice addressed to Pentheus. Teiresias has said (311–12):

And even if you have a mind to be, you are not mindful, for your mind is sick.

A few lines later (332) Cadmus says to him:

Now you are astray and your thoughts are thoughtless.

With his epigrammatic jibe, Pentheus once again directs at Dionysos the sort of comment that really applies to himself. His response to Dionysos' invitation (or interpretation) is to renew the projection and say 'This way of thinking does not belong to me, it belongs to you.' From then on he is doomed to breakdown. There is an echo, surely deliberate, when Pentheus, having been turned into a maenad, says to Dionysos (824):

. . . for from of old you are someone clever.

Now he means it, and sees that it has been true all along, but too late to save his sanity.

All this projection is because Pentheus cannot tolerate diversity in himself. In this connection, it is worth giving a thought to Pentheus' ancestry. His great-grandfather and great-grandmother were Ares and Aphrodite, a marriage of opposites if ever there was one. They had a daughter named Harmonia, who married Cadmus and was Pentheus' grandmother. So ideas about the struggle to harmonise opposites and make them fruitful are there from the start, implicit in Pentheus' family line, and the theme keeps appearing in the text of the need to tolerate difference. At the very beginning of the play Dionysos refers to Asia (17–19),

Which lies along the salt sea with its beautifully towered cities full of Greeks and barbarians mingled together.

97

Throughout, Dionysos tries like this to undo the polarising ideology of Pentheus' totalist mentality. But Pentheus is determined to keep separate what Dionysos would bring into coexistence. For him, the fact that he is Greek and Dionysos barbarian can only be a matter of confrontation (483). When Pentheus goes mad and, as a maenad, becomes a follower of Dionysos, the projected aspects of himself have returned with a vengeance. Now Dionysos says (859–62):

> And he shall know the son of Zeus, Dionysos who is a god with divine authority, most terrible and yet most gentle to mankind.

Gentle? Having driven Pentheus mad, and being about to kill him? The point is that because Pentheus needs to insist that the Other is all bad, he cannot conceive of Dionysos' gentleness, and so is left with nothing but the terror.

Scholars have puzzled, in the scene of Pentheus' breakdown (912ff.), about how Dionysos effects the change in him. Hypnosis has been invoked; Dodds (1960: 172) gives arguments against this. A.W. Verrall (1910) suggested that Dionysos has made Pentheus drunk or drugged him, with which Winnington-Ingram (1948: 117) is prepared to agree. It is unnecessary, however, to invoke extraneous causes. What we are shown is something latent in Pentheus' mind becoming manifest, as his efforts to maintain the defensive splits and projections collapse. The nature of his hallucination is particularly interesting (918–19):

> I seem indeed to see twin suns, two cities of Thebes.

This need not be ascribed to drugs or alcohol. It is the split in Pentheus' world becoming visible. He has been trying, unconsciously, to keep two aspects of reality, and of himself, so far apart that he does not have to know about both of them. Now this attempt is breaking down. As both come into view at once, the makeshift unity of his world disintegrates and the fragmentation of Pentheus' psyche declares itself.

There is an exquisite pre-echo of this at the end of the scene before, when Pentheus leaves the stage with his madness already taking hold. As they go inside for him to be dressed as a maenad he says to Dionysos (843):

> We shall go into the house . . . and I shall decide what to do.

This sentence is ungrammatical. Greek has not only singular and plural but a dual number, a form used specifically to refer to objects in twos. When there are two things or people the dual is not obligatory; the plural is also correct but using the dual emphasises the twoness. Here, in 'We shall go into . . .' (literally 'Going into . . .') the participle 'going' is in the dual; Pentheus is referring to himself and Dionysos as a pair. Following this we expect 'we shall decide', also in the dual. Instead we hear 'I shall decide' in the singular. Because the participle and verb do not agree in number some editors have emended the text. Dodds (1960 ad loc.) and Winnington-Ingram (1948: 104) accept the original reading, saying that the grammatical inconsistency may reflect Pentheus' indecision. But Euripides' use of the dual has more specific significance for Pentheus' state of mind. The particular way his words fall apart grammatically is a precise reflection of the way his mind is falling apart, as he slides between seeing reality as single and double.

We can acknowledge that we are bound sometimes to hurt those we love, and we can accept the responsibility and bear the guilt this brings, only if we have developed confidence that our love is greater than our destructiveness; that although we may wound the objects of our love, they will go on loving us more than they hate us. In Pentheus we discover a character terrified of doing damage that is irreparable, and leaving himself with a world ruined for ever. Afraid of absolute destructiveness within himself, he unconsciously organises his personality around rejecting the aspect of himself he so much fears. The totality of the rejection means that when he meets that aspect of himself he is helpless to accommodate it. The encounter becomes, indeed, absolutely destructive.

Tragedy itself is thought to have originated from religious ceremonies in honour of Dionysos, and K.I. Arvanitakis (1998) has taken *Bacchae* as a paradigm play for studying the nature of Greek tragedy, and of tragedy in general. Although his focus is different, it is interesting that, for Arvanitakis also, 'Pentheus' tragic flaw consists in his repudiation of contradictory dualities and his inability to mourn' (1998: 955): to mourn, in Arvanitakis' view, for a lost, primally undifferentiated, state of being, which he was unable to give up and move on from.

The serenity at the close of *Oedipus at Colonus* is a far cry from *Bacchae*. It is achieved, however, by successful handling of the same challenge that Pentheus was unable to meet. When Oedipus arrives in Colonus seeking asylum, 'the long companionship of time' (7–8) has still not lessened his pollution. The villagers respond automatically (226): 'Depart directly from this land!' For Theseus, however, Oedipus imposes the same necessity for choice that Dionysos placed on Pentheus, and the action turns on how Theseus will respond. In their initial encounter there is already evidence that the person of Oedipus holds meaning for Theseus. He tells Oedipus that he knows who he is (553):

I know you, son of Laïus . . .

Oedipus begins his response to Theseus (607):

Dear son of Aegeus . . .

Common usage as this is, it sets up an alignment between the two characters. The perfect tense, in the Greek, of 'I [have come to] know you' implies the completion of a process. Some internal consideration of Oedipus'
identity is already under way, and Theseus has arrived at a recognition
of Oedipus. At one level this might simply mean that Theseus has been
working out who the stranger must be. But the personal meaning that the
figure of Oedipus holds for Theseus becomes explicit when he says that he
of all people should understand Oedipus' story (560–7). 'I myself' is placed
at the end of its line (561) for emphasis. Oedipus' gratitude for the 'nobility' of Theseus' response (569) echoes the reference to his own 'nobility' (8)
as having helped him bear his sufferings with patience. The language of
both characters thus shows this to be a meeting of like with like. Theseus
points to the similarity of their life histories, and in a memorable phrase
(567–8) puts his own and Oedipus' identities into conjunction:

> I am a man too, and I know the difference between us lies only in the
> fortune of the morrow.

Theseus evokes closely parallel worlds, in striking contrast to the way
Pentheus immediately distances himself from Dionysos.

The connection between Theseus and Oedipus is underlined at various
points in the play. Theseus asks when he will learn what benefit Oedipus
brings to Athens and Oedipus replies (582):

> When I die and you become the one who buries me.

Oedipus stresses that the protection Athens will receive from him after his
death depends on his resting-place being known to nobody but Theseus
(1522–32), and at the end he sends even his daughters away so as to share
his last moments with Theseus alone (1643–4). When Theseus says that bury-
ing Oedipus is a small thing to ask, he is sharply contradicted (586–7):

> Consider, though! On the contrary, it is no small matter.

The manuscripts tell us that Theseus replies (588):

> Do you mean for your descendants or for me?

This is usually emended to

> Do you mean for your descendants and for me?

on the grounds that Theseus' natural concern would be whether his bury-
ing Oedipus will make trouble between Oedipus' descendants and himself.
I am not so sure. What the manuscript text may reveal is Theseus coming
to realise the seriousness of his personal involvement. The confrontation
becomes angry, with Theseus telling Oedipus not to be stupid; he is in no
position to be temperamental. Oedipus snaps back that Theseus should be
quiet until he knows what he is talking about. Theseus replies (594):

> Explain then. It's true I shouldn't speak unless I understand.

Contrast this with Pentheus' response when Dionysos wanted him to pause
for thought.

The difference between the capacities of Theseus and Pentheus to respond
to the Stranger is very clear, but who does the Stranger represent for Theseus?
We have seen that when he first meets Oedipus, Theseus recalls the resonance between their histories (562–8). Like Oedipus, he too was abandoned
by his father and brought up in a foreign city, learnt that he was not who he
had thought he was, went journeying, killing monsters on the way, and
discovered his true father.[4] When their final parting comes their lives overlap
again, as Oedipus makes his purification at the place where Theseus and
Peirithous had sworn their pact before they descended to Hades to carry
off Persephone (1593–4). Where Theseus once departed from this world,
Oedipus is about to do the same. What Theseus does not mention, in his
recollection of the parallels between them, is that he also was accidentally
responsible for his father's death; not with his own hand like Oedipus, but
indirectly, when he forgot to change the colour of his sails.[5] Along with this
near-patricide, there is also near-incest in Theseus' story. He does not
commit it himself, though there is a touch of the incestuous about marrying
the sister of the fiancée he had abandoned.[6] This wife, however, is Phaedra,
whose illicit passion for her stepson Hippolytus is the most famous such
relationship in ancient literature after Oedipus' own with Jocasta. Her
desire was not fulfilled and Hippolytus was not her own son, so this is
still only an approach to incest. Phaedra hanged herself none the less, just as
Jocasta did.

---

4 Theseus was illegitimately fathered in Troizen by Aegeus, King of Athens. He was brought
   up in Troizen in his mother's family until, on learning who his father was, he travelled
   to Athens, putting various brigands and murderers to death as he went, and presented
   himself to Aegeus.
5 It was arranged that the ship which took Theseus to Crete as a prospective victim for the
   Minotaur should, on its return, wear black sails if he were dead but white if he were still alive.
   Theseus forgot about this and his father, seeing the ship with black sails, killed himself
   by leaping from a cliff.
6 Ariadne, whom Theseus left on Naxos while returning from Crete to Athens.

The myth of Theseus thus embodies the central elements of Oedipus' story but in a muted, incompletely realised form (Green 1980). Theseus is confronted, in Oedipus, with something he has been warding off throughout his life – successfully, for he has not, after all, done what Oedipus did – but which has persistently tried to break through and is finally demanding recognition. Oedipus represents the irruption into his world of an alternative, 'polluted' self, the inhabitant of a parallel universe. He might do as Pentheus did: make use of splitting to emphasise all that is different in Oedipus from himself and, by projection, insist that Oedipus inhabit someone else's territory, not Theseus' own. Sophocles shows us, however, a man who has achieved the developmental task that Pentheus could not. Theseus can accept the Stranger. Sophocles does not soften the option by diluting the horror of the pollution or by removing the arrogance and imperiousness which contributed to Oedipus' downfall. All that is still there. Nor does Theseus accept Oedipus by idealising him. He tolerates the conflicting feelings which Oedipus arouses, as well as the aspects of himself that Oedipus represents. He does not need to split either his perception of the other, or of his own self, and the generosity which this makes possible is rewarded by the blessing which Oedipus brings for Athens. If we can recognise and accommodate the Stranger as Theseus does, not only do we avoid the fate of Pentheus, but what we had been afraid of may turn out to bring unlooked for enrichment to our lives.

Behind the sort of reading of these plays that I am offering, lies the question of what contribution psychoanalysis can make to our understanding of works of literature. In their consulting-rooms, analysts are used to people offering partial views of themselves. Patients reveal what they are able to, but that is only the tip of an iceberg, and the analyst listens for what is not finding a way into words. It is tempting to do the same with fictional characters, and to use what is shown as a basis for thinking about what is not. What can Iago's infancy have been like? What kind of fantasy life does Lady Macbeth have? But characters in a play do not exist beyond the text. They are, so to speak, a tip without an iceberg. John Gould makes the point clearly, saying that since any character is a construct of language and gesture on the part of the author, 'the language of dramatic persons does not give clues to or "express" their personality, their inward and spiritual being: it *is* their personality, and their being' (Gould 1978: 44). Lionel Trilling likewise points out that there is nothing behind a play itself, giving rise to it as an unconscious wish gives rise to a dream. 'Hamlet', he writes, 'is not merely the product of Shakespeare's thought; it is the very instrument of his thought' (Trilling 1951: 52). Samuel Beckett was once asked how the role of Mouth in *Not I* should be approached. The play's director wrote:

'We're assuming she's in some sort of limbo. Death? After-life? . . .' Beckett replied:

This is the old business of author's supposed privileged information as when Richardson wanted the lowdown on Pozzo's background before he could consider the part. I no more know where she is or why thus than she does. All I know is in the text. 'She' is purely a stage entity, part of a stage image and purveyor of a stage text.

(Harmon 1998: 279, 283)

Even in these restricted terms, we might do better to refrain from seeing fictional characters as individuals in their own right. In discussing Aeschylus' *Agamemnon*, Gould (1978: 59) comments on Clytaemnestra's 'inverted, monstrous sensuality'. But he then points out that the play is permeated with the language of perverse sensuality, and suggests that Clytaemnestra expresses not an individual character so much as 'the world of the play' itself. Dramatic characters may, perhaps, best be understood in this way, not as distinct entities marked out from each other but as particles of the organic whole that is the drama.

Karen Chase, writing about the delineation of character in the Victorian novel, also looks 'beyond individual character in order to ask how a fiction as a whole attempts to organise emotion' (1984: 39). She finds psychoanalysis well placed to examine this. Psychoanalysis, she says,

overthrows the sovereignty of the individual subject, allowing us to conceive the personality not as an atomistic unit but as a play of complex and competing processes, structures of relative autonomy which function as psychological agents but not as psychological wholes. To share this conception is to become less eager to regard fictional characters as stable entities and more willing to recognise that a given character might function as a process rather than a personality.

(Chase 1984: 32)

Emotional organisation is what psychoanalysis sets out to study. It has an understanding of character formation and of psychic conflict, and a language in which to discuss these. The analytic session provides a framework within which the complex and competing psychic structures that make up an individual mind can express themselves safely and find a response. Drama also offers a framework, one which can safely contain the interactions of embodied fictional representations of discrete psychological structures, or 'voices'. When characters in a play or novel touch us with a sense of emotional truth, psychoanalytic awareness can help us understand where our feeling of recognition comes from, and how it is that a construct of language and gesture can move us so profoundly. To say that Theseus achieved a developmental task which Pentheus did not, is a statement about their adult selves, as the text describes them. The contribution psychoanalysis

103

can make is to try to elucidate, with its particular understanding of psychic development, the emotional truthfulness of the dramatic representation. The collision of Pentheus and Dionysos offers an extreme example of a kind of unconscious, intrapsychic conflict we have all really had to deal with, while the meeting of Theseus and Oedipus shows us something each one of us has struggled to achieve in becoming the people that we are.

7

The Oedipus complex as a lifelong developmental process: Sophocles' *Trachiniae*

Universal Problem Solved with Triangles!

'Scientific Notes' headline:
The Independent, 16 March 1999

The Oedipus complex

Although the Oedipus complex is at the heart of psychoanalytic theory, Freud never set out a systematic account of it (Laplanche and Pontalis 1973: 283). It tended to appear in whatever he was writing about, but always by way of its connection with what he was discussing at the time. Exactly because it so pervaded his thinking, what we have is a series of partial views of it. All the same, there has emerged from this what one might call a basic version of the theory. It has a beginning, a middle and an end. To start with, the infant has no Oedipus complex. Then it develops possessive sexual feelings towards the parent of the opposite sex. Hostility arises towards the parent of its own sex when it realises that its desire is opposed by that parent's superior claim. Fear of castration makes the infant admit defeat, and 'the object cathexes are given up and replaced by identifications' (Freud 1924: 176). Relinquishing, under the threat of castration, its desire for the parent of the opposite sex, and instead identifying with the parent of the same sex, prepares the child to make, in due course, its own sexual relationship outside the family. Once the Oedipus complex, including its re-emergence at puberty, has been worked through in this way, it is resolved and disappears. Such a story may be temptingly straightforward, but it was seen from the beginning to be too simple, and analytic theorising, including Freud's own, about the Oedipus complex can be understood as a continuing reconsideration of this basic account.

I shall look briefly at some of the problems that have prompted that reconsideration, in order to arrive at the central point of this chapter. This is the importance for psychic development of triangularity in its own right, not simply of triangular sexual relationships. The Oedipus complex, I am suggesting, needs to be understood in terms of the variety of different ways in which sexuality may be related to a triangular structure. New manifestations of this may appear throughout the life cycle, and continuing to work them through may be important if later life is to be rewarding. Seen in this way, the Oedipus complex becomes a lifelong developmental challenge.

The ground I cover here is circumscribed but, within it, significant space is given to the French analytic tradition, whose contribution can be under-appreciated, or may simply be less known, by English-speaking analysts. Amongst others who have surveyed the Oedipal landscape more widely, Gregorio Kohon (1999: 3–69) and Dana Birksted-Breen (Breen 1993: 1–48) give particular emphasis to French psychoanalysis in their discussions.

The end, middle and beginning of the story have all been questioned. James Strachey (1961), considering the translation of '*Der Untergang des Oedipuscomplexes*' as 'The Dissolution of the Oedipus Complex' (Freud 1924), debates whether 'dissolution' is too strong a word. Although Freud (1923: 32) had already written of the 'demolition' of the Oedipus complex and speaks unequivocally, in the 1924 paper, of its 'destruction' and 'abolition' (1924: 177), Strachey doubts whether the situation can be so absolute. Hans Loewald (1979) discussed Freud's use of language in more detail and noted Freud's own recognition that his opposition to Rank's ideas about birth trauma might have influenced his choice of terms. Freud did see that Oedipal elements could survive into adult life, and might do so to some extent in everyone. But he thought that a failure for the complex to dissolve was central to neurosis, and the more that its features persisted into adulthood, the more vulnerable would that person be.

Freud also came across difficulties in the middle of the Oedipal story which implied problems for its ending. These were to do with the different meanings of castration for the two sexes. For the male infant it is the threat of something that he does have being taken away, while for the female it is the discovery that she has never had something nor ever will have it. This difference means that the male and female Oedipus complexes cannot be mirror images of each other. In fact there is an opposite relation, for boys and girls, between castration and the Oedipus complex. 'Whereas in boys the Oedipus complex is destroyed by the castration complex, in girls it is made possible and led up to by the castration complex' (Freud 1925c: 256). This also implies a radical difference, for the two sexes, in the later stages of the complex. For the boy, it is understandable that the threat of castration should abruptly terminate his sexual attachment to his mother. For the girl, by contrast, castration is not a threat but a fact, and one which, aligning her with her mother, allows the attachment to her father to continue, so her wish for a baby from him need not be extinguished. An article on the pre-Oedipal period by Ruth Mack Brunswick (1940) is particularly significant for its provenance. It is based on her records, annotated by Freud, of discussions she and Freud held from 1930 onwards. In it she says:

> Once in the Oedipus complex, the normal woman tends to remain there; the Oedipus complex of the woman undergoes no such widespread destruction as that of the man. On the contrary, it remains and forms the normal basis of the erotic life of the woman.
>
> (Mack Brunswick 1940: 296)

It would be strange, however, for normality to depend in one sex on the destruction and in the other on the persistence of the same psychic structure. Loewald concluded, as have others, that, even after its working through has been consolidated in adolescence, the Oedipus complex

> rears its head again . . . during later periods in life, in normal people as well as in neurotics. It repeatedly requires repression, internalisation, transformation, sublimation, in short some form of mastery, in the course of life – granted that the foundations for such repeated mastery are established during latency and that the forms and levels of mastery are likely to vary with changing levels of experience and maturity. Seen in this light there is no definitive destruction of the Oedipus complex.
>
> (Loewald 1979: 386)

Another complication to the middle part of the story came with Freud's observation that the child's feelings were ambivalent towards both parents. The little boy, instead of simply feeling desire for his mother and jealous hostility towards his father, would also feel an affection towards his father that made his mother into the rival. Freud described this as the negative Oedipus complex. He thought the 'complete' complex, comprising positive and negative versions, occurred in the majority of people, but that the positive version needed to predominate for normal emotional development. He was uncertain whether the negative complex was due to innate bisexuality, or whether the boy was identifying with the mother, in her desire for the father, as a solution to the failure of his rivalry with the father (Freud 1923: 33–4). For Melanie Klein ambivalence was even more a primary aspect of the Oedipus complex. She sees the infant relating to part-objects

107

(breast, penis as substitute for breast), gradually perceived as belonging to whole-objects (mother, father). These objects may, in the infant's fantasy,[1] threaten retaliation for its aggressive impulses against them, so that it seeks security from an ideal, loving object instead. 'Each object, therefore, is liable to become at times good, at times bad. This movement to and fro between the various aspects of the primary imagos implies a close interaction between the early stages of the inverted and positive Oedipus complex' (Klein 1945: 409). The good and bad feelings, towards a now good, now bad, object, constitute the positive and negative versions of the complex. This is gradually worked through by establishing a single object, to which the infant has a unitary relationship that can carry the ambivalence: in short, the establishment of the depressive position. That is why, in Klein's thinking, the Oedipus complex and the depressive position are so inextricably linked (Klein 1952: 79–80, 1957: 196). Regularly, she refers not to the Oedipus 'complex' but to the Oedipus 'situation', the Oedipus 'development' or Oedipus 'tendencies' (e.g. Klein 1928: 191, 1945: 406ff.). These formulations may reflect the intrinsic connection she makes with the depressive position. A 'position', although it needs to be achieved, is never resolved in the sense of being superseded or disappearing. It is a psychic configuration which persists, and may need to be worked through in different ways, throughout life. Klein's reference to the Oedipus 'situation' implies what Loewald spelt out so clearly – that it is a psychic configuration of exactly that sort.

As to the beginning of the Oedipal story, analytic thinking has been dominated by the debate between the classical view, dating the onset of the Oedipus complex from around three years onwards, and the Kleinian view which dates it significantly earlier. To see this as a disagreement about chronology, however, misses the point. It is not that both sides are looking at the same thing and disagreeing about when it occurs. The onset of the Oedipus complex has different meanings for Freud and for Klein. Freud dated it when he did because for him the Oedipus complex was connected to genital sexuality and so its onset coincided, by definition, with the child's arrival at the genital phase of development. Klein, on the other hand, believed that before the genital stage the infant was already fantasising, in pregenital terms, about the parents doing oral and anal things together (Klein 1927: 175–6). The disagreement is not essentially about chronology, but about Klein's detaching the Oedipus complex from genitality.

The article by Mack Brunswick, already referred to, is interesting in this connection because it suggests that Freud also became less definite about the genital/pre-genital and Oedipal/pre-Oedipal distinctions. Mack Brunswick writes:

1 On the spelling of 'fantasy', see Chapter 1, note 3.

Three great pairs of antitheses exist throughout the entire libido development, mingling, overlapping, and combining, never wholly coinciding, and ultimately replacing each other. Infancy and childhood are characterised by the first two, and adolescence by the third. These are 1) *active–passive* 2) *phallic–castrated* 3) *masculine–feminine*. Schematically, but schematically only, these follow upon one another, each characteristic of a given stage of development.

(Mack Brunswick 1940: 297–8)

This implies a continuity between active–passive and phallic–castrated, a continuity revealed clearly in Mack Brunswick's account of the phallic mother. The active–passive dynamic governs the beginning of life. An infant is born into a state of passive helplessness, with active capability located in the mother, and this dependence is gradually modified as the infant acquires its own capacities (Freud 1926: 137ff.). A mother, says Mack Brunswick, who cannot stand aside from her active role to allow the infant's developing autonomy, but insists instead that all activity stay located in herself, becomes the phallic, castrating mother who denies the child its sexuality.

Mack Brunswick also specifically attributes to Freud himself the suggestion that the terms 'active' and 'passive' would be more comprehensive and accurate for the Oedipus complex than 'positive' and 'negative'. This leaves the boy still active towards his mother in his positive Oedipus complex and, in his negative one, passive towards his father. But the girl's positive Oedipus complex has become her passive one. 'According to this new terminology, the pre-Oedipal sexuality of the girl becomes her active Oedipus complex with the mother as its object. Her passive Oedipus complex has the father as its object' (Mack Brunswick 1940: 299). It does not make sense, of course, for the girl's *pre*-Oedipal sexuality to be her Oedipus complex. Mack Brunswick must mean that the girl's active Oedipus complex towards her mother is to be found in her pre-*genital* sexuality.

Before the infant arrives, then, at the genitally orientated triangular situation, there is an already developing context of pre-genital triangularity. Semantic arguments aside, about whether or not to call it the Oedipus complex, there might be considerable agreement that this is the case. Klein had detached triangularity from genitality, but pre-genital triangularity remained, for her, intrinsically bound up with sexuality. For the development of structure, however, triangularity in itself is what matters. Geometrically speaking, two points on their own make only a linear world with a single dimension. There is no such thing as shape, but only degrees of closeness or separation. The presence of a third point yields another dimension, and structures become possible. The infant's gradual discovery of triangularity is what makes possible the evolution of its psychic structure. Two dyadic relationships, between oneself and two different other points, do not make a triangle. The lines AB and AC do not yield a shape until the line BC is drawn. What is structuring for the infant is the awareness of a relationship between the two *other* points, a relationship that it has to contemplate without being part of. Klein focused predominantly on the pre-genital sexual content of the infant's fantasies about the parents (the lines AB and AC) and, where the two parents were concerned, on the fantasy of a combined parental object (the merging of points B and C). The effect was that, for some considerable time, Kleinian thinking was unable to place much emphasis on triangularity. More recently, it has taken fuller account of the line BC, and given importance to triangularity in its own right (Britton 1989).

If one thinks less in terms of the content of infantile fantasy, however, and more, so to speak, in terms of its geometry, one can none the less re-read some of Klein's formulations in relation to the emergence of triangularity. If the good breast stops being good, different things may happen. At one stage the infant's experience will be that the good breast has been replaced by the bad breast. Later on, disappointment with the breast makes the infant turn instead to the penis as a substitute (Klein 1945: 408–10). The shift, if the good breast fails, from persecutory fantasies about the bad breast, to hopeful fantasies about the penis as an alternative source of nourishment, is a significant step in development. My present emphasis, however, is on another kind of difference between these situations. They both appear to involve three objects: infant, good breast, bad breast; infant, breast, penis. But structurally speaking, the bad breast and the penis occupy crucially different positions. In the first situation the apparent third term, the bad breast, is only the second term with the sign reversed. It appears in place of the good breast. The infant's good relation to the good breast, and its bad relation to the bad breast, are two dyadic relationships, but the good breast and the bad breast do not, by definition, coexist. They cannot relate to each other. There can be no line BC, and no triangle. The later stage is different, because the penis is a true third element. Breast and penis do not obliterate each other. The infant wishes to incorporate either the breast or, if it stops being available, the penis instead. Now, though, it is not just a question of the infant's having or not having what it wants. The fact that breast and penis coexist faces the infant with a new possibility. The two objects, instead of either of them being available to the infant, may be engaged in a relationship of their own to each other. Klein describes fantasies in the infant about the breast and about the penis which, in their mirroring of each other, amount to a fantasy of just such a relationship. She says that the child's resentment at the mother for withdrawing the breast is intensified now, because the mother does not let the child have the father's penis either. Compounding the injury, the mother incorporates the father's penis herself (Klein 1932: 195). The infant also fantasises parental intercourse as consisting of the father's incorporating the mother's breast (Klein 1932: 40, 195). Neither breast-object, the breast itself or the penis, is there for the infant. Instead the two breast-objects are used reciprocally, by the whole objects of which they are part, to make a relationship with each other.[2] Once again, my emphasis is not on the content, but on the geometry, of the infant's fantasies. The fact that breast and penis have the capacity to make this relationship represents the line BC, which brings the triangle into being. This is what constitutes the foundation, and makes possible the development, of psychic structure.

This re-reading of Klein in terms of triangularity, rather than, primarily, the content of fantasy, is informed by the French analytic tradition. There, more than anywhere else, psychoanalysts have articulated the structural importance of triangularity itself, as distinct from the expression of sexuality in triangular relationships. Claude le Guen, for example, writes that the father first appears, for the infant, as the stranger who disrupts the duality of the mother and infant. He deprives the infant of the mother *as partner in a couple.*

> The child's perception of the stranger's non-identity vis-à-vis the mother brings home the latter's absence. Experiencing the loss of this first object is precisely that which allows it to be recognised as the first object. However, the stranger himself is not cathected as an object, he is only at the source of its revelation: he implies the loss of the mother; he both censors the mother and reveals her. As pure negativity, i.e. the negation of a presence and the affirmation of an absence, we can call him 'non-mother'. His appearance stirs up in the child a desire for the mother's presence, and at the same time, a wish for the destruction of the non-mother.
>
> (le Guen 1975: 371)

The infant's wish for the mother's presence and for the destruction of the father is not because of sexual rivalry, even of a pre-genital sort. At this stage the father is simply the presence which deprives the infant of the dyadic mother. His identity, as yet, consists only in being the non-mother. Serge Lebovici (1982) has written similarly of the need to distinguish between Oedipal sexuality and triangular object relations. As Juliet Mitchell put it:

> For Freud, the learning of difference is the learning of humanity (one's human-ness). The concept of difference Freud is referring to is not, in

2 The fantasy of a combined parental object, according to Klein (1952: 79 fnn. 1, 2), is liable to precede representation of the parents as separate individuals in intercourse.

the first instance, directly expressive of sexuality, but we shall see how it comes to be inextricably tied up with it.

(Mitchell 1974: 382)

Keeping this distinction clear makes it possible to see how sexuality in object relations comes, from an early stage, to be mapped on to triangularity, rather than being the motor that operates it. In this way it produces the evolving manifestations of the Oedipus complex.

The passage by le Guen quoted above emphasises again that triangularity is what generates structure. When the father disrupts the mother–infant dyad, the mother that the infant has known so far is not there any more; and it is in this experience of her absence that the infant discovers her as an object. This is close to Freud's account of hallucinatory wish-fulfilment, and of how reality-testing grows out of it. Reality perception develops when hallucinatory satisfaction fails. The reality of the object is perceived, at that point, through recognition of its absence (Freud 1900: 550–72, 1911b). The implication, although le Guen does not spell it out in this passage, is that the infant recognises *itself* as an object at the same moment, also through the experience of the mother's absence. Although these ideas are to be found in Freud, it is part of Lacan's enduring legacy to have spotlighted their significance. It has, again, fallen chiefly to French psychoanalysis to explore how psychic structure, including the infant's sense of its own identity, is constituted around the experience of lack and of absence.

An important concept in this way of thinking is the 'symbolic father'. This does not refer to a person. It denotes, rather, the function of the third term in the triangle. The actual father carries this function, but a third term may also impinge on the dyad in other ways, and the concept 'symbolic father' applies to these as well. Mitchell's (1974) book *Psychoanalysis and Feminism*, already referred to, was influential in making these ideas available in English. Particularly valuable for this discussion is the chapter 'The different self, the phallus and the father' (Mitchell 1974: 382–98). In it she quotes two passages, from Lacan and Maud Mannoni.

> The Symbolic father is to be distinguished from the Imaginary father (often . . . surprisingly distant from the real father) . . . The Symbolic father – he who is ultimately capable of saying 'I am who I am' – can only be imperfectly incarnate in the real father. He is nowhere . . . The real father takes over from the Symbolic father.
>
> (Lacan, seminar of March–April 1957,
> quoted in Wilden (1968: 271))

> Only the Symbolic dimension (the third element which intervenes in the dual relation of the child to the mother) can enable the subject to

disentangle his words from all the snares and fascinations in which he has been lost at certain stages of his existence – to disengage them too from all the struggles for face or struggles to the death which are specific to dual situations.

(Mannoni 1970: ix)

The 'symbolic father' refers to anything that manifests the function of converting a dyadic relationship into a triangular one. This may be posited from the beginning of life, since even in the earliest mother–infant relationship the infant is relating to a mother who has her own relationship to the infant's father. This is so whatever the external situation, even if the actual father is missing from the family. It is the mother's internal, psychic relationship to the father that is in question. The mother is the only member of the parent–infant triangle that has a bodily relationship to both the others, and the relation of her body to the father is prior to its relation to the infant. Her place within the mother–infant couple is only possible for her as a member of another couple. The existence of that other couple in the mother's mind means that the mother–infant couple always contains a third presence.

This idea has been developed in various ways. For Denise Braunschweig and Michel Fain (1975) the Oedipal mother belongs to two couples, one involving her baby's father, the other her own father. The infant has an excited fantasy about an Oedipal couple which is, according to them, at once its mother and father, and its mother and *her* father. Julia Kristeva writes:

> The loving mother, different from the clinging mother, is someone who has an object of desire; beyond that, she has an Other with relation to whom the child will serve as go-between. She will love her child with respect to that Other, and it is through a discourse aimed at that Third Party that the child will be set up as 'loved' for the mother. 'Isn't he beautiful?', or 'I am proud of you', and so forth, are statements of maternal love because they involve a Third Party; it is in the eyes of a Third Party that the baby the mother speaks to becomes a *he*, it is with respect to others that 'I am proud of you', and so on.
>
> (Kristeva 1987: 34)

It is important to grasp that Kristeva is talking here about the mother's internal world, before the infant's external relationship with the father has developed. André Green puts his cards squarely on the table.

> I would maintain, for my part, that there is no such entity as a baby with his mother. No mother–child couple exists without a father somewhere. For even if the father is hated or banished by the mother, erased from

her mind in favour of somebody else, of her own mother or father, the child nevertheless is the product of the union of the father and mother. Of this union he is the *material, living, irrefutable proof.* There are mothers who want to wipe out any trace of the father in the child. And we know the result: a psychotic structure. Thus we can assert that ultimately *there is no dual relationship.*

(Green 1978: 294)

The first sentence of that quotation appears deliberately to contradict Winnicott's (1952: 99) classic statement that there is no such thing as a baby *without* a mother. Green is, in fact, a great admirer of Winnicott's ideas, but the whole passage seems to run counter to Winnicott's (1956) description of primary maternal preoccupation, indeed to any view of a primary mother–infant dyad. Green, however, is discussing what is needed for such absorption to be normal, and for mother and infant eventually to emerge from it successfully. His point is that absorption in duality should not involve destruction of the third term, the symbolic father, that is somewhere present in the mother's mind: the other member of the other couple she belongs to. Kristeva, just after the passage quoted above, writes:

Any borderline person ends up finding a mother who is 'loving' for her own sake, but he cannot accept her as loving himself, for she did not love any *other* one. The Oedipal negation of the father is here linked with a complaint against an adhesive maternal wrapping, and it leads the subject towards psychic pain dominated by the inability to love.

(Kristeva 1987: 34–5)

The presence of the symbolic father is necessary if primary maternal preoccupation is to be not a static fusional state but the departure point for processes of development.

The function of the symbolic father is to initiate triangularity, within which the child's pre-genital sexuality expresses itself in ways that can, if one wishes, be called a 'pre-Oedipal triangle' or an 'early Oedipus complex'. If such expressions make for confusion, they can be avoided; it is a matter of terminology. As the symbolic father comes to be located more and more in an actual caring male figure, and as the child's sexuality continues to develop, triangular structure becomes a substrate for the genital sexualities of mother, father and child, and the classical Oedipus complex, as Freud described it, comes into being.

To look at the Oedipus complex in this way is to see it as a continuing developmental process. From the beginning of life triangularity and sexuality are brought progressively into relation with each other. Characteristic impulses, anxieties and conflicts pervade that relationship, at first inchoately and then in a more developed way. But there is no end-point – not even a final, fully developed form of the Oedipus complex – to be arrived at. Triangularity and sexuality continue throughout life to be interrelated in all sorts of different ways. Oedipal elements in adult life should not be seen only as residues of childhood development, but as aspects of human relationships that belong to the entire life cycle from birth to death. The term 'Oedipus complex' refers to a lifelong developmental task, whose later manifestations are an essential part of progress towards a fulfilling old age.

Trachiniae

I turn now to Sophocles' tragedy *Trachiniae*, or *Women of Trachis*, with a reading of it that is connected to these ideas about the Oedipus complex. Of the seven surviving plays by Sophocles it is probably the least known and studied. It deals with the return home of Heracles, and his death when he puts on the robe which his wife Deianira has mistakenly poisoned with the blood of the centaur Nessus. Heracles was one of the great Greek heroes, but he usually appeared on the stage as a comic figure. The play's theme is sufficiently out-of-the-way for tragedy to make us wonder what moved Sophocles to write about it. Despite what psychoanalysts might think, *Oedipus Tyrannus* was not written to illustrate the Oedipus complex but because the theme aroused an intense artistic response in Sophocles. Given that, the same theme might be expected to appear elsewhere in his work. It does turn out to be important in *Trachiniae*, and other parallels between the two plays are worth noting. Both deal with a shift from ignorance to knowledge, brought about by the gradual but relentless revelation of an oracle's real meaning. As a result a great leader of his people is ruined and his wife commits suicide. Some of the apparent difficulties in *Trachiniae* become clearer when we see that, here too, Sophocles is pursuing themes we have come to call 'Oedipal', but from an angle that belongs particularly to this play.

First, a summary of the play. The characters are:

HERACLES, son of Zeus and Alcmena
DEIANIRA, wife of Heracles
HYLLUS, their son
IOLE (silent), daughter of Eurytus, king of Oechalia
LICHAS, a herald
A messenger
Deianira's old nurse
An old man
CHORUS of young Trachinian women

115

The action takes place in Trachis in front of the house of Heracles and Deianira. In the prologue Deianira describes her marriage to Heracles. He defeated her other suitor, the river-god Achelous, whom she describes in monstrous, inhuman terms. Heracles, the son of Zeus and a mortal woman, Alcmena, is constantly absent on his labours. He has now been away for 15 months and nobody knows where he is. The nurse suggests sending Hyllus, the son of Deianira and Heracles, to look for him, but Hyllus turns out to have just heard that he is in Euboea, campaigning against the city of Oechalia, ruled by Eurytus. Deianira is startled; Heracles once told her about a prophecy that he would either die in Oechalia or spend the rest of his life in peace.

The Chorus comfort and encourage Deianira, and a messenger arrives with the news that Heracles is alive and victorious. The herald Lichas enters, leading a group of captive women, and explains the events of Heracles' absence. Being humiliated in an argument with Eurytus, he killed his son Iphitus. He expiated this with a period of slavery to the Lydian Queen Omphale, but then returned to Eurytus' city of Oechalia and sacked it. That is the expedition from which he is now coming home. Deianira notices a beautiful and dignified woman among the captives, and Lichas is evasive about her identity.

When Lichas and the captives go indoors the messenger tells Deianira that Lichas has not told her the whole truth. Heracles did not conquer Oechalia just for the sake of revenge. He fell in love with Eurytus' daughter Iole and Eurytus refused to give her to him. That is why he sacked Oechalia and, sure enough, the captive woman whom Deianira noticed is Iole herself whom Heracles is bringing home, not as a slave but to be his new wife. Lichas reappears and, when confronted, confirms this.

Deianira has a love-charm to use on Heracles. On her wedding-day the centaur Nessus made a sexual assault on her, and Heracles shot him with an arrow dipped in the bile of the Hydra. The dying Nessus told Deianira that his blood, with the Hydra's poison in it, would act as a love-charm to stop Heracles ever desiring another woman more than her. She asks the Chorus for advice, and with some misgiving decides to use the magic. She gives Lichas a robe, dipped in the centaur's blood, for Heracles to wear when he makes his sacrifice of thanksgiving for victory.

Having sent Heracles the robe Deianira finds that the wool she used to smear the charm on to it, once exposed to the sun, has shrivelled up and crumbled to dust. Perhaps the charm is actually a poison. She asks herself why, after all, the centaur who was dying because of her should have shown her a kindness. She says that if the poison that killed Nessus also kills Heracles, and she is responsible for this, she will die too. Hyllus now arrives and tells how the robe, in the heat of the sacrificial fire, fastened

116

itself around Heracles and began eating into his flesh. He attacks Deianira with furious hatred, denouncing her for murdering his father. She goes silently into the house.

The Chorus now understand the prophecy. The peace, and rest from his labours, which it promised Heracles, is the peace of death. They lament Deianira's mistake and sympathise with her anguish. All this, they say, is the work of Aphrodite.

The nurse comes out and describes how Deianira, distraught, rushed through the house, finally stabbing herself with a sword on her marriage-bed. Hyllus, learning that his mother had sent Heracles the poison unwittingly, thinks he has driven her to suicide, and is consumed with guilt. The nurse describes him embracing his mother's body in passionate grief.

Now Heracles is borne in on a litter. He has spasms of unbearable pain. He asks Hyllus to end his suffering by killing him and wishes death for Deianira who did this to him. He demands that Hyllus bring her to him so that he can kill her in revenge. Hyllus tells him she has killed herself already and explains that she thought Nessus' blood was a love-charm. Heracles sees that another prophecy has been fulfilled. Zeus had told him he could only be killed by someone who was already dead, and this is what Nessus has done. He makes Hyllus swear to fulfil his final commands. The first is to build a funeral pyre and burn him on it. His second command is that Hyllus should marry Iole. Hyllus is horrified at both commands, but eventually consents. The funeral procession departs and the play ends.

The focus of the play is the relationship between Deianira and Heracles. The action springs from conflicts within that relationship and Deianira's attempt to repair it. Yet these two characters never meet on stage. Some commentators have seen this as a structural weakness, but that is surely a mistake. The play falls into two parts, before and after the death of Deianira, but the overwhelming sense of the effect that she and Heracles have on each other binds it together. Their failure to meet in person represents literally their failure to connect emotionally.

The most important link between them, and the most important visible element in unifying the play, is their son Hyllus. He is essential to both parts of it through his relationship, first to his mother, and then to his father. Moreover his relation to each is about the other. In the first part, he and his mother are preoccupied with his absent father, while his contact with his father in the second part revolves around his dead mother. So the play's structure places the central two-person relationship within the context of a triangular one. There is, moreover, a further set of triangular relationships running through the play, showing that, powerful and dominant as a two-person sexual relationship may appear to be, it can only be understood, or properly worked out by the lovers themselves, in terms of triangular relationships between the generations.

Deianira arouses our sympathy, but not Heracles. We hear throughout the play of his greatness and his victories, but Sophocles imbues these references with a raw physicality which reveals Heracles as a man whose life has revolved around violence. He is 'savage-minded' (975). We see what this means when he demands that Hyllus shall bring Deianira to him so that he can kill her with his own hands. Heracles cruelly insists that Hyllus should personally force his mother out of the house, so that he can see whether Hyllus is more pained by his father's agony or by watching his mother die (1066–9). When Hyllus finally manages to tell Heracles that Deianira was trying to use a love-charm because of Iole and has committed suicide out of grief and guilt, Heracles makes no comment. There is no word of sorrow, no compassion or forgiveness for Deianira. He makes no further reference to her at all, but speaks only of the oracle about his own death. When he emphasises the violent, unapproachable natures of the monsters he has killed (1090ff.), we cannot help thinking that although he has rid the country of them, his callous, egocentric nature is the same as theirs. The Chorus remember his victory over Achelous in terms which minimise any difference between them, and the savagery they share is contrasted with the gentle nature of Deianira.

> Then there was thudding of fists and clang of bows
> and confusion of bulls' horns;
> and there was contorted grappling,
> and there were deadly blows from butting heads
> and groaning on both sides.
> But the tender girl with the lovely eyes sat far from
> them on a hillside,
> waiting for the one who would be her husband.
> So the struggle raged, as I have told it:
> but the bride over whom they fought
> awaited the end pitiably (517–28).

Deianira hopes Heracles will save her from Achelous, but she seems frightened of the violence of whichever suitor will win and claim her. She awaits the outcome of the fight 'stricken with fear lest her beauty should bring pain to her' (25).

This emphasis on Heracles' savagery goes unmitigated. We shall see later that, when he instructs Hyllus to burn him on the funeral pyre and to marry Iole, Heracles is restoring the natural order; and the union of Hyllus and Iole will give rise to the great family of the Heraclidae. But Heracles himself says nothing of such things, and shows no concern for Hyllus or awareness of what he is demanding of him. There is no new-found understanding on his part, no Aeschylean 'learning through suffering' (*Agamemnon* 177). Sophocles did have the option of finally ennobling Heracles. The popular myth was that Zeus lifted him up from the blazing pyre to live on Olympus with Hebe as his bride, and Sophocles mentions this story elsewhere (*Philoctetes* 727–9). Such a reference was there for the making, but Sophocles avoids it.

One theme of the play, then, is the interaction between two aspects of mankind: the untamed primitive savagery which Heracles embodies, and the civilised sensibility represented by Deianira. Freud viewed civilisation as being in constant tension with the archaic force of the drives, and Deianira's hope of containing Heracles' ferocity within the ordered restraints of domestic life, portrays this struggle. But Heracles' essential nature remains, just as the drives themselves cannot be modified. The task is to harness them, by sublimation, defence or compromise-formation, to constructive purposes. This Deianira tries to do, but her own unconscious savagery gets the upper hand.

Sexuality, above all, is the arena where this struggle is played out. However else the play is understood, there is no doubt that it is a tragedy of sexual passion. The Chorus say specifically that Achelous and Heracles fought because of sexual desire for Deianira and that Aphrodite was both referee and victor of the contest (497, 514–16). It is as Heracles' sexual partner that Deianira fears Iole will replace her. The two of them will be under the same blanket awaiting Heracles' embrace (539–40). She may retain the status of wife but she fears Heracles will be called 'the younger woman's man' (550–1). When Deianira leaves the stage to kill herself the Chorus say again that it is the work of Aphrodite (860–1), and when she prepares to stab herself Deianira's language is full of sexual connotations (920–2).

Although the action of the play is driven by sex, Deianira's desire for Heracles is not straightforward. Nessus' story that his poisoned blood is a love-charm is, given the situation, so implausible that the audience must wonder why on earth she believed him. When the wool has shrivelled, but the deadly gift is already on its way, she herself asks

> From what possible motive, in return for what,
> could the dying beast have shown me kindness, when he
> was dying because of me? No, he beguiled me,
> only to destroy the man who shot him. But I
> have come to understand now when it is too late (707–11).

Some such awareness was trying to express itself in her anxiety before she sent the robe, when she asked the Chorus if they thought she was acting rashly (586–7). Sending Heracles the robe contains both her love and her rage towards him. She tries to deny her hostility, saying there is no point in fighting against Love:

> For he rules even the gods as he pleases, and
> he rules me – why not another woman like me?
> You see that I would be altogether mad
> to blame my husband because he suffers from this sickness,
> or that woman. She has been guilty of nothing shameful,
> and she has done no harm to me (443–8).

But this is much too reasonable. If Deianira had been more conscious of her conflict between love and fury, she might not have had to act out the unconscious murderous impulse. Her conflicts, however, are not simply because of Heracles' relationship with Iole. There are many indications in the play that sexuality is problematical in itself. Even in speaking of Heracles' feelings for Iole with such apparent acceptance, Deianira calls them a *nosos*, a sickness (445). This reference becomes more and more important as the play goes on. Hyllus, describing Heracles' agony in the poisoned robe, refers to him as *tou men nosountos*, 'having a *nosos*' (784). The word is used repeatedly thereafter (852, 882, 981, 1013, 1115), most notably by Heracles himself in his final lines (1260). His physical *nosos* reflects the emotional *nosos* which brought it about. At the onset of Heracles' agony, his reaction was to curse Deianira's 'bed with its evil intercourse' (791). At that moment he was not cursing her jealous revenge but the nature of their sexuality together.

Sophocles indicates clearly Deianira's ambivalence about sexuality. When, at the beginning of the play, she tells how she married Heracles, she says that she experienced *nympheiōn oknon algiston* (7–8), 'the most agonising fear of marriage'. *Algistos*, which Sophocles uses to describe her fearfulness, has the specific meaning of 'painful'. It can refer to physical or mental pain, but fear of what will happen to her body cannot be absent from her use of the word in this context. Her declared fear was of Achelous. His monstrous appearances as a bull, a serpent and a man with a bull's face, are full of phallic imagery, and she prayed for death rather than be his sexual partner. We have noted, however, the similarities between Heracles and Achelous, and how terrified Deianira seems of the whole contest. She is afraid of marriage itself, and when she says that Heracles' victory was a good outcome she immediately adds 'Or was it?' (27). This highlights beautifully the conflict that sexuality arouses for her. So far we have been shown her fear of its primitive, uncontrollable power. But she is also afraid of the dependence on Heracles which marriage to him entails. 'Or was it a good outcome?' leads on to her endless worry because he is always away and she does not know what is happening to him. When she says that being Heracles' bed-partner makes her vulnerable, she is talking both about her fear of his sexuality and about her dependence on him.

Deianira pointedly addresses the Chorus as unmarried women, virgins who cannot understand her anxieties (148). When the messenger reports that Heracles is alive and victorious the Chorus give thanks, but in language that has a certain irony. They call for cries of joy within the house because it is *mellonymphos* (207), 'ready for marriage'. The audience must suppose that this refers to the reunion of Heracles and Deianira. But the coming union of Heracles and Iole, which so far has not been revealed, is also ironically foreshadowed. The element *nymph-* in *mellonymphos*, which here is presented as the cause for joy, is the same root as in *nympheia*, the word Deianira used in telling of her agonising fear of marriage. The Chorus give thanks to Apollo and Dionysos and also, significantly, to Artemis and '*geitonas te nymphās*' (215), the 'neighbouring nymphs'. '*Nymphē*' has the two meanings of 'nature-spirit' and 'young bride', and here it means the former. But this comes only seven lines after *mellonymphos*, and to repeat the same word-root, this time in conjunction with Artemis, the virgin goddess, re-emphasises the tension between virginity and sexuality.

The ideas set out in the first part of this chapter suggest that the conflicted sexuality between Deianira and Heracles needed to be worked out, not just in terms of the two-person relationship, but in the light of its triangular context. Although the play is unified by the figure of Hyllus and his relationship to each of his parents, the situation only allows him to relate separately to each of them (the lines AB and AC). The link between them, which would be the line BC, fails. This failure of triangularity is the underlying structural motif of the play itself.

The action opens with a mother and son at home together and the father absent. Sophocles stresses the importance of the missing father–son relationship. In her opening speech Deianira says (31–5):

> We have had children now, whom he sees at times,
> like a farmer working an outlying field,
> who sees it only when he sows and when he reaps.
> This has been his life, that only brings him home
> to send him out again, to serve some man or other.

The Greek legendary hero was not meant to be a New Man, practising for the Augean Stables by taking his turn at the washing-up. But the image of crops growing conveys vividly the growth and development of children and how Heracles has not been part of that for Hyllus. When the Chorus enter and encourage Deianira about Heracles' safety, they remember that he is the son of Zeus and say, optimistically, that Zeus would not be careless of his children (140). This is the first of many references throughout the play to the relationship between Zeus and Heracles. Coming so soon after Deianira's comment on Heracles' lack of involvement with his own son, it has an ironic twist. We know that Zeus will not save his son but instead allow him to die in agony. (The play closes with the mysterious words 'There is nothing of this which is not Zeus.') The early, emphatic references to parent–child, and particularly father–son, relationships set out one of the play's main themes.

Hyllus has grown up with his mother, his father being effectively absent, and Sophocles shows how the sexuality that should have been there between the parents has been destructively replaced by sexualisation between mother and son. When Hyllus denounces Deianira, he describes Heracles, as the poison of the robe eats into him, cursing the sexuality that brought him and Deianira together. Hyllus evidently concurs with Heracles, and is thus himself cursing his own parents' sexuality. When Deianira leaves the stage Hyllus says with savage irony (819–20):

> And the delight
> she gave my father, may she find the same herself.

On finding his mother's dead body, however, and believing he has driven her to suicide, he is stricken with grief and guilt. Sophocles has the nurse describe the way he embraces her body in terms that would suit a lover. He falls upon her lips and presses his side to hers (938–9). Sophocles' word order, *pleurothen pleurān pareis*, brings their two bodies up against each other. This is all the more striking given Deianira's last words, reported by the Nurse a few lines earlier.

> O my bed, O my bridal chamber, farewell
> now forever, for never again will you take me
> to lie as a wife between these sheets of yours (920–2).

Sophocles gives Deianira, throughout this reported scene, a vocabulary with deliberately sexual overtones. Sex is what she is saying goodbye to. But a few lines later it is not her husband but her son who embraces her dead body, on the marriage-bed, like a lover.

Deianira and Heracles have not been able to sustain their side of a triangle. The indications of Deianira's conflicts over sex have already been noted. Heracles' part in the failure is represented by his chronic absence and also, of course, by his choice of Iole. Deianira makes a point of the age difference between herself and Iole (551), and it is important to recognise that Heracles has chosen a woman who belongs to his son's generation. Oedipal conflict is most commonly thought of in an upward direction: the child's desire and jealousy directed towards its parents. But there is also the downwardly directed conflict which belongs to the parents. As children reach maturity, sexuality relates itself to triangularity in fresh ways. Parents have their own incestuous desires and fantasies. Just as children have to give up their unrealisable desires, so parents have the later task of relinquishing their own, and giving up the jealousy of their children who do have the chance to realise them in the relationships that they will make. Father and mother must watch daughter and son take partners, and the partners of their children will be men and women beyond their own reach. Working this through is necessary for the parents' sexuality to continue developing, as they age, with a new maturity of its own.

After Deianira's final exit, the Chorus sing of Heracles as Zeus' very own son, using the rare and emphatic word *autopais* (826). Hyllus too makes much of being a true son to his father, but this is tragic irony. For that to have been possible, the Deianira–Heracles–Hyllus triangle needed to be intact. Heracles has not, however, sustained the relationship with his wife and, by not being a proper husband, he has not been a proper father. The sexual breakdown of the Deianira–Heracles bond exposes Hyllus to sexualisation of his own bond to his mother. The father–son relationship, then, is gripped by destruction. Hyllus' only way of being an *autopais* to Heracles is to curse his mother. Moreover, when Heracles makes the demand that Hyllus himself fetch Deianira and watch his father kill her, he prefaces this with (1064–5):

> O my son, now truly be my true born son
> and pay no more respect to the name of mother.

To be a true-born son has come to mean helping his father kill his mother.

The Deianira–Heracles–Iole triangle is set alongside this. Here the failure of the Deianira–Heracles pairing is linked to the inappropriate pairing between Heracles and Iole. For Heracles really to treat Hyllus as his son would have meant helping Hyllus give up his Oedipal attachment to his mother. Instead Heracles himself was unable to give up his own, downwardly directed, Oedipal attachment.

The competitive element in this inverted Oedipal conflict comes out in another triangle, one that is only implied in the play, but important none the less. This is the Heracles–Iole–Iphitus triangle. In Lichas' first, incomplete, version of why Heracles sacked Oechalia, he explains that the enmity between Heracles and Eurytus arose because Heracles was defeated in an archery contest by the sons of Eurytus (262ff.). It was in revenge for this that Heracles killed Eurytus' son Iphitus, and subsequently attacked Oechalia. Then we learn the missing element in the story, which is Heracles' love for and abduction of Iole. Heracles had thus been faced with a couple in the younger generation: a brother–sister couple, the children of his friend. And his reaction is to kill the young man who is superior to him and steal the woman. With the additional triangle Sophocles composes an Oedipal picture of compelling complexity. This triangle is a displaced representation of an older man's jealousy of his own son and rivalrous desire for the younger woman. But Iole, as sister of the son-figure, also represents a daughter. The incestuous component of the sexual rivalry is evident. The Heracles–Iole–Iphitus triangle is thus an exact reflection, upside down, of the son's desire to kill his father and marry his mother. Heracles' insistence on having Iole for himself is driven by his wish to deny castration anxiety; not the castration anxiety of the child, but the version that can present itself in later life, with all the accretions of maturity.

The long scene which ends the play introduces a shift in the quality of the relationship between Heracles and Hyllus, a change related to yet another triangle, between Heracles, Hyllus and Iole. From its beginning the scene is pervaded by the father–son motif. The Old Man who brings in Heracles, still asleep on his litter, addresses three lines to Hyllus about his father, beginning 'O child of this man!' Hyllus replies in three exactly balanced lines, ending with a reference to Heracles' father, Zeus, and when Heracles wakes, his first words are 'My child!' The shift begins when Heracles calls on Hyllus to follow the instructions he will give, specifically invoking the father–son relationship (1177–8):

> On your own, agree to act with me; discover
> yourself the finest rule – obedience to your father.

When he makes Hyllus swear it is 'by the head of Zeus who begot me' (1185), bringing the two father–son relationships into explicit apposition. The first thing he binds Hyllus to do is to take an active part in burning him on his funeral pyre. This is no longer, however, an impulsive wish born from the agony caused by 'your godless mother' (1034–40). It has become a solemn ritual which Hyllus must perform with dignity and no tears 'if you are my son' (1201). His second duty is to marry Iole. Hyllus is naturally horrified by both demands, and commentators too have found them hard to interpret. But there is sense to be made of them. The Heracles–Iole–Hyllus triangle is an undisplaced version of the Heracles–Iole–Iphitus triangle. In making Hyllus marry Iole, Heracles is restoring, but too late, the natural situation. The father gives up his rivalry and acknowledges that the younger woman belongs to his son, not himself. A father who can do this, accepting the implications of his ageing, can go on developing the relationship with his wife and continue being a true father to his son. This exactly matches how a son, accepting that his mother does belong to his father, becomes free to find a woman of his own outside the family, and thus continue as a true-born son. Both father and son have to accept that the son really is superseding his father. This is symbolised by Hyllus' participation in his father's death specifically in his role as son, and by Heracles' declaration that Iole belongs to Hyllus instead of himself.[3]

Trachiniae does show Sophocles' continuing interest in the theme that underlies *Oedipus Tyrannus*, but his exploration of it in this play is on a broader front. It emerged, from this chapter's opening discussion of the Oedipus complex, that every two-person sexual relationship implies triangular relationships as well. Sophocles confirms that this applies both up and down the generations, and also that there are multiple relations between triangularity and sexuality which need working through in different ways at different times of life. The boy does indeed have to give up his desire to possess his mother, and the girl her father. The identifications which allow them to do so are formative elements in their psychic structures, and if this fails to happen they will be left psychologically vulnerable. Working this through, however, is not the completion of a task, but a milestone in a lifelong process.

Clinical material

A supervisee reported that a patient, a single woman living alone with her 18-year-old son, said her son had asked for a cigarette in a graceless sort of way. She had replied 'Eighteen years old, and you still don't know how to ask for something so that you'll get it!' The tone showed that this was not a lesson in manners but distinctly flirtatious. She said her son had then asked for a cigarette so nicely that she couldn't refuse him. The therapist said 'He seduced you!' The patient replied 'Yes he did, didn't he?', with obvious pleasure. As well as the son's Oedipal interaction with his mother, this episode shows the mother caught up in an Oedipal involvement of her own. The relationship with her son should be psychically a triangular one, whether or not there is a father in the household. It seems that the lack of someone, not just in the family but in the woman's internal world, who could be the third point of a triangle, may be causing a problem for this mother, as well as her son, in working through the Oedipal situation.

---

3 In view of this discussion it is interesting that one of the ancient commentators on the play quotes an obscure variant of the story, which has Heracles asking Eurytus for Iole not on his own behalf, but for Hyllus (Easterling 1982: 17).

The following material is from a session with a patient in later life. Mr H was a successful man, well respected in the financial world. He was married for the second time, and had children from both marriages, including two sons. He and his wife were happy together, although he had had intermittent interest in other women, usually younger than himself. The sexual relationship with his wife was satisfying to both of them, but he sometimes felt it lacked a really deep level of fulfilment. He was liable to talk in a derogatory way about himself as an old man who was 'past it' and could not hope to have any sexual or creative drive left.

This session took place when the analysis was well advanced and the material shows Mr H becoming able to grapple with what the last scene, in particular, of *Trachiniae* refers to.

He was speaking about his sons. They had a rich network of relationships. One was successful overseas in the business world and the other was doing well in his profession. His pleasure in them was obvious, but he was talking rather intensely, as though he needed to convince me of it. Then he mentioned a conference where he was not sure how his contribution would be received. He hoped he would impress the colleague, a woman, who had invited him. I picked up the worry about whether what he had to offer was really wanted and said that, alongside his pleasure in his sons' success, he might also feel competitive with them. He told me a colleague in the same department of his firm had recently asked him for some technical advice. He had suddenly realised one of his sons had better access to the necessary information than he did, and referred the colleague to his son. He told me this with a kind of rueful pride. Next he talked about the holiday he and his wife were planning, and then said again that he was nervous about the conference. The woman who had invited him was attractive, single and some years younger than him. He had sexual feelings about her but was quite clear that he did not want an affair with her. This left him confused about what it would be like for him at the conference. I said I thought he was trying to give up an automatic kind of sexuality which again had an element of competitiveness with his sons. Giving that up meant recognising that he could not compete with them, and he did not know what sort of sexual feeling of his own he would be left with. On the other hand, it might be the only way to discover whatever feelings of a different sort were possible between him and his wife. This made him thoughtful and after a while he said, with some relief, that of course the woman had not invited him for a sexual adventure but for what he did have to offer, which was his expertise in the subject of the conference.

The overall connection between this material and the themes of *Trachiniae* is clear enough. But there is a particular point about the woman at the conference. The patient is trying to sort out whether he sees her sexually as an alternative to his wife, and it would be easy to think in terms of a triangle of the two women and himself. But to analyse his confusion what matters is a different triangle, one which is not so obvious at first sight. This has Mr H at one point, his sons at another, and at the third a fantasised woman, the Iole character, whose role is to confirm that he is still as young and potent as ever he was. There was no connection in reality between his sons and the woman at the conference. But the unconscious, late-life, downward-directed Oedipal fantasy was of winning out against his sons in rivalry for the affections of the Iole figure, whom the woman at the conference represents. Before he can go on developing his relationship with his own wife, this fantasy has to be given up. He needs to acknowledge, as he did recognise with the request from the colleague in his firm, that there is someone whose needs are going to be met by his son and not himself. His relief following my intervention was twofold. He realised that he was not obliged to enter an unwinnable competition with his sons. Having recognised that, he could enjoy knowing he did have something which, exactly because of 'the long companionship of time' (*Oedipus at Colonus* 7–8, p. 99), he really had made his own.

Psychoanalysts may once have thought of maturity as a kind of end-state, to be achieved through satisfactory childhood and adolescent development, so that adult life meant getting on with being the mature person one had become. Analytic thinking is now much more aware that later life has its own developmental challenges and opportunities. We have already seen that arriving at one's identity is a process with no conclusion (p. 82). *Trachiniae* highlights the fact that, if resolution of the Oedipus complex is a criterion of psychosexual maturation, that must be understood in terms of the lifelong developmental task which it represents.

8

The logic of play

Some people think football is a matter of life and death . . . I can assure them it is much more serious than that.

Bill Shankly[1]

To move from the last two chapters about plays to this one about play is not just a play on words. Play and plays both depend on a particular area of the imagination where things can be real and not real at the same time. The discussion, at the end of Chapter 6, about the nature of dramatic reality, raised the question of how people who are not real can have such a powerful emotional effect on the audience. That has to do with the paradoxical reality which the play space creates, and psychoanalysis shares with theatre a framework that makes this kind of reality possible (Pedder 1977, 1979).

Play is always at work in psychoanalysis. The classic statement of this is in Winnicott's much-quoted words:

Psychotherapy takes place in the overlap of two areas of playing, that of the patient and that of the therapist. Psychotherapy has to do with two people playing together. The corollary of this is that where playing is not possible then the work done by the therapist is directed towards bringing the patient from a state of not being able to play into a state of being able to play.

(Winnicott 1971: 38)

What Winnicott means is not simple. A sudden expansion of boundaries, unexpected freedom of exploration – these can bring pleasure and excite-

---

1 I could find no original reference for this famous quotation. It seems first to have appeared in a radio interview in the late 1960s with Ian St John, the Liverpool football player, who reported Shankly saying it in the dressing room after a match.

ment. But such episodes in an analysis, valuable and productive as they are, emanate from what play means at a deeper level. It is a tougher idea, that play is central to the nature of psychoanalysis, than may appear at first sight. It is a theoretical statement about the logic of the situation underlying clinical work. Far from being just an occasional aspect of analysis, the play element functions continuously to sustain a paradoxical reality, whose framework allows the analytic process to take place.

The idea of play as a serious and important element in human civilisation is an ancient one. Plato (*Laws* 803–4) said that since man was God's plaything life should be accepted as play. What mattered was to play it as the noblest game possible. In the eighteenth century Schiller (1795: clxxxv ff., 95–9) posited an instinct for play underlying artistic and other cultural activity. Johan Huizinga (1934) traced in detail how play permeates, in surprising ways, even our highest cultural achievements. Freud's concept, which he kept coming back to (Freud 1933: 89 fn. 1), of thinking as a kind of experimental action, puts him in the same company. The idea that thinking allows one experimentally to imagine an action without having to carry it out (Freud 1911b: 221), gives fantasy, originally seen as a defensive avoidance of reality, a positive, creative function as well. Fantasy, symbolism and play are closely related[2]. All three have both regressive and exploratory functions, which depend on their ambiguous, provisional relationship to reality. Freud conceived of thinking as playing with possibilities. There is a poem by Yeats which runs curiously parallel to one of Freud's own examples, expanding the image to show how momentous such play may be.

> Thinking is an experimental action carried out with small amounts of energy, in the same way as a general shifts small figures about on a map before setting his large bodies of troops in motion.
>
> (Freud 1933: 89)

> That civilisation may not sink,
> Its great battle lost,
> Quiet the dog, tether the pony
> To a distant post;
> Our master Caesar is in the tent.
> Where the maps are spread,
> His eyes fixed upon nothing,
> A hand under his head.
> *Like a long-legged fly upon the stream*
> *His mind moves upon silence.*
>
> (Yeats 1936–9: 381)

2 See pp. 175–6 for further reference to this.

Caesar is not 'playing soldiers'; one point of Yeats' poem is just how much is at stake. Caesar is playing a serious war game on the map, and his soldiers' lives the next day depend in reality on his getting it right. That in turn depends on the fact that now, in his tent, he can try out manoeuvres in fantasy, and play with ideas about what to do tomorrow.

As Yeats' poem shows, play is by no means always light-hearted. Robert Caper (1996) has described its importance in how the infant gets to know both the enjoyable and the unwelcome aspects of the world. Jean Sanville recalls telling a famous analyst that she liked a playful quality in his inter-pretations, only to be 'sternly admonished' by him that psychoanalysis was a serious undertaking. Her response was 'I'll have you know – and all of those in this room who have treated children will have you know – that play is serious business' (Sanville 1991: xi). In the concert hall an orchestra will 'play' a composer's 'work'. Play is often fun, but sometimes it feels like hard work, accompanied not by an easy pleasure but a more serious sense of satisfaction and fulfilment. Moments of expansive fun and humour in an analysis, or sudden, playful flights of imagination, arise out of this deeper, continuously flowing, undercurrent of serious play. If playfulness in analysis is not rooted in that deeper level, that is when it can become false and defensive, and the analyst needs to be vigilant for this and not collude with it.

Like fantasy, play refers to many kinds of activity. This chapter tends to focus on the underlying seriousness just mentioned; if this is not grasped the role of play in psychoanalysis may be misunderstood or mistakenly dismissed. But play is playful as well as serious. The problem of trying too hard for a single, inclusive definition is illustrated by a statement like 'play-ing a game by the rules may be derivative of play, but it is not play' (Solnit 1987: 215). It is true that rules may be used defensively to prevent more exploratory sorts of play, but none the less 'games' are 'played'. Rather than seeking definitions, it is more helpful to think in terms of a family of concepts, in a Wittgensteinian sense, which includes play, plays, playful-ness, games, sports and so on. Amongst these, the relation between play and games is, in fact, very important for clinical work, and later in the chapter I shall discuss it in the light of clinical material. Meanwhile, there is the question of what characterises these concepts as belonging to the same family.

There are sports like tennis and rugby which people play. But motor-racing and mountaineering are sports with a significant mortality rate. Is that play? The karate class, described at the beginning of Chapter 1, may shed some light on this. Karate training is not a real fight. But although we were only pretending to fight, we had to pretend seriously. The purpose of the training session was a particular kind of engagement with the other person at a depth, and with a seriousness, that was possible in no other way. Both karate and psychoanalysis allow something to be explored which would otherwise be impossible. What makes it possible is, for each of them, the framework within which they are practised: for karate the structure of the training class, for psychoanalysis the framework of the session. This family of concepts lies along a spectrum which runs from playfulness through to games and sports, which themselves vary from being relatively playful, open and flexible to being serious, tough and potentially dangerous. At one end of this spectrum might be a baby discovering how to play peek-a-boo with its mother and, at the other end, Formula One motor racing. No wonder definitions are unhelpful! But what is universal is the idea of a framework. The element of play undergoes all sorts of transformations across this spectrum, but the sense of a framework, almost intangible at one end, rigidly codified at the other, persists throughout. This is what characterises the activity as having a play element in one form or another.

The first appearance of play in Winnicott's writings also shows the significance of the framework. In his paper 'The observation of infants in a set situation' Winnicott (1941) describes the 'spatula game'. He would give an infant a metal spatula to play with, and he observed a regular sequence in the infant's responses. If pathological anxieties of one sort or another were present, the normal sequence of responses would be disrupted in certain typical ways. Winnicott describes part of the infant's behaviour as follows:

> he holds it [the spatula] to my mouth and to his mother's mouth, very pleased if we *pretend* to be fed by it. He definitely wishes us to *play* at being fed, and is upset if we should be so stupid as to take the thing into our mouths and spoil the game as a game.
>
> (Winnicott 1941: 54)

The playing is important to the infant, but it is spoiled if the grown-ups take it too seriously; or, to be more accurate, if they take it seriously in the wrong way.

If the analogy between karate and psychoanalysis is surprising, a parallel between karate and the spatula game may seem stranger still. The infant pretends to be really feeding the grown-ups; their part is to make the pretence real too, by pretending to be fed. But if they take the spatula into their mouths and really try to feed from it they spoil the game. The feeding can be treated as real provided it is not really treated as real. If that does happen, it stops being real at all. George Moran described a mother who, when she noticed her child playing with a toy tea set, organised a 'real' toy tea party, herself sitting on a tiny chair and serving real food on toy dishes. 'In this way she intrusively entered and controlled his fantasy play and unwittingly destroyed the quality of playfulness' (Moran 1987: 24). The same paradox is what makes karate training possible. Knowing that we were not engaged in a real fight allowed us to make our attacks with full seriousness and commitment, to make them as real as we possibly could. When we failed to make use of the framework of the class in that way, there was no reality at all and the instructor dismissed us. If, on the other hand, we had lost touch with the pretence like that mother, and started really trying to hurt our opponents, we would have broken the frame in the opposite way and, again, the training situation would have ceased to exist. Both the spatula game and the karate class depend on the same paradox: the activity has to be accepted as real, but this is only possible if we know that it is not real.

Observational studies have looked at how infants develop the capacity to manage these different realities. Robert Emde *et al.* (1997) found that by two years of age infants have two different kinds of psychic reality, one formed by the representation of everyday reality and the other a 'pretend' reality formed by the imagination. The two are not, normally speaking, in conflict but interact in a mutually enriching way. Peter Fonagy and Mary Target (1996a, 1996b) also discuss how infants integrate their imaginative and literal relationships to reality, and they attribute particular importance, for this, to play and to a framework that can sustain play.[3]

The function of the psychoanalytic play frame is to sustain a paradoxical reality that is continuously operative. Play is not for engaging in sometimes, until the work gets too serious and then it has to stop. It is when the work is most serious that it depends most profoundly on the play element, as the following case illustrates.

This is a woman who struggles with a constant fear of betrayal and finds trust almost impossible, because anybody or anything is liable to be a fake. Being alive means being on guard against deception. Her most tormenting concern is how to know whether she herself is a fake person. I think of play, with its ambiguous relation to reality, as being, for her, the psychological equivalent of anti-matter. She has been in analysis for seven years, at first five times a week, then four, and much of the work with her has felt anything but playful. Early on she would assault me with complaints about how useless I was to her with my aloof, uncaring attitude, and would batter me with demands to be told whether I really cared about her or not, telling me in the same breath that whatever I said she knew I did not care. She wanted to be my most difficult patient ever, to be such a problem that I could never stop thinking about her. What mattered to her was not being difficult, in itself, but being, in any way available, the most extreme person

---

3 Psychic reality is a central topic of Chapter 10. The comments there (pp. 175–6) on the connection between fantasy, symbolism, psychic reality and play, are relevant throughout the present chapter.

I had ever had to deal with. This was not for the sake of comparisons. I came to understand that only if she knew she was set apart from all others could she feel she had any identity at all. In response to interpretations she would show no apparent interest in thinking about herself, but turn on me in a rage for not saying the things she insisted that she needed me to say. Behind all this there was real despair. She let me know that she sometimes cut herself and she showed me a scalpel that she carried around with her. She gave it to me to look after for a few days but insisted on having it back again. Any moment of feeling understood by me had to be destroyed as soon as possible. The analysis began to make her aware of how much she did this, and sometimes, in the middle of the destructiveness, she would say 'You do understand, don't you, that it is absolutely necessary for me to be like this with you?' I would say that I did understand that, but if I went on to say anything about why it might be necessary, she would attack me again for making cruel and impossible demands on her. It may seem bizarre to offer this as an example of psychoanalytic play! Whatever chance of success such an analysis may have, however, it is only the play aspect that allows it to be sustained at all.

Gregory Bateson (1955), the anthropologist and biologist, once watched two young monkeys in the zoo playing at fighting, and his comments are reminiscent of the karate class. The monkeys' attacks on each other were the same actions as if they had really been fighting, but Bateson realised that, in addition to the signs of aggression, the monkeys must also be giving out signals about those signs themselves, signals which located the fighting in a play context instead of its being actual combat. Play becomes possible when organisms no longer respond automatically to another organism's behaviour, but are able to communicate about the nature of their behaviour and about its context. This is what makes play the milestone in the development of civilisation that Huizinga and others have recognised.

Bateson expresses the logic of the monkeys' play situation as follows. 'Expanded, the statement "This is play" looks something like this: "These actions in which we now engage do not denote what those actions *for which they stand* would denote"' (Bateson 1955: section 4). The playful nip, for example, denotes the bite but it does not denote what the bite itself would denote. My patient and I both have to understand, somewhere in our minds, that, even though she may give me what feel more like savage bites than playful nips, they still denote a murderous attack without carrying the meaning that that murderous attack would actually carry. Bitter and hard to bear as the experience may sometimes feel to both of us, so long as that remains true, the play element is present and the analysis can continue.

To make this possible, patient and analyst have to put a frame around what may accurately be called the interplay between them. That frame is the session, which is both a description of certain practical arrangements and, more importantly, a psychological concept which says that what happens within it is to be considered differently from what happens outside it. The trouble with such psychological frameworks is that they are always at risk of breaking down. Bateson instances the Andaman Islanders, who end a state of war by giving each side ceremonial freedom to strike each other. But these ritual blows of peace-making may be mistaken for the real thing, in which case the peace-making ceremony turns into a battle. This is the exact equivalent of how the analysis I am describing could break down. At times this patient has been afraid she might commit suicide and has needed me to be afraid of it as well. To consider the analysis, at that moment, in terms of play might seem the last thing that was called for. But that would be to confuse play with playfulness. It is our shared knowledge that killing herself would be her way of proving that she is alive, and that she does not, in the end, want to be dead, that lets us receive the full impact of meaning in what she does do. That paradox, which is the paradox of the karate class, is more than ever necessary to sustain the analysis in such an extremity.

A patient may, it is true, become so disturbed as to make in reality a serious attack on herself, or the analyst. If what my patient was meaning by her attacks in the analysis came to be replaced by the actual attack which they denoted, the play frame would have broken down and, for the time being at least, the analysis would have foundered. One might say that the civilisation we were struggling to develop would have collapsed back into a Dark Age. In such a case her impulses, instead of being contained by the framework, would have been enacted. Enactment is a concept that has gained currency in analytic thinking, and in a brief review of its usage, Anthony Bateman (1998: 13–14) calls it a hybrid term which covers a spectrum of ideas including acting out, acting in, actualisation and others. Enactment may be relatively benign or destructive. An extreme form can bring an analysis to a halt but lesser forms may regularly need to be worked through. Denis Carpy (1989) has written about the analyst's inevitable minor actings-out that arise from the countertransference, which have a mutative potential provided the analyst can become aware of their meanings. Bateman comments similarly on the positive aspect of enactment, when the analyst can observe and separate himself from what is happening, and make use of that understanding. At this point, however, he finds an ambiguity:

> What is not clear is how this differs from a normal analytic process in which the analyst constantly tries to differentiate what is his and that which is his patient's, what is projected and what is not. If we are to call this process enactment then presumably the whole of the analytic process is an enactment, rendering the term redundant.
>
> (Bateman 1998: 14)

This is clarified if we see the characteristic feature of enactment as being a greater or lesser degree of rupture of the play framework of the analysis. This means that the paradoxical reality, within which material can be handled as both real and not real at the same time, fails, at that moment, to be sustained. The important question then is whether the framework can be repaired. In occasional catastrophic cases it cannot. In the less serious instances described by Bateman and Carpy, I think the productive element lies in the active repairing of the play framework which they necessitate. Imagine a farmer going round his fences doing whatever bits of work are needed to keep them intact. The ordinary process of analysis goes on in the middle of the field. The conscious mending of the fence-frame after an enactment is something different. Patient and analyst may both need to take part in it, and the positive aspect of enactment comes from the increased awareness of the role of the analytic framework that this brings.

If play is the manifestation of a paradoxical reality, its nature depends on the logical structure of the paradox. The *paradox of the liar* is produced by the statement: 'What I am saying now is false.' If it is true that the statement is false, it is false. If, on the other hand, it is false that it is false, that makes it true. If it is true, it is false; if it is false, it is true. The paradox is produced by the way the statement is framed, so that its truth or falsity is used as evidence for its own falsity or truth. Bateson suggests that it is the operation of that sort of paradox that makes play possible. Consider a frame inside which is the statement: 'What is inside this frame does not mean what it says.'

What is inside this frame does not mean what it says.

Suppose we ask 'Does that statement mean what it says?' If it does mean what it says then, since it is itself inside the frame, it must be the case that it does not mean what it says. If, however, it does not mean what it says, then it must mean that what is inside the frame, which is to say itself, does mean what it says. So this frame produces a paradoxical statement which both means what it says and does not mean what it says. This paradox is the essential basis of play, and the frame is a representation of the play frame, as observed in the karate class, the spatula game, the mock combat of the monkeys and the interplay of the analytic session.

The same kind of paradox could be delineated for transference, framed in the same way as for play. Transference is sustained by a frame within which a statement like 'I am experiencing you as my father' is both true and known not to be true. Klauber (1987) has written of how truth and illusion are inextricably mingled in the transference. He emphasises that the therapeutic value of transference depends not on resolving the illusion but on accepting its paradoxicality. Although there is such a close relation between the play frame and transference, they are not to be equated. Where transference is concerned, what the paradoxical frame sustains is not its manifestations but the possibility of doing analytic work with them. Transference itself develops willy-nilly, an unconscious phenomenon beyond the control of patient or analyst. The analyst does not cultivate the transference, but observes it, and tries to understand it and interpret it to the patient. The play frame, however, needs to be nurtured and looked after. It is the analyst's task to maintain it, protecting it, if need be, against challenges from the patient and sometimes against the analyst's own impulses. As the discussion of enactment showed, the analyst's role as guardian of the play framework is not merely to protect its integrity, but to do so in such a way as to help the patient understand more and more fully how to make use of it. Winnicott's statement, about 'bringing the patient from a state of not being able to play into a state of being able to play', refers to how the analyst is always working for the patient to become more aware of, and more able to use, the constant presence of the play framework which underpins the analytic process. One of the articles that helped renew analytic interest in the concept of enactment is entitled 'The play of transference' (McLaughlin 1987). As James McLaughlin's examples of enactment illustrate, it is when the unconscious manifestations of transference can be embraced within the play framework, which recognises them as being real and not real at the same time, that it becomes possible to work with them analytically.

Matte Blanco's work was mentioned in Chapter 3, and there is a close relation between it and both Winnicott's and Bateson's ideas. Rayner's (1981) description of the child playing on the beach, quoted in Chapter 3 (pp. 49–50), shows how the paradoxical nature of play is related to symmetrical and asymmetrical thinking. Margaret Arden (1984) linked Matte Blanco's work to the ideas of Bateson, and Horacio Etchegoyen and Jorge Ahumada (1990) have examined the connection further. In the article considered here, Bateson was already describing psychological frameworks in terms of the mathematical sets which defined them, and showing that paradox is produced when asymmetrical logical relations are treated as though they were symmetrical (Bateson 1955: sections 16–17). He says, further, that play depends on a special combination of primary and secondary process in which they are both equated and discriminated. This is the same perception that Matte Blanco was to elaborate and develop into his concept of 'bi-logic'.

The view of play in this chapter may not look, so far, very playful. Gabriele Pasquali (1987) and Ronald Baker (1993), writing about the place of humour in psychoanalysis, give examples of the sort of moment when

something unmistakably playful does break through, and they are illuminating about what it depends on. In particular they distinguish between
humour and telling jokes. They point out that humour is spontaneous, and
they both oppose telling jokes in order to make something happen in the
analysis. Likewise, the last thing I mean by play is an analytic manoeuvre
aimed at producing some result or other. But phrases like the 'use' of humour,
and questions of whether it has 'a place in analytic technique' creep un-
avoidably into both articles, as they tend to in all writing on this subject.
One cannot spontaneously 'make use of' something, or spontaneously
apply a technical procedure. Both authors are as clear as they can be about
this, but the distinction takes some hanging on to. When Pasquali presented
his paper at a Scientific Meeting of the British Psycho-Analytical Society
(20 May 1987), however clearly he repeated that it was not about telling the
patient jokes but about the spontaneous emergence of something between
him and the patient, in the discussion he was still criticised for telling jokes.
This failure to head off misunderstanding is reminiscent of Nacht's experience, referred to in Chapter 1 (pp. 13–14). Pasquali and Nacht were both
drawing attention to the need for trust in the analyst's unconscious processes. There is something difficult about the essential point that humour,
unlike jokes, comes apparently out of the blue. As Pasquali puts it,

> The image that the humorous communication conjures up in our mind,
> the image which makes us laugh or smile, if we are free to catch it, is a
> precious portrait of a difficult situation in which we are painfully stuck.
> Only if we can laugh at our 'seriousness' painted with its paradoxical
> elements, can we reach a deeper level of seriousness.
>
> (Pasquali 1987: 232)

This comment on humour contains much that is true of play in general.
The point of 'if we are free to catch it' is that being able to allow humour,
and play, to happen, depends on the degree of trust an analyst has in her
unconscious. Part, at least, of the benefit of this sort of true playfulness in
analysis is that the patient, experiencing how the analyst trusts her unconscious, is helped to become less frightened of his own.

The analyst's unconscious, though she is less automatically governed by
it than before she became an analyst, remains uncontrollable and unpredictable. To be able to trust that one's unconscious intention towards a patient
is fundamentally benign, means also being able to mistrust oneself; to face
one's hostile impulses and one's own wishes, as an analyst, to avoid truth
as well as to know it.[4] It has already been noted (p. 75) that Klauber follows his description of spontaneous interpretations by emphasising that

4 See Chapter 2 (pp. 24–5) and Chapter 5 (p. 71).

the disciplined understanding out of which they arise is what saves them from being wild analysis. Baker (1993: 956) states the essential point: 'The use of humour in the psychoanalytic situation can only be effective if it is spontaneous but at the same time under control, to the extent that it is in the service of deepening the psychoanalytic process.' This is true, in just the same terms, of play. George Christie (1994) has also drawn attention to the link between humour and play, and his own examples of constructive humour in the therapeutic situation confirm Baker's observation. What distinguishes true psychoanalytic play is that it serves to deepen the analytic process.

When the meaning of the play element in psychoanalysis is understood at this level, its centrality declares itself in fresh ways. Roy Schafer (1976: 22–56) considers the vision of reality implicit in psychoanalytic thought and practice in terms of its comic, romantic, tragic and ironic aspects. These are traditional dimensions of experience in literary and philosophical thinking. Comic does not simply mean funny. The definition of a comedy is not a humorous play, but one with a happy ending. The comic vision of reality emphasises an optimistic view of the future and the hope that difficulties can be overcome. The romantic vision is of a heroic, questing journey culminating, after struggle and adventure, in the achievement of the goal. Both of these have their place in analysis, but Schafer believes the other two elements, the tragic and the ironic, are what specifically characterise the psychoanalytic vision of reality. Of the tragic he writes:

> The person with a tragic sense of life knows the renunciations that are intermingled with the conditions of gratification; the necessity to act in ignorance and bear the fear and guilt of action; the burden of unanswerable questions and incomprehensible afflictions; the probability of suffering while learning or changing; and the frequency with which it is true that only in the greatest adversity do people realise themselves most fully. Of all the perspectives on human affairs, the tragic is by far the most remorselessly searching, deeply involved and, along with the ironic, impartial.
>
> (Schafer 1976: 35)

Not much scope for play there, it seems! The need not to flinch from that remorselessness is what makes psychoanalysis so hard. The tragic vision is made bearable by its counterbalancing with the ironic, with its

> readiness to seek out internal contradictions, ambiguities and paradoxes . . . The ironic vision considers the same subject matter as the tragic but aims at detachment, keeping things in perspective, taking nothing for granted, and readily spotting the antithesis to any thesis so as to reduce

the claim of that thesis upon us. In this respect the ironic vision tends to limit (not minimise) the scale of involvement in human difficulty while continuing to insist on the inherent difficulties of human existence.

(Schafer 1976: 50–1)

The ironic can, like the other stances, be used in the service of resistance. But it has a profound importance in helping the patient, and the analyst too, to bear giving up omnipotent wishes, the loss of hoped-for gratifications and the failure to reach ideals. It says that reality is indeed to be taken seriously, but within a certain framework; seriously but not too seriously; or, more accurately, seriously but not in the wrong way. Irony has this central place in the psychoanalytic vision by virtue of the element of play which it contains. The irony may be savage and the play may be tough, but none the less what irony does is to handle the negative, the potentially destructive and unbearable elements of experience and tame them, not by denying them but by playing with them.

One side of the coin, then, is how play tames the negative. The child-analytic literature has many accounts of play used to master frightening or traumatic situations by exploring them within a framework that makes them bearable (e.g. Arlow 1987: 34ff.). The *fort-da* game with the cotton reel (Freud 1920: 14–15) is an example, and even the simplest, funniest peek-a-boo game is an experiment with the possibility that the mother might disappear. All progress means leaving something behind. The tragic aspect of reality is always facing us, in one form or another, with the need to confront the negative (Green 1993), and the regressive aspect of play helps to work through the mourning for those losses that any process of development involves.

The other side of the coin is the excitement of play, its exploratory quality, the curiosity about what will happen next. Development is frightening because we give up something safe and familiar in favour of we know not what. But this will be balanced, unless the anxiety is too great, by the excitement of discovery and a hope for what the unknown may have to offer. For interest in the unknown and curiosity about it to overcome fear of it, for exploring it to feel safe enough, there must be a containing framework that can be trusted. For the child, this is the parental couple; eventually, the internalised parental couple. The child needs to feel that the parental couple can tolerate, and enjoy, its curiosity without needing to reject it as an intrusion, while still maintaining their own boundaries. In psychoanalysis, if the play element is to function properly, it is the analytic couple that the patient must be able to trust in this way; again, eventually, the internalised analytic couple.

These are truly two sides of one coin. We cannot bear loss unless there is enough hope in the future; and exploring the unknown means being able to contemplate losing what we do know. These interrelations are shown by the later course of the analysis of the patient mentioned earlier. She was able to stay in her analysis, using the play frame in the fearsome way I described, and within the analytic framework she became able to bear real experiences of loss. Lying on the couch came to feel too dangerous and she sat opposite me instead. This was safer and the analysis could continue, but giving up an experience which, although terrifying, had felt so intense, was still a loss and cause of grief to her. Sometimes, instead of just letting the grief be swallowed up in fury, she was able to stay in it and find a way to express it. It was difficult to let go of the anguish, however, because any hope for the future was so uncertain.

She has regularly demanded to be told personal facts about me and my life outside the analytic setting. It infuriates her that I take these questions as needing to be understood rather than answered, even though she says explicitly that she is not interested in the information. But it has gradually become possible for moments of understanding to last for longer. One demand was to know if I discussed her with a colleague. She saw that this was connected to how she longed to feel that her parents shared real concern for her, but moving on from that archaic longing was not easy because of the lack of a trustworthy internal couple who could make it safe enough to risk the unknown. The wish for the analysis to provide her with a static, 'perfect' relationship seems, a lot of the time, a safer alternative. But not always. As I have resisted her demands for information about my ordinary reality, her paradoxical way of wanting and not wanting the information at the same time has become clearer to both of us, and the battles which the demands provoke contain more potential. We saw, for example, that behind one of her demands to know if I were married there lay, not jealousy of my wife if I had one, but the hope that I did have a stable relationship of my own, so that she could have a life without looking after me.

But the battles are necessary. It is a condition of any development that the interaction between us stay as sharp-edged and emotionally violent as ever. When I wondered whether she felt she came to her sessions more for my benefit than hers, she very nearly broke off the analysis. I had intended an interpretation about her feeling obliged to look after my emotional needs, but what she heard me say, it turned out, was that for her to think that she could, in any way, have anything worth while to offer me, was pathetic rubbish. A few days later she came up with a vivid image of her parents as science fiction monsters who had got inside her ('The Invasion of the Body Snatchers') and infiltrated themselves into her personality so completely that she could not distinguish between her own self and theirs. This self-awareness, however, still had to be couched in the form of an attack on me for the outrageous idea that it might ever be possible for her to change.

She is able to refer back to earlier in the analysis when, as she has put it, covering my walls with blood was the only way of making me notice her; and I can interpret this as meaning that it was her only way of knowing, herself, that she was alive. But the idea of losing that way of being angers and grieves her. She feels less alive, not more, from being understood, if it seems to make things easier, and therefore less intense, between us. The idea that intensity and destructiveness might not be the same thing remains difficult.

As we have learned, however, to make use of the framework in ways that are closer to karate than the spatula game, more directly playful moments are able to surface out of it. In one session she reminded me of two episodes in the analysis. Fairly recently, I had said something which indicated some knowledge of the anatomy of the female genitals. On the other occasion, years previously, a comment of mine had, she now told me, implied to her that I took it for granted I could always, with some well-practised automatic routine, bring a woman to orgasm if I wanted to. Having recalled these, she now played with the picture of me exploring a woman's genitals, 'burrowing through the pubic undergrowth on a Darwinian expedition'. The way she conjured this up was, in fact, rather funny. It mattered for me to see beyond this and I said 'But when I get there what am I going to do? Bring the woman to orgasm in a mechanical, depersonalising way that will actually be quite horrible.' And she said 'Absolutely' in a sombre voice. She is afraid that the analysis which she wants to be special and unique is, for me, just a routine performance. It was important that her humour should not stop us recognising her fear of being with an analyst who might coldly manipulate her when she was at her most open and vulnerable. She sometimes demands to know if I have what she calls a 'fast lane' in my life, beyond the measured, thoughtful side of me that she sees. This is because she finds it hard to imagine how opposites can be held together in a unity, and so, if I do have a 'fast lane', she cannot conceive how the two different aspects of me could be connected. I would therefore be 'cheating on her' by not bringing my whole self into the analysis. This reflects her own difficulty in knowing how to integrate the complicated, different aspects of her own self. Given all of this, for her to be able to see something as funny and horrible at the same time, without either of those mitigating the other, was a significant experience.

Another time she asked me, in her abrupt, apparently out of nowhere sort of way, 'Are you married to a Jew?' She herself is Jewish, and her Jewishness is important to her. I was at a loss, in the middle of a hard session, for how to respond. Then words came to me and it felt possible to risk them. I said, looking straight back at her, 'It does sometimes feel like it.' She looked at first as though she could not believe I had said it, then looked shocked, and then creased up with laughter, eventually being able to say 'That was very funny.' This was unconventional psychoanalysis, but I realised on reflection that her question and my answer had contained a richness of unconsciously condensed comment on the analytic relationship between us, which would have been killed by any attempt to spell it out. The elusive genuineness of such moments is hard to convey, but when playfulness is earned, as that had been on both sides, it can carry a lot of meaning.

This case sheds light on the relation, mentioned earlier, between play and games. One thing to be said about games is that the nature of the outcome is known in advance. Not the outcome itself, of course, but what the end-point of the game consists of: win, lose or draw; so many points scored; reaching or not reaching some goal. The nature of the outcome is what defines the game, and the rules are there to keep that definition in place. Games are certainly one form of playing, but their structured quality allows them to be used as a defence against the unpredictability of a different kind of play (Caruth 1988). The only kind of playing this patient knew, to begin with, was to play, in deadly earnest, an unpleasant game with me. That meant she was keeping us constrained within a certain range of interactions, using an imposed, although unconscious, set of rules which limited what we could do with each other to exchanges based around cruelty and hostility. Such a game may be necessary, and the analyst may have to accept that playing it like this is the only way for that person to feel safe enough. As Winnicott (1971: 50) put it: 'playing is always liable to become frightening. Games and their organisation must be looked at as part of an attempt to forestall the frightening aspect of playing.' My patient needed to allow us virtually no let-up from her game for several years, because any idea of a wider range of emotional interaction was too frightening to imagine. An important moment arrived when she could put into words that making someone an object of her hatred was the greatest expression of love she could imagine. This paradox was, for her, a simple description of how she related to people. It let us understand why the game had to be made as hateful as possible: her ability to love was the stake she was playing for. To understand this made the game no longer a defensive structure only, but also an expression of desire and hope.

The degree of support that patients are able to lend their analysts in sustaining the play frame varies. With some, who find it hard to make sense of what play means, the analyst has to do it virtually single-handed, and sometimes in the face of attack. This may need to continue for a long time, before what has seemed to the patient like a wilful denial of ordinary reality on the analyst's part can be perceived as holding a space open for new sorts of experience. Here are two examples of how more overt playfulness can enter into the analytic process. Both became possible only after long and arduous analytic work. It happens that in each one there is pleasure in word-play, but they feel rather different because they represent the two sides of the coin. The first example has its roots in the past but is forward-looking and exploratory, while the second, although it looks to the future, is more reflective of loss that needs coming to terms with.

A patient had begun to be able to express his curiosity about me. For a long while he was hardly able to know that he had any. Then came a time when he tried to look at me, to notice what I was wearing and to think about what mood I was in. Doing this made him terrified. When he looked at my face he saw monsters looking back at him, in my face itself and standing behind my chair. (Throughout the period described here he was coming four times weekly, but sitting facing me.) These monsters were not hallucinations, but the experience was real enough for him almost to run out of the room. We could relate this to the family atmosphere of his early life, where there was a sense of something deeply wrong which he could not let himself be aware of, let alone curious about. If he had done, the unconscious fear was that he would see his parents as monsters.

A year or more further on in the analysis, with a lot of work done in that time, he had a dream in which I was telling him, of my own accord, personal details about my life and relationships. This felt inappropriate and in the dream he was upset about it, thinking he had lost me as his analyst. There were two aspects to this dream. One was the curiosity it did show about the kinds of thing I was revealing. The other was an anxiety about whether I could stand up to his curiosity and preserve the analytic boundary in the face of it; or even, worse still, whether my emotional needs might drive me to use him for some kind of comfort or reassurance of my own. This related directly to his mother who said of him, as a little boy, that he was 'born to serve' her. When this link was made he could say that during the last year he had been intensely curious about my private life, but could only bring that into the open now that he felt I would not attack him for it, but not yield to it either.

Then he said, looking intently at me: 'This is different, isn't it, from when I used to look at you and see monsters?' He paused, thought, and said to himself: 'See monsters . . . see monsters? . . . sea-monsters!' and began laughing. He was imagining sea-monsters in the room and said, laughing and puzzled at the same time, that they seemed benign. He thought of Small Porgys in Kipling's (1902) 'The butterfly that stamped'. (Small Porgys was a friendly sea-monster that smiled at travellers.) He said again, between laughs: 'How did this room suddenly get full of benign sea-monsters?' By now we were both laughing. There was something wonderfully surreal about this first-floor room in north-west London, all of a sudden filled with smiling sea-monsters. When the laughter had passed he looked at me again and said 'Where on earth did *that* come from? How did the monsters I used to see in you turn into Small Porgys?' I said I thought he was having the experience, which it seemed he had not found with his parents, of us as a couple who had confidence in the framework of their relationship, so that the small boy in him felt safe enough to let his curiosity and imagination run riot in the way it could not do during his childhood. This response was connected with my own confidence that the psychoanalytic quality of our relationship, built up over many years, was strong enough for this playfulness to be analytically safe. His letting go of the playfulness in order to think about where it had come from confirmed this, and in the next session he said he had looked again at 'The Butterfly that Stamped' and been reminded that Small Porgys ate up the food that Suleiman-bin-Daoud had prepared for all the animals in the world. There was evidently something not so benign around as well, which needed exploring.

A woman began her analysis with a profound but undefined dissatisfaction with herself. It gradually emerged that she was utterly unable to use her imagination. She could not wonder about anything, speculate, fantasise or, indeed, have any visual images in her mind at all. Through analysis this changed and she discovered in herself a strong vein of creativity. This took several forms, visual and otherwise, including, at one stage of her analysis, a particular kind of playing with words. For example, she was interested in the phrase 'The pen is mightier than the sword.' This became 'The pen-is mightier than the s-word.' The point about the s-word was the shape of the letter 's'. Its rhythmic curve stood for a deep, inward sense of the rhythms of her femaleness which, however, she felt could not withstand the might of the penis. 'Mightier' was 'my tear' – her grief at the failure of her femaleness. That became also 'my tear' – the laceration of her vagina that she feared from the too mighty penis. She hoped I 'might hear' all this, but she was afraid that instead I would fall victim to her anger against the penis. Michael (which she knew was my name) was 'my kill'. This was able to change, though, as she gained trust in her femaleness as something creative. She could make use of the 's' in the s-word to transform 'my kill' into 'my skilled person' (Michael Parsons) who might, after all, be able to help her. When we came to consider ending, she did not know, at first, if separation felt possible. 'Apart' was all one word. As she did become able to see us as separate and to think she could go on developing away from me, she also felt I would go on being 'a part' of her and she hoped she would have become 'a part' of my life too.

She had found her own idiosyncratic way of playing with words as objects and symbols at the same time. It was emotionally intense, with a different feeling from the sea-monsters. There were more tears than laughter. There was also not much interpreting, at the time, on my part. When

I thought she was defensively caught up in the word-play by way of avoiding anxieties in other areas, I turned out to be wrong. As for explicating the word-play itself, she was usually ahead of me. I sometimes made transference connections to other relationships in her life, but what she mostly needed was for me to be there while she played in this serious, sometimes painful way, investigating herself and her experience of the relationship between us.

The papers on humour discussed earlier tended to focus on what comes from the analyst. The examples just given appear to be of playfulness initiated by the patient. But it is not so one-sidedly simple. Pasquali and Baker criticise the telling of jokes because the analyst does it to the patient unilaterally. Instead of arising between them it is imposed by one on the other. The examples in their papers of humour as contrasted with joke-telling show clearly that the humour did not come from the analyst alone, but arose between patient and analyst. The same is true of the play in these examples. This highlights the already clear connection between the play frame and transitional space. The paradoxical space in which children's play occurs is a more developed version of the infant's transitional space where paradox is not to be challenged. The continuing availability of that same intermediate space throughout the whole of life is a central theme of Winnicott's (1971) *Playing and Reality*.

Play in the analytic relationship takes place by the evolution of shared experience in an intermediate space, where patient and analyst have the possibility of finding, by a mixed process of invention and discovery, new ways of knowing and of being known which their starting-point gave no means of predicting.

9

Creativity, psychoanalytic and artistic

Man's greatness is always to recreate his life, to recreate what is given to him, to fashion that very thing which he undergoes.

Simone Weil (1947: 157) *Gravity and Grace*

Freud begins his essay 'The Moses of Michelangelo' by acknowledging his difficulty with works of art:

This has occasioned me, when I have been contemplating such things, to spend a long time before them trying to apprehend them in my own way, i.e. trying to explain to myself what their effect is due to. Wherever I cannot do this, as for instance with music, I am almost incapable of obtaining any pleasure. Some rationalistic, or perhaps analytic, turn of mind in me rebels against being moved by a thing without knowing why I am thus affected and what it is that affects me.

(Freud 1914b: 211)

Freud finds it difficult to appreciate a work of art if he cannot understand it in his own rational, analytical terms. He is interested in unconscious processes provided they are analysable. He wrote similarly of dreams:

There is often a passage in even the most thoroughly interpreted dream which has to be left obscure; this is because we become aware during the work of interpretation that at that point there is a tangle of dream-thoughts which cannot be unravelled and which moreover adds nothing to our knowledge of the content of the dream. This is the dream's navel, the spot where it reaches down into the unknown.

(Freud 1900: 525)

146

Freud is saying that what cannot be analysed cannot add to our knowledge, and must therefore be left on one side. One can see why Trilling (1951: 48) thought he did not understand the nature of artistic meaning. But Freud's choice of language suggests something more encompassing than what he purports to say. However baffled he was by his own response, the *Moses* did affect him powerfully, and to speak of the dream's 'reaching down' implies some kind of contact, analysable or not, with the unknown. The Greeks called Delphi 'the navel of the earth' because it was, for them, a unique point of contact with archaic mystery. Our own navels are a living symbol and reminder of our lives before we were born. Even as Freud seems to reject the unknowable, he reveals his respect for it.

The interest in creativity, that accompanied his ambivalence in the face of it, is evident in Freud's work, and psychoanalytic writing about art and literature has always been abundant. There is much less, however, about creativity in the field of psychoanalysis itself. Perhaps this is another expression of the tension between rigour and freedom. The unfathomable quality of creativity might seem to mask all too easily a departure from established theory and reliable clinical technique. The emotional resonances, the halo of associations around technique and creativity, pull in opposite directions. Technique is a clear and disciplined guide. This may feel reassuring, or constricting; but it is, at least, safe. Creativity is undisciplined and full of subjectivity, but spontaneous and life-enhancing. Analysis needs them both, but they seem to endanger each other.

The polarity shows itself early on in analytic literature. Freud's papers on technique have many remarks about not applying rules as rigid dogma, and the need for flexibility. His rules for beginning the treatment, for example, are 'recommendations'. He opposes any 'mechanisation of the technique' (Freud 1913a: 123). The overall impression on reading these papers, though, is that Freud is giving instructions, more than showing how to explore possibilities. The instructions have become basic to the clinical method of psychoanalysis. But the tension remains, between the scope for clinical creativity which Freud appears to imply, and the way his writing can in fact feel like a prescription to be followed. The difference between obeying rules and following principles was emphasised in Chapter 1 (p. 17). Freud sets out to indicate principles, but his anxiety about whether they would be properly adhered to lets him seem all too easily to be laying down rules.[1]

He acknowledged this in his response, already mentioned in Chapter 4 (p. 54), to a paper Ferenczi (1928) wrote out of his unease over exactly this

1 See the discussion in Chapter 5 (pp. 77ff.) of conflicting elements in Freud's personality. The correspondence mentioned in note 3 to that passage refers to Freud's papers on technique.

issue. Ferenczi writes with admiration of Freud's systematising of technique. But what provoked the paper was his wish to examine what remains after that: the indefinable something which depends on the individuality of the analyst. The word he finds to describe this is 'tact'. He writes: 'The analyst, like an elastic band, must yield to the patient's pull, but without ceasing to pull in his own direction, so long as one position or the other has not been conclusively demonstrated to be untenable' (Ferenczi 1928: 95). Tact used so as to make the analyst's insights acceptable to the patient is one thing. What Ferenczi describes here, however, is the analyst's allowing himself to yield, to be moved by the patient, not so that the patient shall necessarily come to agree with him, but to allow some new position, unknown so far to either patient or analyst, to emerge. Ferenczi sent the paper to Freud for comment. When his paper was published he appended Freud's response (Ferenczi 1928: 99), and Jones also quotes Freud's letter to him.

> The title is excellent and deserves a wider provenance, since the Recommendations on Technique I wrote long ago were essentially of a negative nature. I considered the most important thing was to emphasise what one should *not* do, and to point out the temptations in directions contrary to analysis. Almost everything positive that one *should* do I have left to 'tact', the discussion of which you are introducing. The result was that the docile analysts did not perceive the elasticity of the rules I had laid down, and submitted to them as if they were taboos. Sometime all that must be revised, without, it is true, doing away with the obligations I had mentioned. . . . All that you say about tact is assuredly true enough, but I have some misgivings about the manner in which you make those concessions. All those who have no tact will see in what you write a justification for arbitrariness, i.e. subjectivity, i.e. the influence of their own unmastered complexes. What we encounter in reality is a delicate balancing – for the most part on the preconscious level – of the various reactions we expect from our interventions. The issue depends above all on a quantitative estimate of the dynamic factors in the situation. One naturally cannot give rules for measuring this; the experience and the normality of the analyst have to form a decision. But with beginners one therefore has to rob the idea of 'tact' of its mystical character.
>
> (Jones 1958: 270–1)

The ambivalence in Freud's response is evident. As soon as he has acknowledged 'elasticity' he has to reassert 'obligations'. He is afraid Ferenczi is introducing something which cannot be contained in the framework of metapsychology. This would make it, he thought, subjective and irrational. Ferenczi had not the least wish to make psychoanalysis irrational and writes aggrievedly, in his comment on Freud's response, that his principal aim in writing the paper was precisely to rob tact of its mystical character. But they are not in disagreement so much as at cross purposes. Freud's referring to 'tact' as 'making concessions' misses the whole point of Ferenczi's paper. Ferenczi was discovering an interpretative stance similar to the one Klauber arrived at in the second of his two papers on interpretation discussed in Chapter 5. But Freud could only respond to him, as it were, out of Klauber's first paper.

Fenichel's introductory lectures on technique at the Vienna Psychoanalytic Institute carry the debate further. He acknowledges that psychoanalysis cannot dispense with intuition and empathy (1941: 3–6). His continual emphasis, however, is again on the metapsychological framework, and he writes scathingly of analysts who

> misuse the idea of the analyst's unconscious as the instrument of his perception so that they do hardly any work at all in analysis but just 'float' in it, sit and merely 'experience' things in such a way as to understand fragments of the unconscious processes of the patient and unselectively communicate them to him. There is thus lacking the oscillation from intuition to understanding and knowledge which alone makes it possible to arrange in a larger context the material which has been understood with the help of the analyst's unconscious. Only in this way can we get a picture of the whole structure of the individual which, even though it is always of a provisional nature and alterable at any time according to new analytic experiences, still determines the order and nature of our interpretations. The so-called 'tact', which determines when and how a given matter is to be revealed to the patient, seems to me . . . quite determinable in a systematic way and therefore teachable in a proper degree through comprehension of the definite dynamic changes which take place in the patient during the analysis.
>
> (Fenichel 1941: 5)

This is Freud's reply to Ferenczi writ large. Fenichel implies that Ferenczi's 'tact' and his yielding elasticity add nothing to the theory of technique and are actually conducive to dangerous errors.

Suppose we go back to the question that ran through Chapter 3 about who gets taken by surprise during an analysis. Fenichel would take it for granted that it is the patient, when the analyst 'reveals' things to him. Of course the analyst does make unexpected discoveries about the patient. But the sense of shock which induces a sudden, new experience of reality, which makes one come psychically alive, that experience which is so essential to psychic change: Fenichel's account always has the analyst helping it happen in the patient. One feels that if a student of Fenichel's were touched by a sudden sense of mystery, or startled by an expansion of his own awareness, this would mean he did not know his theory as well as he should have done in the first place. In another set of introductory lectures for students, however, Symington writes:

> Truth in psychoanalysis emerges between the analyst and the patient, and in the moment of understanding there is a change in both. The glimpse of truth demands that a preconception is abandoned in both, for both have come to the encounter with their own preconceptions.
>
> (Symington 1986: 19)

This is a different view of the analyst's relation both to the patient and to his or her own knowledge. It is not just the patient but the analyst too who must be open to surprise.

All analysts would agree that it is important to tolerate the state of not knowing, without irritably trying to escape from it. This is Keats' often quoted 'negative capability' (Gittings 1970: 43 – letter of 21 December 1817). For all the apparent agreement, however, analysts may not mean at all the same thing by this. Not knowing may be seen as a temporary setback to be patiently endured until the analyst's knowledge catches up with her. Or it may be seen, very differently, not as something to be tolerated *faute de mieux*, but as necessary in principle, because without the loss of what we thought we knew the previously unsuspected truth cannot make itself visible. If creativity is the discovery of what we had not known we were looking for, or the making of something, up until now, un-imagined, it calls for a special sort of vulnerability. To be open to the shock of creative discovery means putting ourselves at risk and being ready to give up, with no certainty about the future, ways of seeing which up until now have served us well.

A crucial question, however, for the analyst: does such vulnerability belong in the actual encounter with the patient? Many would say that the analyst should have confidence in her theory as it stands and apply it sys-tematically in her clinical work, as representing her best knowledge to date. If she is vague and indefinite with her patients she will do them no good. The vulnerability, the loss of what she thought he knew – that belongs, on this view, in the laboratory of her conceptualising and not in the consulting-room. The second understanding of negative capability is sometimes criti-cised in this way, as though it represented an idealisation of uncertainty. But being willing to wait, accepting the state of not knowing as a space that the unexpected can enter into, is a very clear position. Vagueness and uncertainty are generated, rather, by the desire for a certainty that is not there. In Chapter 3 (p. 48) it was emphasised that Bion's +K state of mind is not an insistence on knowing, but a willingness to know, which implies also a willingness not to know. The willingness to wait, with the patient, in that clear position of acceptance towards the unknown, is another manifestation of the analyst's trust in her own and the patient's unconscious processes.

Freud's realisation of the role of fantasy following his abandonment of the seduction theory, and the new view of countertransference which developed in the 1950s, were major conceptual advances. Even such theoretical landmarks, however, were only possible because Freud and, for example, Paula Heimann (1950) found their assumptions questioned in the consulting-room. However much hard conceptual work outside the session was needed to formulate these advances, the foundations of what had seemed secure were shaken in the encounter with the patient. It is hard to sustain a distinction between undeviating use in the session of theory as it exists, and willingness creatively to re-examine it outside the session. Analysts need to be vulnerable to the loss of what they thought they knew, to giving up their preconceptions, while they are with their patients as well as when they think about them in the safety of their absence.

The place of creativity within the clinical situation, however, is no straightforward matter. Consider the session described in Chapter 4 (pp. 59–61) in which the patient became agitated and confused about his tears, shit, semen and urine, and then talked about Bach and Mozart. It was an important session in which the fear of his chaos and destructiveness became less overwhelming. Notice, though, how my technique could be criticised. The hostility to me early in the session is unmistakable. When the patient says his teacher is useless not to notice how destructively he is playing the violin, it might seem obligatory to interpret that he will find me useless if I do not recognise his destructiveness towards me. Instead I made a comment about Mozart's music. This led to his noticing for himself his feelings towards me and seeing the discrepancy between his fantasy of me and the reality. A discovery that a patient makes for himself like this is more valuable than something interpreted. But suppose nothing had come of my remark. What did happen could not be foreseen and might easily not have happened. It is all very well for me to pass up an opportunity of interpreting, for the sake of his having his own realisation. If no such realisation occurs, however, my not taking up the negative transference might well look like a mistake, and leaving a creative space for the unexpected might appear as just a failure of technique. In the session mentioned in Chapter 5 (p. 70), I did not see how to make a transference interpretation. Instead I found myself speaking, apparently inconsequentially, about abstract painting. This somehow led to the patient seeing the transference connection for himself without breaking the experience of the present moment. But again, suppose it had not gone like that. I might have been left apparently inflicting on the patient an inappropriate and intrusive association of my own, to no purpose.

Freud and Fenichel, with their insistence that analytic technique should be rationally derived from well-founded theory, and Ferenczi, with his stress on the analyst's individuality and intuitiveness, were responding in different ways to the same dilemma. Is creativity to be trusted as it happens, or only after the event when its results have been cautiously evaluated? The pitfalls in both directions, of wild analysis one way and lifeless rigidity the other, are evident. But more thought has been given to one side of the dilemma than the other. There is a large literature on the theory of psychoanalytic technique, but much less on the theory of psychoanalytic creativity.

Milner's work, which has contributed so much to the understanding of artistic creativity (Milner 1950, 1987b), also sheds light on analytic creativity. The autobiographical writings discussed in Chapter 2 investigate a state of mind which allows a deeper awareness of the truth, precisely by giving up the assumption of knowledge and by opening one's vision to the unlooked for and unthought of. In Milner's receptivity towards the Answering Activity she is clearly in touch, at a profound level, with the creativity of her own unconscious. What the Answering Activity arouses in her is that same mixed sense of recognition and surprise produced by whatever is truly creative. She does not categorise this experience. The Answering Activity is certainly part of herself, but it has also a sense of 'otherness' which makes the experience extraordinary. Milner's not seeking to reduce this otherness represents just that acceptance of the unfathomable which Freud could not achieve in front of Michelangelo's *Moses*. Milner does not put aside what she cannot analyse. She accepts, without challenging the paradox, that the Answering Activity is both herself and something other. It is like the navel of a dream, reaching down into, or emerging out of, the unknown.

Her classic paper on symbolism (Milner 1952) shows how this quality of mind can allow creativity into an analysis. The paper's original title, 'Aspects of symbolism in comprehension of the Not-Self', expresses better than its revised one the connection with the Answering Activity. Milner opposes the view of symbols as defensive substitutes for an unwelcome reality. She emphasises their creative potential, which comes from their being malleable but also having a texture and consistency of their own that must be respected. In one way we create them; in another way we discover and make use of them. Milner illustrates, from her analysis of an 11-year-old boy, what this means in the clinical situation. She had to let herself become a 'pliable medium' for him. He needed to be able to create her in his mind, and at the same time to discover and make use of her. Her analytic activity consisted partly of interpreting, and she makes it clear that this always remained an essential element, but partly also of a particular kind of attentiveness to her own state of mind. She needed to keep herself in a state which facilitated his experience of her as a pliable medium of that sort. The detail of the material shows how she enabled him to experience her as partly an aspect of himself, created and controlled by him, and partly something other than himself that had its own responses. She functioned for him, in fact, as an answering activity. The paper itself, and references to the case in *Eternity's Sunrise* (Milner 1987a: 150–1), shows that she was able to do this through being in contact with her own Answering Activity. There is a parallel here with Ferenczi's image of the elastic band pulled from both directions, but Milner demonstrates even more clearly how she helped the creativity of the analysis to manifest itself in the patient as well as in herself. The pliable medium, partly an aspect of her patient, partly independent of him, and the partly created, partly discovered symbol, and Milner's own Answering Activity, all share the quality of being both Self and Other. This idea runs throughout her work, and accepting its paradox is what allows her creativity to emerge.

Milner's description of her work has evident connections with Winnicott's concept of potential, or intermediate, space, referred to at the end of the previous chapter. This is an area of experience intermediate between the inner world of the individual and the external world of shared reality. The area of play, with which that chapter was specifically concerned, is one example only of how intermediate space, in Winnicott's view, pervades human experience. In this chapter I shall explore how this concept offers a fresh understanding of the nature of creativity.

The most systematically worked out psychoanalytic views of artistic creativity have been Freud's own, and the view, based on Kleinian ideas, of art as a reparative activity emanating from the depressive position (Segal 1952). In his earliest reference to the subject, Freud suggests that in *The Sorrows of Young Werther* Goethe was defending himself against suicidal feelings, and says: 'The mechanism of creative writing is the same as that of hysterical phantasies' (Freud 1897: 256). Broadly speaking, this remained his view, expressed in a series of writings such as 'Creative writers and day-dreaming' (Freud 1908), 'Leonardo da Vinci and a memory of his childhood' (Freud 1910) and Lecture 23 of the *Introductory Lectures on Psycho-Analysis* (Freud 1916–17: 358–77). He thought that, like us all, the artist suffered from unfulfilled wishes that could not be acknowledged because the desires they expressed were forbidden. The artist, however, escaped a neurotic outcome of this conflict, not just by the regular sublimations available to ordinary people, but by a particular gift of shaping the forbidden, unconscious fantasy so that it could avoid censorship and be visually or verbally represented. This affords pleasure, and not only to the artist, because it gives other people too some kind of access to their own unconscious fantasies.

Freud is often accused of pathologising creativity. But there are two ways to read this theory. Is the artist a feeble fellow who has only just managed not to be a neurotic invalid? Or is he a hero who finds a construct-ive solution to a universal conflict, not available to most of us but in which his art allows us to participate? Sometimes Freud does see an achievement in the work of the artist.

> The artist, like the neurotic, had withdrawn from an unsatisfying reality into this world of imagination; but, unlike the neurotic, he knew how to find a way back from it and once more to get a firm foothold in reality. His creations, works of art, were the imaginary satisfactions of uncon-scious wishes, just as dreams are; and like them they were in the nature of compromises, since they too were forced to avoid any open conflict with the forces of repression. But they differed from the asocial, nar-cissistic products of dreaming in that they were calculated to arouse sympathetic interest in other people and were able to evoke and satisfy the same unconscious wishful impulses in them too.
>
> (Freud 1925d: 64–5)

Often, however, Freud seems closer to the first view.

> An artist is once more in rudiments an introvert, not far removed from neurosis. He is oppressed by excessively powerful instinctual needs. He desires to win honour, power, wealth, fame and the love of women; but he lacks the means for achieving these satisfactions. Consequently, like any other unsatisfied man, he turns away from reality and transfers all his interest, and his libido too, to the wishful constructions of his life of phantasy, whence the path might lead to neurosis.
>
> (Freud 1916–17: 376)

In describing the hero of Jensen's novel *Gradiva* he writes of his

> entirely unscientific . . . imagination, which could show itself not only in his dreams but often in his waking life as well. This division between imagination and intellect destined him to become an artist or a neurotic; he was one of those whose kingdom is not of this world.
>
> (Freud 1907: 14)

For all Freud's scientific detachment, it is hard not to feel a devaluation of artistic endeavour in comments such as these.

In *Civilisation and its Discontents* Freud maintained that 'the substitutive satisfactions, as offered by art, are illusions in contrast with reality' (Freud 1930: 75). It was the same view of art, as false representation in place of truth, that made Plato exclude it from his ideal city-state. In his book *Art and Artist* Rank (1932) offered a very different understanding. He had just that positive perception of artistic creativity, as something both individually and socially valuable, which Freud could have found more of in his own theory. Rank's separation from Freud in the early 1920s was one of the dramatic splits in the history of psychoanalysis, and their views in this area are one index of the differences between them. Freud saw artistic achievement as grounded in the need to avoid pathology. The need is a real one, of course, and if civilisation is based on mastering the drives, the conflicts they arouse will always be present. Nevertheless the implication is that the freer of conflict a society manages to be, the less need it will have of art. A society that was truly successful in its sublimations, and not caught up with avoiding neurotic solutions, might have no artists in it at all.

Close to that passage in *Civilisation and its Discontents* there is a discussion of work, which shows the same ambiguities as Freud's view of art. For him work also was essentially linked to the renouncing of instinctual satisfaction in favour of the compromises and sublimations on which civilisation depends. It is not enjoyable in itself, but something to be tolerated for a greater good. The more we can 'heighten the yield of pleasure' (Freud 1930: 79) which we gain from work, the more tolerable it will be, and the more effectively it will control our instincts. Freud recognises that

> A satisfaction . . . such as an artist's joy in creating, in giving his phantasies body, or a scientist's in solving problems or discovering truths, has a special quality, which we shall certainly one day be able to characterise in metapsychological terms.
>
> (Freud 1930: 79)

So far, however, this kind of satisfaction, like Michelangelo's *Moses*, seems to escape Freud's metapsychology. He goes on:

> Professional activity is a source of special satisfaction if it is a freely chosen one – if, that is to say, by means of sublimation, it makes use of existing inclinations, of persisting or constitutionally reinforced instinctual impulses. And yet, as a path to happiness, work is not highly prized by men. They do not strive after it as they do after other possibilities of satisfaction.
>
> (Freud 1930: 80 fn.)

Freud does try to explain the positive satisfaction that can be found in work, but only in terms of residual access to impulses that have found a way to avoid complete repression. This rather negative form of satisfaction makes it understandable, perhaps, that people do not 'strive after' work.

But here is something written about Pushkin by a close friend of his, Prince Petr Vyazemsky.

Deep within him there lay concealed a moral strength, protective and saving . . . This strength was love of work, the necessity of work, the insuperable necessity to express himself creatively, to force out from himself sensations, images, feelings . . . Work was for him the shrine, the font in which sores were healed, courage and freshness overcame the feebleness of exhaustion, his weakened powers were restored. When he felt the onset of inspiration, when he got down to work, he was calmed, he became courageous, he was reborn.

(Edmonds 1994: 5)

This is about a creative artist – at work. Certainly we can see the artistic work being used to ward off symptoms of exhaustion, weakness and agitation. It was 'the font in which sores were healed'. Freud might have had the same view of the 'saving' quality of his art for Pushkin as he did for Goethe. The 'moral' strength of Pushkin's work could reflect a superego whose sublimations work in the direction of civilisation. What is so interesting, however, is that even while this passage corresponds in such ways to Freud's ideas, what it conveys most strongly is the sense of a man who, when he was working, when he was creating, was at that time being most completely his own self. This is the special quality of satisfaction that Freud was plainly aware of in the artist's or scientist's creativity, but which he could not fit into his metapsychological scheme.

It does fit well, though, with Rank's view of how the artist expresses his being in his work (Chapter 1). It also fits with Abraham Maslow's (1954) concept of the self-actualising person. When Maslow examined the characteristics of people who seemed especially fulfilled in the development of their personalities, one thing he found they had in common was a particular attitude to their work. It tended to be in the service of others, or of a cause outside themselves. It was precious to them, like a responsibility to which they were dedicated. Above all, the nature of the work was not accidental. It arose from a person's particular quality as an individual, and the idea of being engaged in a different sort of work seemed to these people like a kind of contradiction in terms (Maslow 1967). What such people do, one might say, is who they are. Freud once wrote to Oskar Pfister about what his own work meant to him.

I cannot face with comfort the idea of life without work; work and the free play of the imagination are for me the same thing. I take no pleasure in anything else. That would be a recipe for happiness but for the appalling thought that productivity is entirely dependent on a sensitive disposition. What would one do when ideas failed or words refused to come? It is impossible not to shudder at the thought. Hence, in spite of all the acceptance of fate which is appropriate to an honest man, I have one quite secret prayer: that I may be spared any wasting away and crippling of my ability to work because of physical deterioration. In the words of King Macbeth, let us die in harness.

(Meng and Freud 1963: 35)

To reduce this to 'heightening the yield of pleasure' so as to render work tolerable would be a travesty. It is tempting to respond to Freud's reductionism as Pfister responded to 'The Future of an Illusion' (Freud 1927): 'You are much better and deeper than your disbelief' (Meng and Freud 1963: 122).

Segal (1952) has elaborated in Kleinian terms a view of creativity that is more positive than Freud's. Where he sees the need to create art as a defence, which a person who is freer of neurotic conflict would not require, she relates it to a universal process of development. Segal sees artistic creativity as an expression of the reparative impulse arising in the depressive position, when the infant looks for ways to repair the damage caused, in reality or fantasy, by its destructiveness. She has related this idea to various individual works, mostly in the field of literature. Sometimes it is applied to the artist's psychic conflicts which generated the work (e.g. Segal 1984). On other occasions the theory is applied more to the conflict portrayed in the work of art, with less emphasis on the artist's own internal state (e.g. Segal 1974).

Segal's and Freud's are both theories of motivation. They hypothesise unconscious needs which initiate creativity, but they do not deal with the creative process itself. In this way, they both take a functional view of creativity. Even though Segal roots her theory in the processes of normal development, it is still a matter of meeting the needs of a particular developmental stage, by finding ways of putting damage right or making the guilt for it bearable. Both theories make creativity itself secondary to the developmental function that it serves.

Winnicott's ideas, by contrast, allow a view of creativity that is primarily to do with the nature of the creative process itself. Although his observations about creativity are mentioned from time to time in the literature, it is striking how little systematic use has been made of them to articulate a theory of creativity, although the makings of one are plainly there in his writings (Winnicott 1971: chs 5, 7). Interestingly, those who do read him in this way have mostly come fresh to Winnicott as an outsider to their own traditions – Americans such as David Schecter (1983), Peter Rudnytsky (1993) and Jerome Oremland (1997); and Susan Deri (1984), a Hungarian analyst who moved to the United States, among whose early teachers in Budapest was Michael Balint.

As mentioned earlier, the essential concept in the view of creativity I am putting forward here is the area of experience that Winnicott called potential, or intermediate, space. To grasp what an advance this offers in the understanding of creativity, we must go back to Ernst Kris (1952). It is noticeable, when Kris introduces his idea of 'regression in the service of the ego' (1952: 177), how anxious he is about it, adding '*si licet venia verbo*' as a plea for tolerance of his audacity. Kris was departing from Freud's view of art as the avoidance of pathology, to propose it as a healthy, autonomous ego-function in its own right. To take something that appeared so obviously pathological, in an adult, as regression to primary process, and claim it as the very thing that freed art from its link to pathology, was bold indeed. Elsewhere in his book (1952: 167, 312) Kris is repeatedly at pains to clarify what he means by the ego's being in control of regression and making use of primary process, as opposed to being overwhelmed by them. The work of Silvano Arieti reveals again how problematic this idea, of a non-pathological relation between primary process functioning and creative activity, was thought to be. Freud (1911b) had set primary and secondary process in opposition to each other and, when Arieti aimed to interpret 'the processes by which the primitive unites with the highest levels of the psyche to produce the process of creativity' (Arieti 1967: ix), he could only conceptualise this by postulating a new notion of 'tertiary process' (Arieti 1967: 329).

Winnicott's framework, on the other hand, does not assume a necessary opposition between internal fantasy and external reality-testing. Intermediate space is an experiential realm whose particular quality is to unite these two. Winnicott spelt out its essential feature most clearly with regard to transitional space in infancy and the transitional objects which occupy it.

> Of the transitional object it can be said that it is a matter of agreement between us and the baby that we will never ask the question: 'Did you conceive of this or was it presented to you from without?' The important point is that no decision on this point is expected. The question is not to be formulated.
>
> (Winnicott 1971: 12)

Winnicott repeatedly insists that the paradox which this involves must be accepted. 'The baby creates the object, but the object was there waiting to be created and to become a cathected object' (Winnicott 1971: 89). Respecting this paradox, of an area of experience that is not challenged in respect of its subjectivity or objectivity, is what gives the 'space' its 'potential'.

The second key aspect of Winnicott's concept is that this area of experience, with its particular mode of psychic functioning, is available throughout the whole of life. Transitional space in early infancy may be its best recognised manifestation, but the realm of play in later childhood is another version of intermediate space, and depends on acceptance of the same paradox. Chapter 8 showed that the play space, in adult life, is what makes psychoanalysis possible. More broadly, this area is where all sorts of cultural activities are located, amongst them artistic creativity, and aesthetic and spiritual experience (Winnicott 1971: chs 5, 7, 8). Winnicott stated plainly that although certain functions of intermediate space may belong to particular epochs in a person's life, it is a single, lifelong area of experience and activity. This space opens with the blend of discovery and creation by which the infant constitutes its own identity and that of the world around it. Its closing seems harder to think about, but some analysts have tried to address it (Hildebrand 1988; Limentani 1995). The following passage on the creativity of later life is noteworthy.

> I would like to bring together, at this point, the notions of Elliott Jaques (1965), with whose basic tenet concerning the universality of a midlife crisis at the age of 37 I cannot agree, but whose notion of different types of creativity at different times of life, i.e. hot from the fire creativity in youth versus sculptured creativity in later life, I find sympathetic; and George Pollock (1982), who in his various papers on creativity in later life has made very convincingly the point that later life work has to do with mourning for one's own losses and the transmutation of these through creative processes as one ages. I hold that there are grounds for suggesting that as well as there being primal fantasies concerning birth and the primal scene there are also primal fantasies concerning one's own death and that these often become central to and are expressed in many ways in the creative work of artists, particularly as they age.
>
> (Hildebrand 1988: 356)

Peter Hildebrand's ideas, of age-specific primal fantasies and that the approach of death may open up a new sort of creativity, recall Chapter 7, which suggested that Oedipal triangularity, while remaining structurally the same, needs to be worked through in different configurations throughout a lifetime.

All creativity, in Winnicott's view, is intrinsically connected to the creativity of the infant by which it becomes itself. It is interesting to go back to Rank with Winnicott in mind.

> This creativity begins with the individual himself – that is, with the self-making of the personality into the artist . . . The creative artistic personality is thus the first work of the productive individual, and it remains fundamentally his chief work, since all his other works are partly the repeated expression of this primal creation.
>
> (Rank 1932: 28)

What Rank says here of the artist, that by his creativity he constitutes his own self, Winnicott would say of all of us. Rank's 'repeated expression of this primal creation' asserts the same continuity as Winnicott does when he says that 'an intermediate area of experience which is not challenged (arts, religion etc.) . . . is in direct continuity with the play area of the small child who is "lost" in play' (Winnicott 1971: 13). Winnicott summarises:

> This intermediate area of experience, unchallenged in respect of its belonging to inner or external (shared) reality, constitutes the greater part of the infant's experience, and throughout life is retained in the intense experiencing that belongs to the arts and to religion and to imaginative living, and to creative scientific work.
>
> (Winnicott 1971: 14)

Immediately after that passage, Winnicott (1971: 14) writes: 'It is not the object, of course, that is transitional'. This is profoundly important. The significance of the transitional object is that it represents a process, a movement from one state to another. It embodies 'betweenness'. In that sense, it is transitional. But *what constitutes the object is the unfolding of the process*. This does not apply only to an infant's transitional objects. Oremland (1997) had the interesting idea of inviting a painter, a theatre director, a sculptor and a businessman, to respond to his ideas on creativity, and of including their responses in his book. The painter was Françoise Gilot, who wrote:

> In common parlance, a work of art is an object, but this is a difficult concept for the artist to entertain, at least as far as one's work is concerned. I offer the following metaphor. If a person walks on the wet sand of a beach, the purpose is to go from one end to the other. In doing so footprints are left behind as the objective proof of the action taken. Are the footprints objects? In the same way works of art are traces of an artist's quest. They are objective clues, but are they objects? They become objects as they are beheld, heard, appreciated or rejected by others.
>
> (Gilot 1997: 125)

This is true, in precisely the same terms, both of the art object and the transitional objects of infancy. Oremland's theatre director, Carey Perloff, tells of a production of Euripides' *Hecuba*. In this play, the Chorus live in tents which, at the climax of the play, have to be suddenly torn down on stage. Perloff had cast, as the Chorus, a group of singers called 'Kitka'.

> What was the stage life of these women, the Kitka singers, going to involve? How was I going to imbue a group of non-actors with the imaginative life necessary to fill their performances on stage? How could

we personalise the tents to such a degree that when at the end of the play they are torn down by the Thracian ruler, the audience experiences a true violation? As we were talking, an idea occurred to me seemingly out of nowhere but utterly complete. The action of the Chorus in this play would be to build their structures themselves in live time during the course of the play. Whatever 'scenery' the audience saw would evolve from the women themselves . . . Weeks later came an important workshop in which we tested the efficacy of this idea. We led Kitka into a room filled with flotsam and jetsam: wet nets, pieces of wood, long strips of cloth, shells, some jewellery, etc. We asked them to create shelter for themselves out of what they found. For an hour and a half we sat and watched, captivated, as a whole life began to be lived in the room. Long rows of women on their knees began wringing out wet netting and passing it down the line to be placed in piles. Big arcs of cloth were thrown into the air to catch onto wooden planks wedged into benches to provide support. Bits of raffia were carefully woven into the cloth and nets to create an entire tissue covering the wooden frame. Finally, flowers, jewels, and bits of personal clothing were artfully arranged around the 'doorway', along the crest of the structure, and bordering the floor. When it felt complete, the women went inside the 'tent', closed the door flap, and slowly began to sing a lament.

Through a simple task, these non-actors had found a deeply personal connection to a real life experience, without any verbal communication among each other or coaching from us. It was an incredible moment. Rather than a series of tents, which is what I expected, they created a single structure that encompassed them all because that is where the need was most deeply felt.

(Perloff 1997: 136–7)

When that tent was torn down, the effect on the audience must have been shattering, because it was not just an object, but the *making* of the object, that was destroyed.

The object that is a process and the process that becomes an object are like a figure-ground drawing. (Note that the word 'drawing' itself refers to both object and process.) What is in view is the same, but one look shows the figure, another shows the ground. Bollas (1987: 13–29) describes the 'transformational object' in similar terms. In early infancy, he says, the infant experiences the mother, not as an entity but in terms of the changes that she brings about for, and in, the infant. 'The mother is less significant and identifiable as an object than as a process that is identified with cumulative internal and external transformations' (1987: 14). This experiencing of the mother as a process of transformation 'lives on in certain forms of object-seeking in adult life, when the object is sought for its function as a signifier of transformation' (1987: 14). At first sight the distinction between object and process might seem clear enough. But where does my fist go when I open it? The answer depends on seeing that, as well as being a thing, the fist was the activity of clenching the hand. Latecomers who only got to the theatre in time for the end of *Hecuba* would assume that they were seeing an object, the tent, being destroyed. And so they would be. But they might be baffled by the powerful effect on the audience around them, because they would not know that, in the form of the tent, they were also watching the destruction of an extraordinary process. The distinction between the analyst, and what the analyst does, was challenged in Chapter 1, and the concept of psychoanalysis as vocation, in the sense that what the analyst does is who she or he is, has developed into a main theme of this book. The analyst, and what the analyst does, are object and process. One look shows one, another look, the other.

This connection back to the analytic situation shows artistic creativity, and creativity in psychoanalysis, to be closely connected after all. Milner's work with the 11-year-old boy is an example of analytic creativity appearing in the potential space between patient and analyst. Her description, however, could just as well be an account of artistic creativity. The boy used her as a pliable medium that he could mould however he wanted, except that she also had qualities of her own to be taken account of. So his being able to make things out of his pliable medium depended also on his discovering things about it at the same time. The artist has just such a relation to his or her artistic medium. The mixed process of invention and discovery is the same.

True art and true analysis share the same sense of a game played for high stakes. What if this analysis or this work of art should fail? Perhaps pathology will break through. But for writing *The Sorrows of Young Werther*, maybe Goethe would indeed have had a suicidal depression. Or, following Segal, the artist may be left with a world of irreparably damaged internal objects. But there is an even more fundamental danger, which is to be alone in a void empty of any objects at all. Art which has this at stake is not about repairing damage, but about bringing something into existence and sustaining it in being. The reflection of this in analytic terms is not the depressive position but the transitional space in which we create and sustain both our objects and our own selves.

Near the end of his life the Greek novelist Nikos Kazantzakis wrote of himself:

What struggle was in that handful of clay! It was kneaded . . . it became mud, became a man, and began the ascent to reach – to reach what? It clambered pantingly up God's dark bulk, extended its arms and groped, groped in an effort to find His face.

And when in these very last years this man sensed in his desperation that the dark bulk did not have a face, what new struggle, all impudence and terror, he underwent to hew this unwrought summit and give it a face – his own!

But now the day's work is done; I collect my tools. Let other clods of soil come to continue the struggle. We mortals are the immortals' work battalion. Our blood is red coral, and we build an island over the abyss.

God is being built. I too have applied my tiny red pebble, a drop of blood, to give Him solidity lest He perish – so that He might give me solidity lest I perish.

(Kazantzakis 1965: 18)

The person who wrote those words is struggling not against neurosis or damage to internal objects, but against the threat of not being. As with Milner and the Answering Activity, it is not clear, even to him, whether what he is struggling to create and keep in being is himself or something other. He is inhabiting a space where that distinction does not obtain.

The landscape painting of John Constable might seem far removed from Kazantzakis' existential struggle. But Constable's creativity also depended on his finding a space intermediate between what was presented to him from without and what he conceived of from within. Constable's relationship to his native Suffolk landscape was intimately bound up with his father's desire for his son to succeed him in the family business. Constable's father was a prosperous grain merchant, a trade which naturally involved deep and detailed technical knowledge of the countryside and how it worked: the land itself, windmills and water-mills, storage of grain, river transport and so on. In the paintings from his early years in Suffolk, Constable is always using his countryman's eye and the technical knowledge of farming, boatbuilding and river management, that he imbibed as his father's son. The act of painting, however, was a rejection. Constable's decision not to follow in his father's footsteps, to be an artist instead of a merchant, caused a rift between them that was never fully healed.

A comparison of two paintings illustrates his refusal. *Golding Constable's Kitchen Garden* (Figure 1) is a view from the back of the family home, over the kitchen garden, farm buildings and wheatfield. All this was part of his father's extensive property. *View from Golding Constable's House* (Figure 2) shows the same landscape, with the windmill on the skyline, the rectory buildings with the wood to the left of them (Constable's fiancée was the rector's granddaughter), and the fence in the middle distance. But Constable has obliterated his father's garden and farm buildings, replacing them with his own creation of a field with a track and a cowherd driving his cows along it.[2]

---

2 Ann Bermingham (1987: 99) discusses the dating of these paintings, and whether the view had changed in reality. She concludes that it had not, and that Constable was deliberately transforming his father's landscape.

Figure 1 John Constable *Golding Constable's Kitchen Garden*

Figure 2 John Constable *View from Golding Constable's House*

Aggression is an important element in creativity. This is not just because it causes damage, in reality or fantasy, which then has to be put right by some creative work of reparation. Segal's view, for example, needs to find room for the fact that aggression, as well as having to be dealt with reparatively, within the depressive position, is also essential, prior to that, for bringing the depressive position into being in the first place. Aggression has a fundamental, positive, role in establishing to begin with the space in which creativity can occur. Winnicott's (1971: ch. 6) expression of this was that the subject destroys the object, the object survives destruction, and the

Figure 3 John Constable *Dedham Vale, Morning*

subject can then use the object. The apparent contradiction in this is puzzling. How can something that is destroyed survive, when not surviving is what being destroyed means? But if Winnicott was talking in terms of fantasy, and asserting that, when an overwhelming fantasy of destruction turns out not to be true, this releases the object in question to be made use of in fresh ways, why did he not say that? The answer, I think, is that he was referring, in a precise and specific way, to something that happens in intermediate space; and the nature of intermediate space is that the worlds of objective reality and of fantasy are not separated. His formulation should not be understood as contradictory but as paradoxical, reflecting the paradox that defines the quality of intermediate space.

Constable destroyed the landscape that was presented to him by his father, in a way that seems to correspond to Winnicott's description. The two paintings just mentioned illustrate this. The point is not the destruction of that particular view in those particular paintings. Their importance is in indicating a process in Constable's mind. For example, *Dedham Vale, Morning* (Figure 3) shows a landscape that seems, on the face of it, not to have been in the least destroyed. It is an accurate piece of topography, and Constable has even put in a milestone inscribed with the name of the landscape. He seems intent on showing the viewer what this particular bit of Suffolk is really like. It is a working landscape. The figures are going about their business as part of a rural community, and we see how the community operates. There is the everyday business of bringing cows in from the fields, the land is organised for farming, and prominent in the distance is the church, around which community life revolves. To be able to paint this, however, Constable had to destroy the landscape *as an object to be related to in the way his father intended for him.* Having done so, he found the landscape survived, and this let him put it to extraordinary use. This painting shows, what is more, that he brought to his handling of the landscape that survived, just the kind of detailed, technical knowledge and skill that his father had wanted him to bring to bear on the one that was destroyed. Not only has the object that was destroyed survived, but the activity related to it has also survived. Constable brings the transformed activity to bear on the transformed object. He destroyed the identity offered to him, but it survives, refound in his identity as an artist.[3]

The visual space which Constable embodied on his canvases is derived from the intermediate space in which his images were conceived. Because of the nature of that space, Constable's paintings are able to look, not either outward *or* inward, but outward and inward at the same time. This gives them their remarkable blending of detailed, objective realism and emotional expressivity. In individual works, the accent may appear to be on one or the other. *Dedham Vale, Morning,* for example, declares its relation to the outside world. *Hadleigh Castle* (Figure 4), on the other hand, painted shortly after his wife's death, has an emotional power that belongs more obviously to Constable's inner world. The painting has no fixed viewpoint. Artist and viewer are disturbingly 'suspended in the void' (Parris and Fleming-Williams 1991: 314). This seems very much a landscape of the imagination. These two paintings illustrate how Constable's artistic space can represent both external reality and the subjectivity of his inner world, without division between them. They are always combining and interpenetrating each other. To question whether Constable's landscapes are naturalistic or imagined would have, as with the transitional object, no meaning.

The sky stirred Constable's creativity in a particular way. When he married and settled in London he felt the loss of the Suffolk landscape. But the sky remained, and the studies of it that he made following the move reveal its importance to him at that time. His painting of clouds had always shown an extraordinary quality of observation, which he could also convey in language:

> immediately upon these large clouds appear numerous opaque patches, which, however, are only small clouds passing rapidly before them, and consisting of isolated pieces, detached probably from the larger cloud.

---

3 Seamus Heaney opened his first published collection (Heaney, 1966) with the poem 'Digging', in which he recognises that his work as a poet replicates the work his countryman father did with a spade.

Figure 4 John Constable *Hadleigh Castle*

These floating much nearer the earth, may perhaps fall in with a stronger current of wind, which as well as their comparative lightness, causes them to move with greater rapidity; hence they are called by wind-millers and sailors 'messengers', being always the forerunners of bad weather. They float about midway in what may be termed the *lanes* of the clouds; and from being so situated, are almost uniformly in shadow, receiving only a reflected light from the clear blue sky immediately above, and which descends perpendicularly upon them into these *lanes*. In passing over the bright parts of the large clouds, they appear as 'darks'; but in passing the shadowed parts they assume a gray, or pale, or lurid hue.

(Constable 1833)

This passage accompanies a mezzotint, in Constable's 'English Landscape' series, whose original, painted not long before the move to London, is the oil-sketch *Spring – East Bergholt Common* (Figure 5). The windmill shown is the very mill where the young Constable worked, carving his name as a 16-year-old on one of the beams – 'J. Constable 1792'. That is where he learnt to read the clouds, and now he looks at the sky through the know-ledgeable eyes of the miller he has refused to be. But he is also, and in the same act, looking at it with the inner vision that made him make that

167

Figure 5 John Constable *Spring – East Bergholt*

refusal. The sky was, for Constable, 'the chief organ of sentiment' in a land-scape (Beckett 1968: 77). In this painting his meteorological observation fuses with a deep inner experiencing, to produce a sky which is objective, yet, at the same time, a powerful exploration of feeling – a sky that exists in a space neither internal nor external.

It is not just the artist who inhabits a potential space. If looking at a painting is to be truly a looking into what the artist has created, it demands the viewer's own creative participation. Aesthetic experience is, in fact, a form of aesthetic activity, which calls on the viewer to enter a potential space as well.

The Annunciation is one of the central, enduring images of the Western artistic tradition. It presents to us a young woman discovering her capacity for motherhood. There are two people, Mary and the angel, in a vivid, sudden relation to each other. The first relationship, through which a woman discovers herself as a mother, is an identification with her own mother. The angel's transmission to Mary of the knowledge of her motherhood may be seen as a representation of that relationship. In this two-person view of the Annunciation the angel stands for the young woman's mother, the image for her of the mother she will become. This is not something a mother can simply tell her daughter. That she too can be a mother is a complicated piece of knowledge which evolves in the girl as she becomes a woman. The child pushing her pram and feeding her doll is doing what her mother does. She cannot yet imagine being what her mother is. That requires a new relationship to herself and her body, with an awareness that her maturing sexuality can bring a baby into existence. The Annunciation can also be seen as a discovery in solitude, representing the moment at

Figure 6 Carlo Grivelli *Annunciation with St. Emidius*

which this complex new awareness of herself emerges into the woman's consciousness. This view sees the angel as an aspect of Mary: her own knowledge of herself as a potential mother, declaring itself for the first time as a conscious perception. The sexuality that is part of this self-awareness implies another relationship. The woman identifying with her mother identifies with her as a woman who has become a mother through a sexual relationship with a man. A third person, then, is also implied by the angel's presence. His relation to Mary portrays the shared sexuality which has created the baby. The Annunciation typically shows Mary in an interior, symbolic of the woman's body, into which the angel enters with his message from outside. The penetration is sometimes even more explicit. In Crivelli's *Annunciation with St. Emidius* (Figure 6), for example, the Holy Spirit enters into Mary down a shaft of light through an aperture in the wall of her house.

The significance of the angel is continually shifting. It is Mary's mother, it is an aspect of her own self, it is the baby's father. Whatever meaning we give to the angel, we negate something different which it also means. However we view the Annunciation at any one moment, there is someone missing from the scene and we are called on, unconsciously, to bring forward from our awareness the aspect of it which that particular view has left

169

out. This protean quality, which keeps demanding our own creative participation, is part of what makes the Annunciation so compelling an image. Are we responding, then, to what the painting presents to us or to what we bring to it from our imaginations? But the image binds the two inextricably together. To force them apart, by asking that question, would destroy our experience of the painting. Our own aesthetic activity, like the artist's creativity, arises within that intermediate area, which stands in a direct line of development from the transitional space of infancy.

The concept of potential space offers an understanding that embraces artistic, psychoanalytic and other forms of creativity, and aesthetic experience as well. Freud, Segal and others have contributed to understanding the emotional needs and conflicts that may motivate the creation of particular works of art. This view, based on Winnicott, is of the creative process itself. It does not see that process as being secondary to anything, nor as any kind of corrective or compensatory activity, but as a central expression of what it means to be human.

10

Psychic reality, negation and the analytic setting

We only suffer reality to *suggest*, never to *dictate*.
Charlotte Brontë (1849: 207)

'Maintaining an analytic stance' means actively holding on to a particular frame of mind. Most commonly it refers to how psychoanalysts are with their patients, but it also applies to the state of mind needed for thinking analytically or reading analytic writings. Whatever the situation, there is work involved in sustaining it. There is a sense of tension – slight, maybe, but constant. There is always a tug in the opposite direction, a pull away from the analytic state of mind. When we look at something which is not quite within our normal range of vision and try to focus on it, the muscles of accommodation in our eyes have to work harder than usual and we become conscious of keeping a steady tension in them as we work to keep the object in focus. It is not painful or difficult. We might not even call it a strain. But the effort, the tension, of not letting the focus slip, is there. Keeping oneself attuned to the realm of psychic reality rather than ordinary reality requires a particular sort of effort. There is a resistance to be overcome.

A patient told me how, as a girl, she would be frightened of burglars in the night and wake her father. He would reassure her that there weren't any burglars. This would make her more agitated, not less, and she would tell him she was afraid of dying, or of nuclear war. He would again reassure her, rather irritably now, that she was perfectly well, and there wasn't going to be a nuclear war. The reason this was so unhelpful to her is that she wanted him to meet her at the level of psychic reality where her fear was real, and the necessary question was 'So what is she *really*, that is to say *psychically*, afraid of?' He, however, was meeting her in terms of ordinary reality which showed him, and made him say to her, that there was nothing really to be afraid of. In order to see that there *was* something to be afraid of, and then to think about what it might be, he would have had to negate his ordinary way of thinking.

Contrast this with Freud's attitude to the delusional self-reproaches of the melancholic. He says in 'Mourning and melancholia':

> It would be equally fruitless from a scientific and a therapeutic point of view to contradict a patient who brings these accusations against his ego. He must surely be right in some way and be describing something that is as it seems to him to be.
>
> (Freud 1917: 246)

Freud is doing what my patient's father could not. He sets aside the automatic, ordinary response: 'That's absurd. Of course you're not like that!', and asks in what way it is not absurd. But this respect for reality at the psychic level is an unusual, non-habitual way of thinking which requires a distinct negating of our automatic attitudes.

Freud first mentions what he came to call psychic reality in the *Project*: 'Indications of discharge through speech are also in a certain sense indications of reality – but of thought-reality not of external reality' (Freud 1895: 373). In *The Interpretation of Dreams* he says: 'If we look at the unconscious wishes reduced to their most fundamental and truest shape we shall have to conclude, no doubt, that *psychical* reality is a particular form of existence not to be confused with *material* reality' (Freud 1900: 620). In the *Introductory Lectures* he says that 'phantasies possess *psychical* as contrasted with *material* reality' (Freud 1916–17: 368); and in the paper 'The Unconscious' he lists, as one of the characteristics of the system *Ucs*, 'replacement of external by psychical reality' (Freud 1915c: 187). The striking thing is that in all these passages psychic reality is defined by the negation of external, or material, reality. The father of the woman who was afraid of burglars would have needed, in order to understand her fears, to negate his own focus on ordinary reality in favour of her psychic reality. If staying in touch with psychic reality means sustaining the tension of negating ordinary reality, these texts suggest that this is not just an incidental necessity, but one that comes from an intrinsic connection between psychic reality and negation.

It might seem, at first sight, that negating ordinary reality must be an avoidance, like denial or disavowal. Negation, however, needs to be disentangled from such concepts. Freud (1925b) described it as being on the one hand defensive but also important in freeing thinking from repression. The first part of this is familiar, but the second part tends to get forgotten. If negation is aligned with other concepts so as to make it automatically counterproductive, no room is left for its double function that Freud was pointing to. Negation can sometimes be a way of avoiding reality, but setting aside ordinary reality is also an essential element in all psychic work, particularly psychoanalytic work. What matters is how the underlying activity of negating is being used, whether to contradict ordinary reality or to disengage from it, for the time being, without rejecting it. In the previous chapter's discussion of the Annunciation (pp. 168–70), for example, it was observed that the significance of the angel is always shifting. Whatever meaning we are attending to at any one time implies the negating of other possible meanings. This is not to say that those other meanings are denied. They are simply being, for the moment, disengaged from and set aside. The not attending to them is what makes space for attending to something else.

The passage quoted above from the *Introductory Lectures* runs, in full: 'The phantasies possess *psychical* as contrasted with *material* reality, and we gradually learn to understand that *in the world of the neuroses it is psychical reality which is the decisive kind*' (Freud 1916–17: 368). Elsewhere Freud describes how there may be 'a domination by an internal psychical reality over the reality of the external world and the path to a psychosis lies open' (Freud 1939: 76). These passages clearly link psychic reality to pathology. In such cases there is a retreat from an ordinary reality that is too painful or conflictual, into a psychic one where conflicts can be negated. The cure will then lie in undoing that defensive negation. As I have just indicated, however, psychic reality is not only a refuge. The opposite may also be true. The starting-point for this chapter was the way that maintaining an analytic stance requires a resistance to the pull of ordinary reality. Particularly when patients do *not* speak from their psychic reality but use *ordinary* reality defensively, the analyst must work all the harder to hold a position within psychic reality, knowing that that is where analytic work is done.

What Freud could do, and my patient's father could not, was to see what was being spoken about in terms of external reality as a representation of something internal. This idea is fundamental, of course, to the whole of clinical psychoanalysis. A patient told me, for example, how the local businessmen in a particular community were getting together to improve the environment and develop the amenities in the area, and how different this was from somewhere else where the local people seemed unable to mobilise themselves and co-operate in that way. I took this as referring to his own internal state, and to his concern whether the different aspects of himself could come together so as to mobilise his own resources and bring about change in him. This commonplace interpretation illustrates rather clearly how external may represent internal reality. The interpretation is made possible by the analyst's being able to see external reality in this way, and to hold on to this understanding as a piece of psychic reality, against the pull of the ordinary meaning of the material. That is not to say that this patient was particularly resistant; he was not. But making any such interpretation means actively setting aside the first meaning of the material that presents itself. The patient must be able to do the same thing, if he is to understand and make use of the interpretation. So this constructive use of psychic reality involves the negating of ordinary reality, just as much as its defensive use does.

The passages from Freud, quoted above, were written years apart and do not hang together systematically. It is not clear whether Freud distinguishes between psychic and internal reality, nor whether ordinary, external and material reality are interchangeable concepts or have different connotations. The idea of psychic reality has been understood in such a variety of ways that it has become an ambiguous and somewhat problematical concept. A whole Congress of the International Psychoanalytical Association was devoted to elucidating it (IPA Congress 1995, 1996), with one contributor denying that it served any useful function at all (Arlow 1996). The concept stays alive none the less, with observational studies of infant development focusing fresh attention on it (Fonagy and Target 1996a, 1996b; Emde *et al.* 1997). Psychic and internal reality may tend to get rather loosely equated, but I want to make a clear distinction between them. Furthermore, the distinction between psychic and ordinary reality is not the same as the distinction between internal and external reality. Ordinary reality includes both the encounters and events that we experience in the external world, and our feelings, hopes and anxieties. These too are experiences we have, or which happen to us. By ordinary reality I mean the ensemble of our internal and external realities, as we experience them. Psychic reality is the realm where we *reflect* on what happens to us. Our psychic reality is constituted by what we *make*, consciously and unconsciously, of our experiences, both internal and external.

For that to happen, for us to have a psychic reality at all, some kind of representation of our experience is necessary. If we have no way of representing to ourselves what we experience, we cannot process it, and we are left with what Bion referred to as beta-elements and Lacan called the Order of the Real. Bion (1962: 3) resisted the idea of saying what alpha-function means, but I think it is very close to the capacity to represent our experience to ourselves, and thus to establish a psychic reality or, in Lacanian terms, the Symbolic Order. Psychic reality is the area where psychic work can be done. Not being able to establish it, for lack of alpha-function, is the mark of psychotic functioning and characterises those personalities described by Bion (1970: 9) who can only feel pain but not suffer it, and so cannot 'suffer' pleasure either. Psychic reality is constituted by the representation of experience, and a large part of the work of psychoanalysis lies in helping patients create a psychic reality, by finding how to represent their experience to themselves so that its psychical transformation becomes possible.

The point of a representation is that it is not the thing itself. It denotes what it is a representation of, but what allows experience to be processed is the separation between the representation in psychic reality and the thing itself in literal reality. The representation is *instead of* the literal reality. Making use of the representation means setting aside, for the time being, the thing of which it is a representation, just as understanding the psychic reality of a patient's communication means setting aside the ordinary reality of its surface meaning.

There is a close connection, in this respect, between psychic reality and symbolism. As Freud's references to psychic reality stress the defensive aspect of it, so symbolism was seen, to begin with, as a form of regression (Jones 1916: 89–90, 95–6 quoting Rank and Sachs), and was defined in terms of its defensive function. 'That symbolism arises as the result of intrapsychical conflict between the repressing tendencies and the repressed is the view accepted by all psychoanalysts' (Jones 1916: 115). But just as psychic reality also establishes, with its negation of ordinary reality, a space in which psychic work can be done, so it came to be recognised that symbolism also has positive functions. Klein, for example, still seeing symbolism in terms of anxiety and conflict, nevertheless wrote: 'Thus, not only does symbolism come to be the foundation of all phantasy and sublimation but, more than that, it is the basis of the subject's relation to the outside world and to reality in general' (Klein 1930: 221). In Milner's paper on symbol formation referred to in the previous chapter (pp. 152–3) she describes how she had

> grown rather tired of being treated by this boy as his gas, his breath, his faeces . . . But when I began to see and to interpret, as far as I could, that this use of me might be not only a defensive regression, but an essential recurrent phase in the development of a creative relation to the world, then the whole character of the analysis changed; the boy then gradually became able to allow the external object, represented by me, to exist in its own right.
>
> (Milner 1952: 104)

The importance of symbolism in developing a creative relationship to the world has since become generally accepted (Segal 1957; Winnicott 1971). This is not a mere parallel between symbolism and psychic reality. A symbol is a particular kind of representation, and it has its symbolic function only in so far as it belongs to psychic reality. If the symbol does not exist in psychic reality, it is equated to the object in ordinary reality, in which case it cannot symbolise the object. There can only be, in Segal's (1957: 53) terms, a symbolic equation. The distinction between symbolisation and symbolic equation underlines the fact that although a symbol refers to the original object, its symbolic function depends on its being detached from it. The symbol at one and the same time points to the object and negates it as it exists in ordinary reality. Without that negation there is no symbolisation.

That a symbol can stand for something because it is not identical to it recalls Bateson's comments (p. 133) on the combat play of the monkeys at the zoo, which stood for fighting by virtue of not being actual fighting. It was also noted in Chapter 8 that fantasy, symbolism and play share an ambiguous, unfixed relation to ordinary reality. This gives all of them important roles in establishing psychic reality (pp. 129, 132).

There is an issue which I mention in passing, in order to keep clear of it. A particular emphasis was given to the concept of representation, from the 1960s onwards, by Sandler and his co-workers at the Anna Freud Centre (Sandler 1987: chs 4, 5, 15). Sandler's concept of the 'representational world' has been much discussed. Whether it successfully clarifies such notions as internalisation, introjection, projection, and identification, whether or not representations have a motivating function, what connection they have with the drives: these and other questions have been debated, particularly by ego-psychologists who see the idea of representation as a Trojan horse from the object-relations camp (Perlow 1995: 85–98). My present point, which is simply that reflecting on experience implies being able to represent it, is not part of that controversy.

The material about the local businessmen illustrated how external can represent internal reality. In psychoanalysis, there is one external situation which functions in a very particular way as a representation of internal psychic structure, and that is the psychoanalytic situation itself. For the patient to come every day and lie on the couch free-associating, with the evenly attentive analyst seated behind, all within the framework of the session, is not only a way of finding access to the mind and its contents. It is that, of course, but this might be called the weak version of the point at issue. The strong version is that the structure of the analytic setting is itself a representation of internal mental structure. It not only gives access to the structure of the mind, it embodies it.

Two examples which illustrate what it means, to say that the external structure of the analytic setting represents aspects of internal psychic structure, are provided by the dream-state and the Oedipus complex.

The analytic setting as a representation of the mind in a dream-state was explored by Bertram Lewin (1955). He comments that the analytic setting arose historically from the setting for hypnosis, Freud being led to develop it when certain patients proved not susceptible to the hypnotic state. So a relation between the structure of the analytic setting and sleep, censorship and resistance has been there from the beginning. Despite the shift away from hypnosis, the analytic patient's narcissistic withdrawal of attention from the outside world still corresponds, said Lewin, to the narcissism of sleep, with its complete withdrawal of cathexis from external reality.

Lewin is using 'narcissism' not as a symptomatic description of pathology, but as a metapsychological description of a self-absorbed state of mind. He observes that psychoanalytic interest in dreaming has centred on comparing the formation of dreams with the formation of neurotic symptoms, and on how mechanisms such as condensation and displacement are put to the same use in both. He points out that this comparison, which has been clinically so fruitful, has steered psychoanalysis away from its initial interest in the metapsychology of dreaming. 'The study of the patient as a quasi-sleeper or quasi-dreamer was completely subordinated to the therapeutic and theoretical study of his symptoms . . . The patient on the couch was *prima facie* a neurotic person and only incidentally a dreamer' (Lewin 1955: 169). Freud (1900: 102) himself commented that free association resembles the state of mind that precedes sleep, and if the patient on the couch is a quasi-sleeper or a quasi-dreamer, it is free association that corresponds to the uncensored activity of the unconscious, pushing forward to express material which in turn provokes censorship. The conflict between free association and resistance, so fundamental to the analytic setting, exactly represents the intra-psychic conflict and censorship that give rise to the latent and manifest content of dreams. One might also compare the analytic constraint against action to the neuromuscular inhibition during sleep, which makes possible the continuance of the dreaming state. The analyst, whose awareness makes bridges between the latent and the manifest material, is in the position of the sleeper's ego that can articulate the dream work, finding disguised expression for the unconscious wishes (Khan 1974: 36). The analyst works in the reverse direction, however, trying to see through the defences, not keep them in place, and is therefore an 'awakener' rather than a guardian of sleep (Lewin 1955).

Green has also touched on the analytic setting and the dream-state but, in addition, has shown how the setting is a representation of the Oedipus complex:

> The symbolism of the setting comprises a triangular paradigm, uniting the three polarities of the *dream* (narcissism), of *maternal caring* (from the mother, following Winnicott) and of the *prohibition of incest* (from the father, following Freud). What the psychoanalytic apparatus gives voice to, therefore, is *the symbolisation of the unconscious structure of the Oedipus complex*.
>
> (Green 1984: 123)

The first polarity is the dream situation. With the second and third of his polarities, Green points to another fashion in which the psychoanalytic framework represents psychic structure. I think his statement may be understood in the following way. There are two different kinds of object that the analyst, by virtue of the setting, represents. One aspect of the analytic situation is the peaceful, reliable environment, the lying down, the invitation to say anything and express any wish or feeling, without having to censor it. The analyst who offers these is inviting the patient to regress and be cared for in a state of dependence. But there are other aspects, such as the prohibition on enacting wishes or feelings, the rigour and constraints about session times and payment of fees, and the analyst's refusal to accept at face value what the patient offers him. This is what Friedman (1997: 30) has called the 'adversarial' quality of psychoanalysis, and the analyst who embodies it is a different object for the patient from the one that offers regression. The analyst thus represents two opposite sorts of object at the same time. The patient's wish is to separate them and relate to one but not the other. But these two objects have their own relationship with each other. There is a union between them in the person of the analyst, which the patient is not privy to. The patient has to accept this, and find a way of relating to both of them together, despite the wish to keep them apart and establish a special relationship with just one. The nature of the analytic framework sets up a triangle of conflict between these two objects and the patient, which is the external representation of the internal, unconscious structure of the Oedipus complex.

I want to suggest that this relation between the structure of the psycho-analytic situation and internal psychic structure, illustrated by the dream-state and the Oedipus complex, also holds true with regard to negation. If psychic reality is constituted by representation, and representation depends on an act of negation, that makes negation an essential element in the con-stitution of psychic reality. Here is some clinical material to illustrate the idea that the structure of the analytic setting embodies that activity of negation on which the creation of psychic reality depends.

A woman started four-times-weekly analysis, not responding to my invitation to use the couch but sitting opposite me in the chair. The reason she gave for seeking help was uncertainty about whether to have a baby. Her way of talking was bright, cheerful, often laughing; but her cheerful-ness felt brittle and defensive and an underlying unhappiness was evident. She chatted away, with few pauses and no real silences, and was noticeably unreflective about herself. I was not at all clear what she wanted from me, and when I made an interpretative, or at least a linking, kind of comment, she would consider it briefly, say something like 'Yes, well . . .' and rush back into a narrative of her busy day or complaints about her husband. For several weeks I was struck by how thoroughly she seemed to avoid think-ing about what she was doing in coming to see me. When I brought up the idea of the couch again she dismissed it, mentioning in passing that the couch looked like a bed. Shortly afterwards, in a different context, she made a reference to platonic relationships. It seemed the couch aroused too strong a sexual anxiety of some, as yet unknown, nature.

She became pregnant and was uncertain whether she wanted to keep the baby. She did not want to discuss it with her GP, for fear he would want to take her into some back room of his surgery and do an abortion himself then and there. She knew this was unrealistic, but when eventually she saw an obstetrician there was a similar fear about letting him examine her. She did not know what he might suddenly want to do next. There did not seem to be any clear or specific fantasy, but her anxiety was powerful. By this time I had been able to make some references to the relationship between us, so when this material about the GP and the obstetrician appeared, I said that I now understood that her reaction to the couch showed the same anxiety about what I might secretly have in mind to do with her. She came in to the next session and, without saying anything, immediately lay down on the couch.

I was startled, not just by her doing this, but by the instantly noticeable change in how she talked and in the whole quality of her presence. On her second day on the couch her session went as follows. She said that she suddenly felt like going to sleep; then, ironically, that it would be an expensive sleep! I said that all the same she was probably talking about something she did feel she needed. She said that at home she certainly would not be able to lie down and have an hour to herself. (Pause.) She said she had stretched some of the canvases she had bought. (She is an artist.) Should she stick to her plan of getting them all stretched first, or start a painting now on one of the stretched ones? (Pause.) She said that sometimes, out driving, she just takes a turning on impulse, even if it is not where she is meant to be going. I said something about finding her own direction as she went along. There was a considerable silence. She said, rather suddenly, that this was very different from sitting up. I made a questioning sound, and she said 'Less like conversation.' When she used to sleep over with one of her schoolfriends they would lie in their beds in the dark, just talking about anything, until his mother came in and told them to shut up. All this was in a slow and reflective, almost meditative, vein. I noted that the schoolfriend, like myself, was male. The bedroom, a potentially sexual place that seemed safe for the time being, might represent the analytic room. There was also the anxiety about someone who might try and put a stop to this new way of talking and being. There seemed no need at this point, though, to interrupt her new-found free associating with interpretations.

She recalled talking yesterday about whether to go on seeing the same obstetrician. It was as much to do with the traffic and parking problems around his workplace, as about whether she thought he was a good doctor or not. Well, she said, she had decided like that about coming to see me too. She had always liked my road, for the way it sits rather hidden between two others. She liked my room, the feel of its space. Spaces were important to her. Another analyst she had consulted had a sink in the consulting-room; she didn't like that. Doctors always had sinks and they were full of instruments. I said that here was the same concern again, about

179

what the doctor might do. What would the instruments in the sink be for? She said she had seen things pretty clearly in the other analyst's sink, but she was sure there wasn't anything there really. There was a photo in yesterday's paper of a murder victim, looking beautiful and innocent, with a story that she had in fact been a violent and cruel character. It reminded her of a Cindy Sherman work (an artist whose works contain disturbing images of the artist herself). She said she can never draw herself except in the mirror. I said that she might be afraid of what would appear as she drew herself, unless she looked in the mirror for reassurance. She went back to the schoolfriend, whom she still sees. He could always give things a humorous turn. Even a serious conversation with him, about her pregnancy, had had laughs in it. Maybe she would phone him. But he usually had his answering machine on. What if he didn't pick up, and just left her talking? As she said this she turned on her front, on the couch, and looked at me.

I said I thought I had picked up her message. Lying on the couch not seeing me, she was worried whether I was really there for her, listening and willing to respond. I thought as well that she was looking to see in what way I would respond and what instruments I might be planning to use. For serious talk with me to be safe, that would matter a lot.

Beyond the particular interpretation I also had a sense that she was asking if I could pick up that *kind* of message, if I was ready for this allusive, associative way of communicating. After the preceding weeks, this abrupt change in tonality as she moved from the chair to the couch was as distinct as a suddenly different taste in the mouth. Unmistakably, this was the experience of shifting from ordinary into psychic reality. The quality of my listening had probably helped towards this, but her wondering whether I am ready to follow her, shows that the process is reciprocal. Her move from ordinary to psychic reality not only means that she can talk differently. It also helps my efforts to stay within psychic reality as I listen.

When she lay on the couch for the first time, the way she did it, immediately on entering the room and without explanation, felt like an active negation of what had been going on before. There was another key moment, when she was struck by how different lying on the couch felt from sitting up. It was 'less like conversation'. Again, this is a recognition of the negative. With the disappearance of something which belongs to ordinary, sitting-up, conversation-like reality, space is made for something different. This is simple and apparently obvious, but I want to highlight its significance. Specific aspects of the analytic situation are regularly understood in terms of their functions. Lying down, for example, helps towards a regressive state of mind. Coming four or five times a week encourages an intensity of transference experience, and makes it harder for defences to be constantly re-established. The profound silence of the analyst brings anxieties into the open and, at the same time, has an important holding function. Such observations are true enough but, more generally, the lying down, the frequency and the silence are all examples of how the analytic situation is set up so as to embody the negation of ordinary reality.

If the analytic setting represents in its external structure the internal activity of negation, and if, as I argued earlier, negation is essential to the creation of psychic reality, this means that the structure of the analytic situation represents the process by which psychic reality is constituted. We are looking, in fact, at what makes the psychoanalytic situation psychoanalytic.

This has corollaries when it comes to variations on the setting. There is a familiar debate about whether fewer than four or five sessions a week is a satisfactory analytic situation. Among the many arguments that have been brought forward, it is worth saying that to have more frequent sessions is, quite simply, *more different* from ordinary conversational reality. Lying down to talk to someone you cannot see might be a still greater negation of ordinary reality than talking face to face, however frequent that was. If someone is coming less often, maybe only twice or once a week, it tends to be seen as less appropriate to use the couch. But if the sessions are less frequent, the couch might be *more* important, provided the patient can tolerate it, because it would keep the therapeutic situation still representing as much as possible the negation of ordinary reality.

Heisaku Kosawa, the pioneer of Japanese psychoanalysis, studied with Freud in Vienna in the 1930s, being analysed by Richard Sterba and supervised by Paul Federn. Back in Japan he began analysing patients in the conventional way using the couch. Later he stopped using it regularly and often saw patients sitting up; but not face to face. He still sat out of sight, with the patient's chair turned away from him. Analyst and patient sat in their chairs, both facing in the same direction with the analyst behind. Strange as this may seem, and whatever Kosawa's reasons for giving up the couch, the clinical situation he did use still shows a fine awareness of the need to negate ordinary reality.

The comparison of psychic reality and symbolism showed the same double function in both of them. Both can be used defensively to avoid contact with ordinary reality, but they are also both essential to an alive engagement with it. The reason for this is that they both depend intrinsically on negation, which itself has a double function. It can be used in different, opposing, ways, and the use to which the underlying act of negation is being put, is what determines whether psychic reality or symbolism is being used defensively or constructively. Freud introduces negation as a clearly defensive procedure. 'Now you'll think I mean to say something insulting, but really I've no such intention.' 'You ask who this person in the dream can be. It's *not* my mother.' A moment later, however, he is writing: 'With the help of the symbol of negation, thinking frees itself from the restrictions of repression and enriches itself with material that is indispensable for its proper functioning' (1925b: 236). Negation frees think-ing from repression, Freud says, because the people who say 'I'm not insulting you' or 'It's not my mother' are letting themselves be aware of something they might have obliterated – the aggression, the association to mother – by virtue of saying that it does not count for anything. In itself that is defensive, but it does at least allow the thing in question out of the unconscious and makes it available for thinking about. In that way nega-tion is 'a way of taking cognizance of what is repressed' (Freud 1925b: 235).

The essential factor in this is that

> the intellectual function is separated from the affective process. With the help of negation only one consequence of the process of repression is undone – the fact, namely, of the ideational content of what is repressed not reaching consciousness. The outcome of this is a kind of intellectual acceptance of the repressed, while at the same time what is essential to the repression persists.
>
> (Freud 1925b: 236)

For Freud this thought was by no means new. It is a thread running through his work from *Jokes and their Relation to the Unconscious* (1905b), through 'Formulations on the two principles of mental functioning' (1911b) and the metapsychological papers 'Repression' (1915b) and 'The Unconscious' (1915c) up to this paper in 1925. In all of these he refers to the connection between intellectual judgement and repression, with the idea gradually emerging that conflictual experience can be saved from repression and be available for thinking about, if the emotional aspect of the conflict is sepa-rated from its intellectual evaluation.

Freud's concern was with intellectual judgement, but the converse must also be true of affective awareness. Clinical work in psychoanalysis shows all the time that for someone to stay in touch with feeling, and to let the nature of an emotional state reveal itself, it may be necessary to make the same separation between affective process and intellectual function. This way round, however, it is the intellectual awareness that has to be kept repressed in order for the emotion itself to become conscious. My patient's anxiety concerning doctors and their instruments, for example, could be conscious on condition that she did not know what it was about. This is the converse of what Freud described, but it depends on the same act of negation.

A tangential thought at this point. There is a tag to the effect that 'hysterics cannot think and obsessionals cannot feel'. Perhaps the underlying problem is that hysterics cannot negate their affect, so as to be able to think, and obsessionals cannot negate the ideational component so as to have access to their affect. Should we say 'hysterics cannot stop feeling and obses-sionals cannot stop thinking'?

After describing the negation which allows ideational content but not affect into consciousness, Freud says that one can sometimes succeed 'in conquering the negation as well, and in bringing about a full intellectual acceptance of the repressed' (Freud 1925b: 236). The double function of negation, however, shows that it is not so much a question of conquering negation as of how it is being used in the first place. If negation is being used to establish psychic reality as a realm for developing an engagement with the world, it will not need to be conquered. If, on the other hand, psychic reality is being turned into a defensive refuge, efforts to reduce the negation will indeed be taken as attempts at conquest and resisted.

The difference lies in whether negation is a fixed state to be held on to, or a mobile and flexible activity; whether it is being used to contradict ordinary reality, or provisionally to suspend it, disengaging from it for the time being without contradiction. The second makes it possible to work with the psychic representation instead of the real object, so as to come back to the real object in a new way. The former use of negation sets up a defensive psychic reality to be used as a refuge; the latter use sets up a psychic reality that extends the range of, and enriches, contact with ordinary reality.

The double usage of negation and the double function of psychic reality are related to what Green has called 'the work of the negative'. This concept is developed in his book of that name (Green 1993), and it sheds light on what it means for the use of negation to be free or restricted. All ego-development and any experiencing of ourselves as 'subjects' has to be achieved against an essential background of loss and of absence. We become who we are by how we deal with the fact that we cannot have what we want nor be who we wish to be. Many psychoanalytic ideas need to be understood, according to Green, in terms of how they address this fundamental experience of lack. In considering the '*fort-da*' game at the beginning of *Beyond the Pleasure Principle* (Freud 1920: 14–16), for example, his emphasis would not be first on the '*da*', the child's successful recovery of the cotton-reel, or his mother, but on the '*fort*', his throwing away of the cotton-reel, which is the acknowledgement that his mother is missing. There are two possible ways of dealing with the inevitability of lacking what we want. They are opposite to each other and display opposite forms of the work of the negative (Green 1993: 5ff., 181–2). One of these has a structuring effect on the ego and promotes development. The other is destructuring and hampers it.

Demands to give something up are of many sorts: the infant's not being able to feed the instant it is hungry; failure to achieve an ambition; bereavement by the death of someone beloved. Bearing these means facing the reality of deprivation, or the truth of not being like one's ideal, or accepting the loss of the loved object. If it is possible to make this act of negation, to accept the reality of lack, or of loss, that opens the door, through a process of working-through, to new experience, new ideals and new object-relationships. This is the structuring form of the work of the negative. The same process, in microcosm, is continually at work in what I have been calling the constructive use of negation. All exploration of reality, all movement towards new experiences or new ways of being, all creativity and any kind of symbolic functioning, in fact the whole fabric of psychic development, implies an ability to negate ordinary reality in temporary favour of psychic reality.

Doing this depends on a trust in being able to work through to a new connection with ordinary reality. If there is too much unconscious anxiety about ever being able to do that, this way of using negation may not be possible. In that case, what has been lost cannot be given up, the truth of lack and of absence cannot be faced, displacement and symbolisation are not possible, and negation can only be used to contradict the reality that cannot be borne. This opposite use of negation keeps the door closed to new experience or development. When the work of the negative takes this form, it is destructuring and disorganising to the ego.

These ideas may be recognisable from earlier discussions. Accepting that we cannot be those other selves, who inhabit worlds that our developmental pathways have closed to us (pp. 82ff.), calls for just that structuring 'work of the negative' that Green describes. The tragic vision of reality (p. 138) is the awareness of absence and loss as the constant background of human existence. The ironic vision is what helps to make that bearable so that the work of the negative can take its progressive form, as it did for Constable with his cloud studies, for example, when he settled in London and lost the Suffolk landscape (pp. 166–8).

The destructuring use of negation is discussed in Green's (1983) paper 'The Dead Mother'. He considers the situation of a mother who is absorbed by a bereavement, but who cannot give up that which is no longer there. The classic case involves the death of a child in infancy. The child's life and the mother's relationship with the living child have been negated by death. But the mother cannot allow that; she can only use the function of negation to contradict the truth of it. So she becomes frozen into a relationship with the child's non-existence. As Green (1993: 7) points out, this is what Bion (1970: 17) called a relationship to a 'no-thing'. If nothing is there anymore, accepting the negation of what was there is necessary for relationships to new things to become possible. Failing that, the nothing that is there may itself become the object. This is what happens with the 'dead' mother, who makes a relationship to the 'no-thing' that is constituted by the absence of the dead child.

Green's term for this is 'negative hallucination'. He instances (Green 1997) the patient who said to Winnicott (1971: 23) about her previous analyst 'The negative of him is more real than the positive of you.' A woman who came to me for consultation presented another example. She was in psychotherapy at the time and experiencing great frustration in the therapeutic relationship. She understood about the idea of transference but felt the situation was so unproductive that she was considering breaking off treatment. A crucial episode in her life history had been a passionate love affair with an artist. He had ended the relationship and done so, as she felt, very brutally. When she said she had never got over it, she meant it in a specific way. Although they had not seen each other for years and he was now married and living elsewhere, she said that in her mind the relationship was still just as much in existence today as ever. As we talked it became clear that she was indeed still actively involved in a relationship. But what she was relating to was the void this man had left behind, the gone-ness of what there had once been. He had created, when the relationship broke up, a work of art which, in its particular medium, powerfully embodied his rejection of her. The continued existence of this work of art helped perpetuate in her mind the active, continuing non-existence of the relationship. It was the embodiment of the negative of the relationship, and it was this negative that she was still relating to. The relationship to her therapist as a transference object could not compete with the active aliveness of her relationship to the negative of her ex-lover.

The constructive work of the negative requires a certain psychic mobility, a capacity to shift between negating and affirming, separation and connection. Broadly speaking, the ability to use negation in this provisional, flexible way, so as to establish a creative kind of psychic reality, is an index of well-being. But of course there is nothing cut and dried about it. In his sequence of references to the relation between judgement and repression, Freud is trying to say something about an ebb and flow between different states of mind. We cannot be continuously in touch with the fullness of our experience at all levels, intellectual and emotional. We regularly need to distance ourselves from some part of it in order to address other parts, and to resolve conflicts. As a particular resolution is worked through it becomes possible to reconnect, we hope more richly, with what we had negated and to enter again into the fullness of our experience; until the next time. The depth and quality of our emotional and thinking life thus moves to a kind of tidal rhythm, which we may sense both in the short term, within a single hour or day, and over the years.

The analytic situation opens that rhythm, of movement and fixity in how people negate and reconnect with their experience, to a unique kind of exploration. Analysts themselves are now in touch, now out of touch with their own experience of the session. All analysts know what it is like to feel slow in the uptake. It is chastening to have the penny suddenly drop about what a patient has been trying to convey for a long time. I realised recently that one of my patients was telling me he felt an entire fun-loving, risk-taking side of his personality had been, to use his word, 'engineered' out of existence. Given the decades over which that had happened, and also his present life circumstances, he could see no possibility of ever recovering it. That part of him seemed gone for ever. When the impact of this hit me I thought 'How could I not have understood?!' But I think the sense of tragedy was such that I had to negate the affect (unconsciously at the time) in order first to grasp at an intellectual level what I was hearing about. Only later could I let the full emotional significance of it emerge, and begin to speak out of that awareness.

The psychoanalytic situation makes possible its unique exploration of unconscious mental life by virtue of the fact that its structure, in various different ways, is a representation in external reality of the internal structure it is investigating. This internal structure is thus both unconscious and, at the same time, made visible and audible. In particular, the analytic setting is an external representation of the internal negation which is essential to the establishing of psychic reality. The quality of a person's psychic reality, and the degree of freedom in his or her use of negation, will find a direct representation in the quality of psychoanalytic situation that person can take part in, and in the degree of freedom with which he or she can use its negations of ordinary reality. The more restricted someone is to a fixed and immobilising use of negation, the more the analytic setting will represent, and draw the analyst into, a fixed and immobilised psychic reality; and the more difficult will be the analytic task of establishing a psychic reality in which the constructive work of the negative can take place.

A refinement, however, is needed to conclude with. It is incomplete to say that what makes the psychoanalytic situation psychoanalytic is its being a representation of psychic structure. That is true as far as it goes, but the analytic situation is not a static tableau. By its nature it calls on patients to express themselves, and on the patient and analyst to engage with each other. This makes the analytic situation not just a representation of psychic structure but an expression of it. It is the way psychic structure expresses itself, and cannot not express itself, through the structure of the setting, that makes the psychoanalytic situation psychoanalytic. This is what makes the unconscious visible and audible. The point is not that the analyst looks for something from the patient, within the setting. The analytic setting itself, by its very nature, constitutes a demand for the expression of the psychic apparatus; and this, as Green (1984: 119) has put it, is what makes the setting a psychoanalytic apparatus.

Conclusion

Existence and non-existence generate each other.
Heavy and light complete each other.
Long and short shape each other.
High and deep convert each other.
Before and after follow each other.

Lao Tzu (1985: ch. 2)

11

The dove that returns,
The dove that vanishes

The water does not think of giving it lodging
Nor the moon of lodging there –
How clear the reflection!
From the Japanese
(Leggett 1978: 145)

A comparison between Freud, Klein and Lacan provides Ricardo Bernardi (1989) with the springboard for an illuminating discussion. Their theories are not abstract formulations, but paradigms which offer, or more accurately *are*, ways of viewing, and thinking about, psychoanalytic material. A paradigm, first of all, constitutes a particular way of looking, as Einstein emphasised to Heisenberg (p. 65). Bernardi illustrates this with Freud's, Klein's and Leclaire's Lacanian accounts of the Wolf-Man's dream, showing how differently they perceive the same material. The second effect of a paradigm appears in 'the kind of questions and answers that are particular to each paradigm, and the ideal that inspires these different forms of posing and solving problems, that is to say, paradigms as ways of thinking psychoanalytically' (Bernardi 1989: 344). The word 'ideal' is worth noting for its implication that different paradigms operate according to different values. When he comes to spell out the difference between a theory and a paradigm, Bernardi says: 'While the term "theory" refers essentially to cognitive aspects, in the term "paradigm" notional elements, preconceptions, attitudes, values and fantasies meet together' (1989: 343). He is pointing to the same thing that Klauber emphasised in the second of the two papers discussed in Chapter 5.

> The analyst's spontaneity . . . is the sign that not only have impulses based on drives been recognised, but also their amalgamation with fantasies, feelings and values . . . This mediating role of the patient's

values is crucial in understanding how therapeutic changes actually come about.

(Klauber 1981: 115)

The resonance with Bernardi is striking. Klauber writes explicitly of the need for the analyst to understand 'the changes of [the patient's] values at different periods of his life' (Klauber 1981: 117). The analyst, that is to say, must understand the paradigm shifts that have informed the patient's life.

There is no point in hoping not to be subject to our paradigms. We inhabit them. An analyst's paradigm is the expression of his or her analytic identity. What matters is to be aware, as Bernardi puts it, 'how much they condition our ability to observe and to think' (1989: 350). While opening certain horizons they close off others. 'The area that is most clear in each paradigm is also its blind spot; what they help us to think about is also what they cannot stop thinking about' (1989: 351). Paradigms can, in that way, block the flexible use of negation which, as discussed in the previous chapter, makes psychic work possible. It was stressed in Chapter 3 (p. 46) how important is an attitude towards the unconscious that does not limit us only to ways of looking that we are already familiar with.

Barnaby Barratt (1994) has classified types of analyst according to the paradigms they use. The 'computational' analyst distinguishes clearly between the patient's mind and the analyst's mind, and also between the analyst's working ego and the rest of his mind and personality. It is the analyst's working ego that discovers the truth about the patient, and the analyst uses theory to help the working ego do this and to convey those discoveries to the patient. This is reminiscent of Gray's technique (pp. 20–1) and of the first of Klauber's papers discussed in Chapter 5 (Klauber 1981: 79–90). Barratt contrasts this with what he calls the 'engaged' psychoanalyst, who does not think so much of one person, the analyst, acting on another, the patient, but of a shared process between two people. Truth is not discovered by one person and conveyed to the other, but emerges between them in the course of that shared process. The analyst does not use a particular part of his mind to engage with the patient, while the rest of him acts to safeguard that working part. Instead, as Klauber describes in the second paper (1981: 109–20), the analyst's whole self is involved in the analytic process. This gives theory a different function. The 'computational' analyst uses it to make metapsychological inferences and gain insight about the patient. For the 'engaged' analyst theory acts as a guide and framework to underpin the analysis as a whole, so that the analyst's spontaneous responsiveness remains psychoanalytic in character.

These paradigms imply different kinds of listening. For the analyst who works as Klauber describes in his first paper, the structure of the session is known in advance. It exists from the beginning of the session, unconsciously in the patient's mind, consciously in the analyst's, and is waiting to manifest itself as the session develops. How the analyst listens to the patient, and thus what he hears, will be determined by that preconception. The shift from the first paper to the second makes for a different sort of listening. No longer needing so much to order the material, Klauber has a greater breadth of receptivity. The patient's impact on him is not there just as something to be aware of and monitor, so that his interpretations are not distorted by it. In this paradigm, the analyst's spontaneous response to the patient's impact is what makes his interpretations creative and allows them, in turn, to have a personal impact on the patient. The analyst's listening is not aimed now at protecting him from contamination (Klauber 1981: 90) but at opening him to the effect of the patient on him.

To think of the 'evolution' of Klauber's analytic identity might seem to imply that his later standpoint is more developed and preferable to the first. By no means all analysts would agree. A student whom I once asked to present a comparison of Klauber's two papers did not notice the dates of writing. He assumed that the first had been written later than the second. He saw the second as full of vagueness and uncertainty which, as the analyst got more experienced, clarified itself into, as he perceived it, the more lucid understanding shown in what was in fact the earlier paper. Gray's (1990) and Coltart's (1992) statements, quoted at the beginning of Chapter 2, illustrate how distinctly analysts may align themselves with one paradigm or the other.

To hold the apparent opposites together in a creative tension calls for a suppleness in the analyst's relation to the analytic process of which he or she is part. At those moments, for example, for which Bion (1967: 127) uses the word 'evolution', when something suddenly comes into view about a patient, the analyst needs to have different possible kinds of response available. He may look to see what he can do with the new perception: how to interpret it to the patient so as to show him something about himself. At other times the last thing he wants is to use what he has seen in that way. Instead he finds himself doing as little as he can with it, so as not to get in the way of whatever is coming next. It is not that he does not want the patient to understand himself, of course, but he does not want to *use* what he has seen to *get* him to understand.

Patients too vary in how they relate to the process. A young man in analysis suddenly exclaimed 'Yes! I understand. Psychoanalysis isn't meant to be useful!' This took me aback, until I saw that it expressed a true recognition. He did not mean psychoanalysis was useless, but that what we were doing together was not defined in terms of goals or objectives. Another patient was acting out in a strongly negative transference. She was missing sessions, not paying her fees and appearing to get nothing from her analysis. I thought she was getting ready to break it off. One day I made reference to a time when she had thought I was helpful to her. 'Oh yes', she replied. 'There's a process at work here. No doubt of that.' All at once it was clear that analysis was, after all, going on between us. I once heard an ex-analytic patient say: 'I don't think my analyst was any great shakes, but the process was amazing!'

This sensitivity to the process and trust in it contrasts with the attitude of another patient, a man who, in a somewhat paranoid way, liked to keep ahead of the game both in his analysis and in the rest of his life. He would practically never spontaneously think of the process between us. He desired certain changes. Some were quite specific, such as to sleep better, and to overcome an unreasonable perfectionism which impaired his relationships at work. Other problems were less focal. He did not feel he belonged in the world, and was afraid he would kill himself simply because it made no difference whether he was alive or dead. He had a deep sense of disconnectedness from those he loved. Even with these less defined concerns, though, he had a markedly utilitarian view of what happened in his sessions. Every intervention of mine was liable to scrutiny for what function it served and whether or not it was helpful. When he thought it was not, he would tell me so and wait for me to say something better. He did not understand the idea that something might gradually develop in the space between us, and that we could wait for its value to declare itself in time. His attitude, of course, was itself part of the process between us, and I analysed it as best I could. The point is not that no process was at work, but how different his relationship to it was from the patients mentioned before.

The analyst occupies an internal vantage point with regard to the analytic process, and this vantage point varies. He may wish to capitalise on the process so as to extract insight from it, or he may be more concerned for the process to unfold and find its own direction, regardless, for the moment, of tangible results. Each vantage point is valuable, indeed necessary. They do not exclude each other, and analytic work involves activity emanating from both. The analyst's stance fluctuates, in fact, along a dimension that extends between the two of them in their pure forms. Although patients differ, as these vignettes show, and the same patient will shift his stance from one time to another, they are not generally conscious in these terms of what they are doing. The analyst, on the other hand, needs to be consciously aware of this dimension and move fluidly back and forth along it, sensitive both to the patient's vantage point of the moment and to the long-term needs of the analysis.

The man just referred to, who likes to keep ahead of the game, had not been able to stop his baby daughter crying. He had an impulsive outburst of fury against her. After describing this he went on to a film he had seen about a boy accused of murder. A teacher tried to vindicate him by showing he had been deprived as a child and was subject to outbursts of rage where he was not responsible for his actions. In court the boy refused to accept some lie that was told but screamed out that it was false. This helped get him acquitted. Next the patient moved on to a situation at work. A colleague had done something incompetently and he offered to do it properly himself. Then he realised he had given himself a lot of work which did not belong to him. He said he did not know why he should have told me these three stories together.

If I want to intervene at this point I have various options. I might say something about the helpless rage in him, that he may not be aware of, but which is trying to express itself. This uses my own understanding to get him to see something about himself. I am trying to make the unconscious conscious, having decided myself what it is that needs to become conscious. Secondly, I might look for an interpretation about the care he wants from me and his anxiety that I will judge him, or his fear of rage between us, or his doubts about my competence as an analyst. A direct transference interpretation of that sort would still be trying to get him to see something which I understand but he as yet does not. A third option would be to comment that he is allowing himself the unfamiliar experience of telling me something without understanding why. This points to what he is doing, not so as to reveal its meaning but to open up for him his own experience of himself, and of himself in relation to me. I certainly take note of what I understand about his rage and about the transference, but my overriding concern in this instance is not to close off his experience by using my understanding to assign meaning to it. All three kinds of intervention are valid, and any one might be appropriate according to the analytic moment. But they originate from different vantage points along this dimension.

Freud said more than once that one does not become a good analyst by being too directly concerned to help the patient, but by attending without preconceptions to the process one is engaged in.

> The most successful cases are those in which one proceeds, as it were, without any purpose in view.
>
> (Freud 1912: 114)

> I adopted the expedient of renouncing working by conscious thought, so as to grope my way further into the riddles only by blind touch. Since I started this I have been doing my work, perhaps more skilfully than before, but I do not really know what I am doing.[1]
>
> (Freud 1954: 312)

The analyst's attention is balanced between the process and its objective, and this balancing involves a particular kind of ego-activity. John Padel calls attention to the following functions of the ego:

---

1 Compare the passage from Coltart (1992: 2) quoted on p. 23.

1. Scanning of the field in which one is acting.
2. Division of the field with alternation of attention between at least two features of it and exploration of each from the vantage point of the other.
3. Reuniting of the field (especially that featuring two persons – self and other) and viewing of the field from a third position.

(Padel 1985: 281)

The dimension I am describing has at one end a vantage point which is the process itself, from which an objective may be considered. At the other end the objective becomes the vantage point, determining how the process is viewed. The analyst at work seeks to reunite this field and find a position from which to comprehend both vantage points. The function of this third position is freedom of movement. The analyst may make use of the process to show the patient something about himself, or he may want to foster the unfolding of the process itself, without trying to put it to use. What matters is not to be immobilised in one position or the other.

Dream interpretation might seem, at first sight, a clear instance of the analyst's seeing something the patient has not seen, and then getting the patient to see it too. As Freud (1911a) emphasised, however, interpretation has two meanings. One is what goes on in the analyst's mind, the other, what the analyst says to the patient. If the analyst assigns meaning to the dream in her mind, and puts that meaning into a spoken interpretation, that is at what we might call the 'near' end of the spectrum which makes active use of theoretical insight and interpretative technique. If, instead, she tries to open possibilities for the patient to discover meaning in the dream experience, she moves towards the 'far' end, where absence of preconceptions and openness to the unknown are more important.

A patient dreamed of *filming an army on the march. He was doing it in a risky, adventurous way. Starting from a close up of one soldier's hand, he rose up to see the other soldiers, then all their heads, and then took the camera up on a crane to overlook the entire army in a downward long-shot. All this was in one sequence.* He remembered another dream where *he saw a flight of birds on the ground. They were very pale yellow and remarkably beautiful. They had bald heads.* He said that the birds' heads seemed to go with the soldiers' helmets. He supposed this was phallic imagery about circumcised and uncircumcised penises. This was relevant in relation to other material and probably correct. The interpretation was there for the making that the way he filmed the army represented an erection, and we might have gone on to a fantasy of intercourse as shooting. But what he said, although possibly true, felt stereotyped and lifeless, and I did not take it up. He went on to talk about playing squash the day before. He was playing orthodox shots fairly well, but losing. Then he gave up playing by the book. To his delight his unconventional

194

shots came off and he won. The thing about the film shot in the dream was the exhilaration of doing it in such an adventurous way. I then did take up his link between the birds' heads and the soldiers' helmets, not as an explanation of meaning but simply to comment on his freedom in moving between the two dreams. He spoke of the impact certain images in actual films had made on him, and said that to connect the pale yellow birds and the army on the march seemed somehow beautiful. He realised that the sense of creativity he had had in the first dream, and which he longs for in his own work, was in fact available to him. Simple as this sequence may appear, the realisation moved him deeply.

A contrasting example is the dream of a woman with sexual problems, who thought concretely and showed little conscious capacity for symbolisation. *She was meant to be on a train to Glasgow but her luggage had been stolen by Liverpool football supporters. She was complaining to the inspector. She was desperate because she had packed carefully; all the luggage was essential. It wasn't really so important, though; it was only clothes. Then again it was essential but she could do without certain things: some trousers that made her look fat and a sweater that was too small. She collapsed in tears as she told the inspector about it.* I commented that she seemed uncertain whether clothes were unimportant or essential. She said the sweater would have made her breasts look big and she could not think why she had packed it. Then she remembered the previous evening, when she and her husband took their clothes off in the sauna. It was exciting. Afterwards she had gone naked into the swimming-pool and enjoyed it. Another association was that when she was a girl her father used to go to Glasgow on business. I spoke of myself as the inspector-analyst to whom she was trying to talk about things that disturbed her. I might have stopped there, and not put forward ideas of my own as to what she was trying to talk about. She being the patient she was, however, I thought some definite ascription on my part of meaning to her dream was called for. I pointed out the play on Liver*pool* and said that behind her sexual fears the dream revealed a wish for the excitement of being without her clothes and showing her breasts. I also said that her conflict about her body seemed linked to a wish to be close to her father.

With the man my vantage point was closer to the far end of the dimension. By not getting in the way with an interpretation I heard about the unexpected shots, and this helped him make contact with his creativity. With the woman, however, I thought she needed me, at that time in her analysis, to shift towards the near end, so as to point out the meanings she could not see for herself and show her that there was more going on in her mind than she was aware of.

Consultation might seem, because of the circumscribed nature of the situation, to be *par excellence* an activity of the near end, concerned with specific, more or less definable issues. Here too, however, a range of vantage points is called for. I was once assessing a woman as a prospective training case for a psychotherapy organisation. She responded well to trial interpretations, such as that her work, which was pastoral in nature, might be connected with a wish to heal her own badly damaged family; and that her difficulty in relating to men, including myself during our interview, seemed linked to her tantalising but frustrating relationship with her father. These interpretations clearly registered with her. The making of them and her responses were an important part of the assessment. What also struck me, though, was a gradual, steady evolution throughout the interview. She seemed to become emotionally more available, and to gain a sense of what she might be needing, more from the overall experience of being listened to in a certain way than because of particular interpretations. In fact I made few interventions, and when I came to write up my report it seemed that not a great deal had happened in the session. But I knew perfectly well that a lot had. Her slow but continuous response to my analytic listening made me realise that she was appreciating not just what I said but the vantage point I was occupying. I was not only looking for particular insights or clarifying what she might get from treatment, but also sensing her capacity to participate in a process.

As well as needing my own free movement between vantage points, I had to be open to the position in this woman's mind from which she herself was seeking help. It is by being open to the patient's vantage point that analysts are guided about what vantage point to take up themselves. This may not be conscious, and it is too simple, in fact, to speak of 'taking up' a vantage point. There is a continuous process, in a successful analysis, of patient and analyst discovering, through their interaction, the shifting vantage points they need to occupy.

The story of Noah presents a striking metaphor for the theme of this chapter. Noah is a man threatened by destructive forces. To escape them he has to make a journey which is itself almost as terrifying. Then he learns that the flood waters have abated and he can end his journey. How does he learn this? He sends a dove out from the ark. It comes back with an olive leaf in its mouth. Solid ground is once again available. How much solid ground? Perhaps the dove could bring back something more substantial than just an olive leaf. He sends it forth again. It does not, however, return with yet further information. Instead it vanishes. This is a shock. The dove that returned showed Noah at least the olive leaf. The dove that vanishes shows him nothing. But then we see that in vanishing, it has shown him more. Seeming to abandon Noah, it has found the exact and only way to show him the full truth. The dove that returns and the dove that vanishes, which are the same bird, represent twin aspects of psychoanalysis.

Entrusting oneself to the process, without secretly saying 'provided it takes me where I want to go', because it will take us where we need to go, without our having to know in advance what that means: all that demands faith in the process. Faith is an uneasy concept for many analysts, but in fact it denotes a necessary scientific attitude. Bion (1970: 34–5) makes the point succinctly: 'An "act of faith" is peculiar to scientific procedure and must be distinguished from the religious meaning with which it is invested in conversational usage.' Scientists and philosophers of science know well that science depends on faith. From the seventeenth century when Francis Bacon set out the first modern account of scientific methodology, until our own day, it was accepted that science proceeded by the method known as induction, of drawing general conclusions from numbers of particular instances. Philosophers struggled with the problem of justifying this. Scientific advances showed that induction worked, but there seemed no logical basis for it. Scientists were in the same position as psychoanalysts, entrusting themselves to an unpredictable process, in the faith that it would take them where they needed to go. Popper's (1934) critique of inductivism, and his introduction of the concept of falsification, revolutionised the philosophy of science. But where induction had meant scientists believed their theories on the basis of a process they could not justify, the accurate logic of the falsification principle now made it impossible ever to know for certain that any theory was true. Science was left just as dependent on faith as before.

There is nothing metaphysical about Noah's need for dry land. Sending out the dove is a practical attempt to see whether it is possible to re-establish normal life. The olive leaf is a clear answer, but incomplete. The dove can only show that it has no further need of the ark at all by not returning. Vanishing is the only way for it to show Noah what he needs to know. Noah, for his part, must see that the empty sky is not failure but the completion of what the olive leaf meant. This is practical, scientific understanding which depends on faith.

The olive leaf and the vanishing are different kinds of showing, and sometimes one is needed, sometimes the other. Analysts may talk of 'showing' patients that they are doing a certain thing: attacking, or trying to please, the analyst, or avoiding an anxiety, or enacting something in the session. Whatever it is, the analyst 'shows' the patient that that is what he is doing. This is the dove that returns. The analyst wants to convey his understanding to the patient, so that the patient can benefit from seeing himself in this new way. Such interpretations emanate from the near end of the dimension. Often they are illuminating and helpful, but this kind of showing can also, at other times, seem to impose a view of the analyst's on the patient. An interpretation emanating from the farther end aims to open up the possibility of something happening, without the need to know what that something is going to be. Understanding is not just the acquisition of knowledge; it is the occurrence of an event. Knowledge can, to an extent, be given to a patient. The event can only be allowed and made room for.

If what the analyst says, and also the analyst's silence, may come from either end of this dimension, the same is true of the patient. What matters is for patient and analyst to be in tune as they shift back and forth along it. The consultation example showed how a sense of the patient's vantage point can guide the analyst's. In the second dream example the patient needed, if my judgement was right, to be shown something with an interpretation from the near end of the dimension. If I had offered her an unclosed intervention from the far end, it might simply have confused her. But if the patient is unconsciously seeking a vantage point towards the farther end while the analyst, insisting on operating at the near end, wants the patient to have the same experience of himself that the analyst has had of him, that is when 'showing' becomes an imposition. The analyst may appear to be opening up possibilities for an event to occur, but he has decided in advance what the event is to be.

Bion (1962) thought that raw experience itself could not be dealt with by our mental processes. The elemental units of experience cannot, for example, be thought about, used in dreaming or stored in memory. These raw bits of experience he called beta-elements. They cannot turn into anything else. Nothing can be generated out of them. All they can do is happen to us. For beta-elements to be actively handled and made use of by the mind they must, through what Bion calls alpha-function,[2] become alpha-elements. These are, by contrast, open to transformation.

Suppose that interpretations start their life in an analyst's mind as beta-elements. The analyst comes up against an aspect of the patient's functioning and wants to convey this to him. If he tries to do literally that, however, to convey the experience from himself to the patient, he will be like a removal man trying to shift something from one location to another. Bion describes how psychotic patients try to evacuate their beta-elements into the analyst. Analysts can do the same to patients with their interpretations, if their alpha-function does not act sufficiently on the experience they wish to convey, before they communicate it. The analyst's experience can have no effect on the patient if it remains, simply, the thing that happened to the analyst. To interpret it the analyst must use his alpha-function to give the experience the potential for evolution.

The farther out that the analyst is working along the dimension considered here, the more alpha-process is involved. If the analyst's vantage-point is in the goals of the analysis, he will know clearly enough what it is, about his experience of the patient, that he wants to convey to him. The alpha-element in the interpretation is not all that far transformed out of the beta-element experienced by the analyst and, once transmitted to the patient, it does not need to undergo much further transformation. The patient is

2 See p. 174 for a comment on the meaning of alpha-function.

expected to 'see' what he has been 'shown', as I wanted my patient with sexual difficulties to see what I was showing her about her dream. If the analyst's vantage-point, on the other hand, is in the process itself, his hope will be different. He will want his alpha-function to work further on the beta-element, so as to bring into play an alpha-element with the potential for all sorts of transformations, foreseen, unforeseen, unforeseeable: an alpha-element which, once transmitted to the patient, has an unpredictable life of its own. My other patient 'showed' me, on his own account, what his dream 'meant'. When something told me I should not go along with this, he began to make unexpected shots: unexpected both to himself and to me. Both sorts of vantage point are needed for their appropriate occasions. If the analyst's stance is too far out towards the second when the first is called for, then a patient's specific, focal need of the moment will not be met. If the analyst does not move out along the dimension when he needs to, what looks like a thoroughly insightful interpretation may in fact be handing the patient a left-over, untransformed part of the analyst's experience. Since beta-elements cannot evolve, the patient cannot do anything with such an interpretation. He can only choose between letting it happen to him or not letting it.

A patient who teaches said that whilst lecturing that morning he had suddenly 'taken off'. Original ideas had come into his mind which were exciting both for him and the students. He was due to speak at a conference. Would the magic happen again? There was another speaker on the programme with him, and this might stop it. 'I can do it when I'm on my own', he said. 'If there's a colleague in the lecture room it all disappears into rivalry.' Suppose I sense that this needs to be taken up in the transference. I might formulate the following: 'I think that you see me as a rival, and you are afraid I may spoil your creativity or take it from you.' Let us call that A. Even without further clinical detail, it seems a possible interpretation. It certainly appears to have more to it than, say: 'There are two of us in this room.' We may call that B. It does not look a very substantial intervention, and indeed it may not be. If I am vaguely feeling there is some competitiveness around and think I ought to nudge things along a bit, and therefore decide to say B, then it truly does not amount to much. It could even be heard as aggressive towards the patient. That version of B we may call B1. But consider another possibility. Suppose I think that what is expressed by A is probably true, but I am reluctant to say A because it seems to define something too closely. The range of response it leaves open to the patient is somewhat limited. Then I may try and let my alpha-function work further, to strip away the elements which limit the patient's response while keeping the essence that I want to indicate to him. I might arrive at something like: 'There are two of us in this room'. This is B2. The words are the same, but it is a completely different utterance from

B1, for both analyst and patient. If the patient responds to it by realising that he does see me as a rival, the idea contained in A becomes a discovery for him. If he does not respond in this way, but I still feel the idea behind A is what matters, I can interpret his avoidance of it: 'You seem unwilling to think that you might see me as a rival . . .' The chance of interpreting A is not lost. Other possibilities, however, are also left open. The patient may do something unexpected with my intervention, finding in it what I had not even been aware of saying. The closed horizon of interpretation A is less likely to yield such a shared discovery of something unknown to both of us.

Entrusting oneself to the process might seem a passive idea, and to overlook the work that analysis involves. Notice, though, how much more psychic work it requires to reach B2 than interpretation A. The analyst is not passive, but the nature of the work makes his activity curiously invisible. Bion's (1962: 36) concept of 'reverie' attempts to describe this. Reverie is something the analytic stance has in common with the state of mind by which a mother cares for, and expresses her love for, her infant. It is a contemplation of, and receptivity towards, whatever may come to us from the object of our regard. The patient experiences B2 differently from B1, just as the baby responds not merely to the substance of the food but to the mother's state of mind out of which she feeds it. It is not only because they are made up of different words that A and B2 are different interpretations. The difference between them is not just in what they say, but in where they originate from within the analyst. B1 and B2 consist of the same words, but they also are different interpretations because they have different origins within the analyst.[3] Reverie is essential to alpha-function. Through it the analyst's beta-element experience of the patient can become an alpha-element, available for use in interpretation. If an interpretation is to find an origin further out along the dimension, as it does in moving from A to B2, it will be by further reverie.

'Reverie', like 'faith', is a word with connotations in ordinary usage which may need to be set aside in considering its psychoanalytic meaning. The analyst's reverie is not at all a dreamy vagueness, withdrawn from reality. It is both a state and an activity. Being angry, for example, is a state of mind; but someone being angry is also doing something. The same is true of analytic reverie. The inner state and activity are like a ground bass in music, that sustains whatever is going on, peaceful or turbulent, in the upper voices. It is something the analyst tries to maintain, whatever else he or she may be doing externally. An analyst can be working to formulate an interpretation, grappling with her own emotional reactions, or actively confronting the patient, and still be engaged in reverie. The karate student

---

3 Compare Nacht's (1962) emphasis on the 'deep inner state of the analyst' (Chapter 1, p. 13).

striking the *makiwara* (pp. 19–20) is an example of reverie even in violence. In moving from the near end towards the farther end of this dimension, the analyst entrusts himself or herself more unreservedly to the analytic process, and the degree of analytic reverie increases. Trust in the analytic process is inseparable from the analyst's trust in his unconscious, which is the ground of his analytic identity. Reverie is an act of faith in unconscious process, the same faith that the empty sky demanded of Noah.

Analysts vary in whereabouts from within themselves they work most comfortably. Some find themselves more at home near one end of the dimension, some near the other. Differences of style and personality, and different paradigms of psychoanalysis, will tend to push an analyst this way or that. But the dove that returns and the dove that vanishes are yet one more instance of the tension between opposites that has to be sustained without sacrifice of either. This depends crucially on keeping up a resistance to one's personal inclinations, and to one's own psychoanalytic paradigm, so as to attend to that end of the dimension where one feels less at home: the end of it that one finds *unheimlich* (Freud 1919b).

The karate class, with which this book began, showed the necessary connection between disciplined technique and commitment of spirit. There is an image which traditionally expresses the martial artist's equivalent of the analyst's reverie. His mind should be like the water of a still lake as it reflects the moon. The poem at the head of this chapter is traditionally given to advanced martial arts students, for them to meditate on as part of their training (Leggett 1978: 145). The clarity of spirit which it expresses is founded on an enduring attention to technique. This state, of 'mind like water, mind like the moon', is also what allows technique itself to become, in turn, an expression of spirit. The analyst at work is both repairman and healer, the dove that returns and the dove that vanishes. The inner freedom of movement that this demands is based on constant interplay between a technique that makes possible the refinding of theory, a capacity for reverie, and the resources of a psychoanalytic faith.

Bibliography

Anzieu, D. (1986) *Freud's Self-Analysis*, London: Hogarth.

—— (1989) 'Beckett and Bion', *International Review of Psycho-Analysis* 16: 163–9.

Arden, M. (1984) 'Infinite sets and double binds', *Midwifery of the Soul: A Holistic Perspective on Psychoanalysis*: 9–25, London: Free Association Books (1998).

—— (1998) *Midwifery of the Soul: A Holistic Perspective on Psychoanalysis*, London: Free Association Books.

Arieti, S. (1967) *The Intrapsychic Self: Feeling, Cognition and Creativity in Health and Mental Illness*, New York: Basic Books.

Arlow, J. (1987) 'Trauma, play and perversion', *Psychoanalytic Study of the Child* 42: 31–44.

—— (1996) 'The concept of psychic reality – how useful?', *International Journal of Psychoanalysis* 77: 659–66.

Arvanitakis, K.I. (1998) 'Some thoughts on the essence of the tragic', *International Journal of Psychoanalysis* 79: 955–64.

Bakan, D. (1967) 'Psychotherapist: healer or repairman?', *On Method*: 122–6, San Francisco: Jossey-Bass.

Baker, P. (1997) *Beckett and the Mythology of Psychoanalysis*, London: Macmillan.

Baker, R. (1993) 'Some reflections on humour in psychoanalysis', *International Journal of Psychoanalysis* 74: 951–60.

Balint, E. (1993) *Before I was I: Psychoanalysis and the Imagination. Collected papers of Enid Balint*, eds J. Mitchell and M. Parsons, London: Free Association Books.

Bao Ruo-Wang (Jean Pasqualini) and Chelminski, R. (1976) *Prisoner of Mao*, Harmondsworth: Penguin.

Barratt, B. (1994) 'Critical notes on the psychoanalyst's theorising', *Journal of the American Psychoanalytic Association* 42: 697–725.

Bateman, A. (1998) 'Thick- and thin-skinned organisations and enactment in borderline and narcissistic disorders', *International Journal of Psychoanalysis* 79: 13–25.

Bateson, G. (1955) 'A theory of play and fantasy', *Steps to an Ecology of Mind*, New York: Chandler (1972).

Beckett, R.B. (1968) *John Constable's Correspondence, vol. VI: The Fishers*, Ipswich: Suffolk Records Society.

Berlin, I. (1990) 'The pursuit of the ideal', *The Crooked Timber of Humanity: Chapters in the History of Ideas*: 1–19, ed. H. Hardy, London: John Murray.

Bermingham, A. (1987) *Landscape and Ideology: the English Rustic Tradition 1740–1860*, London: Thames and Hudson.

Bernardi, R. (1989) 'The role of paradigmatic determinants in psychoanalytic understanding', *International Journal of Psychoanalysis* 70: 341–57.

Bettelheim, B. (1961) *The Informed Heart: Autonomy in a Mass Age*, London: Thames and Hudson.

Bhagavad Gita (1962) Trans. J. Mascaro, Harmondsworth: Penguin Books.

Bion, W.R. (1958) 'On arrogance', *International Journal of Psychoanalysis* 39: 144–6.

—— (1961) *Experiences in Groups and Other Papers*, London: Tavistock Publications.

—— (1962) *Learning from Experience*, London: Heinemann, in *Seven Servants*, New York: Jason Aronson (1977).

—— (1967) *Second Thoughts*, London: Heinemann.

—— (1970) *Attention and Interpretation: A Scientific Approach to Insight in Psycho-Analysis and Groups*, London: Tavistock Publications, in *Seven Servants*, New York: Jason Aronson (1977).

Black, D. (1993) 'What sort of thing is a religion? A view from object-relations theory', *International Journal of Psychoanalysis* 74: 613–25.

Bollas, C. (1987) *The Shadow of the Object: Psychoanalysis of the Unthought Known*, London: Free Association Books.

—— (1989) *Forces of Destiny: Psychoanalysis and Human Idiom*, London: Free Association Books.

Borges, J.L. (1962) 'The garden of forking paths', *Ficciones*, London: Weidenfeld and Nicolson.

Braunschweig, D. and Fain, M. (1975) *La Nuit, Le Jour*, Paris: Presses Universitaires de France.

Breen, D., ed. (1993) *The Gender Conundrum: Contemporary Psychoanalytic Perspectives on Femininity and Masculinity*, London: Routledge.

Brenman Pick, I. (1985) 'Working through in the countertransference', *International Journal of Psychoanalysis* 66: 157–66.

Breuer, J. and Freud, S. (1893–5) *Studies on Hysteria*, *The Standard Edition of the Complete Works of Sigmund Freud*, vol. II, London: Hogarth Press (1950–74).

Britton, R. (1989) 'The missing link: parental sexuality in the Oedipus complex', in D. Breen, ed., *The Gender Conundrum: Contemporary Psychoanalytic Perspectives on Femininity and Masculinity*: 82–94, London: Routledge.

Brontë, C. (1849) Letter to Ellen Nussey of November 16, in E. Nussey, ed., *The Story of the Brontës: Their Home, Haunts, Friends and Works. Part Second – Charlotte's Letters*, Idel, Bradford: J. Horsfall Turner (1885–9).

Caper, R.A. (1975) 'Psychological forces supporting totalitarian systems', *Contemporary Psychoanalysis* 11: 161–74.

—— (1996) 'Play, experimentation and creativity', *International Journal of Psychoanalysis* 77: 859–69.

Cardinal, M. (1975) *The Words To Say It*, trans. P. Goodheart, London: Picador (1984).

Carpy, D. (1989) 'Tolerating the countertransference: a mutative process', *International Journal of Psychoanalysis* 70: 287–94.

Carroll, L. (1904) *The Story of Sylvie and Bruno*, London: Macmillan.

Caruth, E. (1988) 'How you play the game: on game as play and play as game in the psychoanalytic process', *Psychoanalytic Psychology* 5: 179–92.

Cavafy, C.P. (1911) 'The god abandons Antony', in E. Keeley and P. Sherrard, eds and trans., *Six Poets of Modern Greece*, London: Thames and Hudson (1960).

Chase, K. (1984) *Eros and Psyche: The Representation of Personality in Charles Dickens, Charlotte Brontë and George Eliot*, London: Methuen.

Chasseguet-Smirgel, J. (1985) *The Ego-Ideal: A Psychoanalytic Essay on the Malady of the Ideal*, London: Free Association Books.

Christie, G. (1994) 'Some psychoanalytic aspects of humour', *International Journal of Psychoanalysis* 75: 479–89.

Coltart, N. (1992) *Slouching Towards Bethlehem . . . and Further Psychoanalytic Explorations*, London: Free Association Books.

—— (1996) *The Baby and the Bathwater*, London: Karnac Books.

Constable, J. (1833) *Various subjects of Landscape, characteristic of English Scenery, principally intended to mark the Phenomena of the Chiar'Oscuro of Nature*, in A. Wilton, *Constable's 'English Landscape Scenery'*: 32, London: British Museum (1979).

Deri, S. (1984) *Symbolism and Creativity*, New York: International Universities Press.

Dodds, E.R. (1960) *Euripides' Bacchae*, 2nd edn, Oxford: Oxford University Press.

Easterling, P.E., ed. (1982) *Sophocles' Trachiniae*, Cambridge: Cambridge University Press.

Edmonds, R. (1994) *Pushkin: The Man and his Age*, London: Macmillan.

Eigen, M. (1993) *The Electrified Tightrope*, New Jersey: Jason Aronson.

—— (1998) *The Psychoanalytic Mystic*, London: Free Association Books.

Eliot, T.S. (1940) 'East Coker', *The Complete Poems and Plays of T.S. Eliot*: 177–83, London: Faber and Faber (1969).

Ellman, S.J. and Moskowitz, M.B. (1980) 'An examination of some recent criticisms of psychoanalytic "metapsychology"', *Psychoanalytic Quarterly* 49: 631–62.

Emde, R., Kubicek, L. and Oppenheim, D. (1997) 'Imaginative reality observed during early language development', *International Journal of Psychoanalysis* 78: 115–33.

Etchegoyen, R.H. and Ahumada, J.L. (1990) 'Bateson and Matte Blanco: bio-logic and bi-logic', *International Review of Psycho-Analysis* 17: 493–502.

Farrell, B.A. (1981) *The Standing of Psychoanalysis*, London: Oxford University Press.

Fenichel, O. (1941) *Problems of Psychoanalytic Technique*, New York: Psychoanalytic Quarterly Inc.

Ferenczi, S. (1928) 'The elasticity of psycho-analytic technique', *Final Contributions to the Problems and Methods of Psycho-Analysis*: 87–101, London: Hogarth (1955).

Ferenczi, S. and Rank, O. (1925) *The Development of Psychoanalysis*, Madison: International Universities Press (1986).

Follett, M.P. (1924) *Creative Experience*, New York: Longmans, Green and Co.

Fonagy, P. and Target, M. (1996a) 'Playing with reality: I. Theory of mind and the normal development of psychic reality', *International Journal of Psychoanalysis* 77: 217–33.

—— (1996b) 'Playing with reality: II. The development of psychic reality from a theoretical perspective', *International Journal of Psychoanalysis* 77: 459–79.

Franco, O. de M. (1998) 'Religious experience and psychoanalysis: from man-as-god to man-with-god', *International Journal of Psychoanalysis* 79: 113–31.

Freud, S. (1895) *Project for a Scientific Psychology*, *The Standard Edition of the Complete Works of Sigmund Freud*, vol. I: 295–397, London: Hogarth Press (1950–74).

—— (1897) 'Draft N', *The Standard Edition of the Complete Works of Sigmund Freud*, vol. I: 254–7, London: Hogarth Press (1950–74).

—— (1900) *The Interpretation of Dreams*, *The Standard Edition of the Complete Works of Sigmund Freud*, vols IV–V: xxiii–621, London: Hogarth Press (1950–74).

—— (1905a) *Fragment of an Analysis of a Case of Hysteria*, *The Standard Edition of the Complete Works of Sigmund Freud*, vol. VII: 7–122, London: Hogarth Press (1950–74).

—— (1905b) *Jokes and their Relation to the Unconscious*, *The Standard Edition of the Complete Works of Sigmund Freud*, vol. VIII: 9–238, London: Hogarth Press (1950–74).

—— (1907) *Delusions and Dreams in Jensen's Gradiva*, *The Standard Edition of the Complete Works of Sigmund Freud*, vol. IX: 7–95, London: Hogarth Press (1950–74).

—— (1908) 'Creative writers and day-dreaming', *The Standard Edition of the Complete Works of Sigmund Freud*, vol. IX: 143–53, London: Hogarth Press (1950–74).

—— (1910) 'Leonardo da Vinci and a memory of his childhood', *The Standard Edition of the Complete Works of Sigmund Freud*, vol. XI: 63–137, London: Hogarth Press (1950–74).

—— (1911a) 'The handling of dream-interpretation in psychoanalysis', *The Standard Edition of the Complete Works of Sigmund Freud*, vol. XII: 89–96, London: Hogarth Press (1950–74).

—— (1911b) 'Formulations on the two principles of mental functioning', *The Standard Edition of the Complete Works of Sigmund Freud*, vol. XII: 218–26, London: Hogarth Press (1950–74).

—— (1912) 'Recommendations to physicians practising psychoanalysis', *The Standard Edition of the Complete Works of Sigmund Freud*, vol. XII: 111–20, London: Hogarth Press (1950–74).

—— (1913a) 'On beginning the treatment (further recommendations on the technique of psychoanalysis I)', *The Standard Edition of the Complete Works of Sigmund Freud*, vol. XII: 123–44, London: Hogarth Press (1950–74).

—— (1913b) 'The claims of psychoanalysis to scientific interest', *The Standard Edition of the Complete Works of Sigmund Freud*, vol. XIII: 165–90, London: Hogarth Press (1950–74).

—— (1914a) 'Remembering, repeating and working through (further recommendations on the technique of psycho-analysis II)', *The Standard Edition of the Complete Works of Sigmund Freud*, vol. XII: 145–56, London: Hogarth Press (1950–74).

—— (1914b) 'The Moses of Michelangelo', *The Standard Edition of the Complete Works of Sigmund Freud*, vol. XIII: 211–38, London: Hogarth Press (1950–74).

—— (1914c) 'On the history of the psychoanalytic movement', *The Standard Edition of the Complete Works of Sigmund Freud*, vol. XIV: 7–66, London: Hogarth Press (1950–74).

—— (1915a) 'Instincts and their vicissitudes', *The Standard Edition of the Complete Works of Sigmund Freud*, vol. XIV: 117–40, London: Hogarth Press (1950–74).

—— (1915b) 'Repression', *The Standard Edition of the Complete Works of Sigmund Freud*, vol. XIV: 146–58, London: Hogarth Press (1950–74).

—— (1915c) 'The unconscious', *The Standard Edition of the Complete Works of Sigmund Freud*, vol. XIV: 166–204, London: Hogarth Press (1950–74).

—— (1916–17) *Introductory Lectures on Psychoanalysis*, *The Standard Edition of the Complete Works of Sigmund Freud*, vols XV–XVI: 9–463, London: Hogarth Press (1950–74).

—— (1917) 'Mourning and melancholia', *The Standard Edition of the Complete Works of Sigmund Freud*, vol. XIV: 243–58, London: Hogarth Press (1950–74).

—— (1918) *From the History of an Infantile Neurosis*, *The Standard Edition of the Complete Works of Sigmund Freud*, vol. XVII: 7–122, London: Hogarth Press (1950–74).

—— (1919a) 'Lines of advance in psychoanalytic therapy', *The Standard Edition of the Complete Works of Sigmund Freud*, vol. XVII: 159–68, London: Hogarth Press (1950–74).

—— (1919b) 'The "uncanny"', *The Standard Edition of the Complete Works of Sigmund Freud*, vol. XVII: 219–56, London: Hogarth Press (1950–74).

—— (1920) *Beyond the Pleasure Principle*, *The Standard Edition of the Complete Works of Sigmund Freud*, vol. XVIII: 7–64, London: Hogarth Press (1950–74).

—— (1923) 'The ego and the id', *The Standard Edition of the Complete Works of Sigmund Freud*, vol. XIX: 12–59, London: Hogarth Press (1950–74).

—— (1924) 'The dissolution of the Oedipus complex', *The Standard Edition of the Complete Works of Sigmund Freud*, vol. XIX: 173–9, London: Hogarth Press (1950–74).

—— (1925a) 'The resistances to psychoanalysis', *The Standard Edition of the Complete Works of Sigmund Freud*, vol. XIX: 213–22, London: Hogarth Press (1950–74).

—— (1925b) 'Negation', *The Standard Edition of the Complete Works of Sigmund Freud*, vol. XIX: 235–9, London: Hogarth Press (1950–74).

—— (1925c) 'Some psychical consequences of the anatomical distinction between the sexes', *The Standard Edition of the Complete Works of Sigmund Freud*, vol. XIX: 248–58, London: Hogarth Press (1950–74).

—— (1925d) 'An autobiographical study', *The Standard Edition of the Complete Works of Sigmund Freud*, vol. XX: 7–74, London: Hogarth Press (1950–74).

—— (1926) 'Inhibitions, symptoms and anxiety', *The Standard Edition of the Complete Works of Sigmund Freud*, vol. XX: 87–172, London: Hogarth Press (1950–74).

—— (1927) 'The future of an illusion', *The Standard Edition of the Complete Works of Sigmund Freud*, vol. XXI: 5–56, London: Hogarth Press (1950–74).

—— (1930) *Civilisation and its Discontents*, *The Standard Edition of the Complete Works of Sigmund Freud*, vol. XXI: 64–145, London: Hogarth Press (1950–74).

—— (1933) *New Introductory Lectures on Psychoanalysis*, *The Standard Edition of the Complete Works of Sigmund Freud*, vol. XXII: 5–182, London: Hogarth Press (1950–74).

—— (1937) 'Analysis terminable and interminable', *The Standard Edition of the Complete Works of Sigmund Freud*, vol. XXIII: 209–54, London: Hogarth Press (1950–74).

—— (1939) *Moses and Monotheism: Three Essays*, *The Standard Edition of the Complete Works of Sigmund Freud*, vol. XXIII: 7–137, London: Hogarth Press (1950–74).

—— (1940) 'An outline of psycho-analysis', *The Standard Edition of the Complete Works of Sigmund Freud*, vol. XXIII: 144–207, London: Hogarth Press (1950–74).

—— (1954) *The Origins of Psycho-analysis: Letters to Wilhem Fliess, Drafts and Notes, 1887–1902*, eds M. Bonaparte, A. Freud and E. Kris, London: Imago.

—— (1961) *Letters of Sigmund Freud, 1873–1939*, ed. E. Freud, trans. T. and J. Stern, London: Hogarth.

Friedman, L. (1997) 'Ferrum, ignis and medicina: return to the crucible', *Journal of the American Psychoanalytical Association* 45: 21–36.

Gay, P. (1988) *Freud: A Life for our Time*, London: Dent.

Gill, M. (1954) 'Psychoanalysis and exploratory psychotherapy', *Journal of the American Psychoanalytical Association* 2: 771–97.

—— (1984) 'Psychoanalysis and psychotherapy: a revision', *International Review of Psycho-Analysis* 11: 161–79.

Gilot, F. (1997) 'A painter responds', in J. Oremland, *The Origins and Dynamics of Creativity*: 123–31, Madison: International Universities Press.

Gitelson, M. (1962) 'The curative factors in psychoanalysis: the first phase of psychoanalysis', *International Journal of Psychoanalysis* 43: 194–205.

Gittings, R., ed. (1970) *Letters of John Keats: A Selection*, Oxford: Oxford University Press.

Glover, E. (1937) 'Contribution to Symposium on the theory of the therapeutic results of psycho-analysis', *International Journal of Psychoanalysis* 18: 125–32.

Gould, J. (1978) 'Dramatic character and "human intelligibility" in Greek tragedy', *Proceedings of the Cambridge Philological Society* 24: 43–67.

Gray, P. (1990) 'The nature of the therapeutic action in psychoanalysis', *Journal of the American Psychoanalytic Association* 38: 1083–97.

Green, A. (1978) 'Potential space in psychoanalysis: the object in the setting', *On Private Madness*: 277–96, London: Hogarth (1986).

—— (1980) '*Thésée et Oedipe: une interprétation psychanalytique de la Théséide*', in D. Anzieu *et al.*, *Psychanalyse et Culture Grecque*, Paris: Les Belles Lettres.

—— (1983) 'The dead mother', *On Private Madness*: 142–73, London: Hogarth (1986).

—— (1984) *Le langage dans la psychanalyse*, in A. Green *et al.*, *Langages: 2èmes rencontres psychanalytiques d'Aix-en-Provence 1983*: 19–250, Paris: Les Belles Lettres.

—— (1993) *The Work of the Negative*, trans. A. Weller, London: Free Association Books (1999).

—— (1994) *Un Psychanalyste Engagé: Conversations avec Manuel Macias*, Paris: Calmann-Lévy.

—— (1997) 'The intuition of the negative in *Playing and Reality*', *International Journal of Psychoanalysis* 78: 1071–84.

Greenson, R.R. (1967) *The Technique and Practice of Psychoanalysis*, London: Hogarth Press.

le Guen, C. (1975) 'The formation of the transference: a reply to the discussion by A. Béjarano', *International Journal of Psychoanalysis* 56: 371–2.

Guntrip, H. (1975) 'My experiences of analysis with Fairbairn and Winnicott', *International Review of Psycho-Analysis* 2: 145–56.

Hanly, C. (1990) 'The concept of truth in psychoanalysis', *International Journal of Psychoanalysis* 71: 375–83.

Harmon, M., ed. (1998) *No Author Better Served: The Correspondence of Samuel Beckett and Alan Schneider*, Cambridge, Mass.: Harvard University Press.

Heaney, S. (1966) *Death of a Naturalist*, London: Faber and Faber.

Heimann, P. (1950) 'On counter-transference', *International Journal of Psychoanalysis* 31: 81–4.

Heisenberg, W. (1971) *Physics and Beyond: Encounters and Conversations*, trans. A.J. Pomerans, London: Allen and Unwin.

Herrigel, E. (1953) *Zen in the Art of Archery*, London: Routledge and Kegan Paul.

Hildebrand, H.P. (1988) 'The other side of the wall: a psychoanalytic study of creativity in later life', *International Review of Psycho-Analysis* 15: 353–63.

Hitchens, C. (1980) 'Oxford's unlikely liaisons', *New Statesman* (London) no. 2557, 21 March: 429.

Huizinga, J. (1934) *Homo Ludens: A Study of the Play-Element in Culture*, London: Routledge and Kegan Paul (1944).

International Review of Psycho-Analysis (1990) Part 4: Milner and Matte Blanco Birthday Number.

IPA Congress (1995, 1996) 39th Congress of the International Psychoanalytical Association, San Francisco, July–August 1995. Pre-published papers, *International Journal of Psychoanalysis* 76: 1–49. Plenary papers and panel reports, *International Journal of Psychoanalysis* 77: 1–148.

Jaques, E. (1965) 'Death and the mid-life crisis', *International Journal of Psychoanalysis* 46: 502–14.

Jennings, E. (1980) 'Into the hour', *Collected Poems*, Manchester: Carcanet (1986).

Jones, E. (1916) 'The theory of symbolism', *Papers in Psychoanalysis*, 5th edn: 87–144, London: Baillière.

—— (1954) *Sigmund Freud: Life and Work*, vol. I, new edn, London: Hogarth.

—— (1958) *Sigmund Freud: Life and Work*, vol. II, new edn, London: Hogarth.

Kardiner, A. (1977) *My Analysis with Freud: Reminiscences*, New York: Norton.

Kazantzakis, N. (1965) *Report to Greco*, Oxford: Cassirer.

Kennedy, R. (1984) 'A dual aspect of the transference', *International Journal of Psycho-analysis* 65: 471–83.

Kenny, A. (1997) *A Life in Oxford*, London: John Murray.

Kernberg, O. (1996) 'Thirty methods to destroy the creativity of psychoanalytic candidates', *International Journal of Psychoanalysis* 77: 1031–40.

Khan, M. (1974) *The Privacy of the Self*, London: Hogarth Press.

—— (1975) Introduction to D.W. Winnicott *Through Paediatrics to Psychoanalysis*, London: Hogarth Press.

King, P. (1978) 'Affective response of the analyst to the patient's communications', *International Journal of Psychoanalysis* 59: 329–34.

Kipling, R. (1902) 'The butterfly that stamped', *Just So Stories*, London: Macmillan.

Klauber, J. (1981) *Difficulties in the Analytic Encounter*, New York: Jason Aronson.

—— (1987) 'The role of illusion in the psychoanalytic cure', *Illusion and Spontaneity in Psychoanalysis*: 1–12, London: Free Association Books.

Klein, G.S. (1976) *Psychoanalytic Theory: an Exploration of Essentials*, New York: International Universities Press.

Klein, M. (1927) 'Criminal tendencies in normal children', *The Writings of Melanie Klein*, vol. I: 170–85, eds R. Money-Kyrle, B. Joseph, E. O'Shaughnessy and H. Segal, London: Hogarth Press (1927).

—— (1928) 'Early stages of the Oedipus conflict', *The Writings of Melanie Klein*, vol. I: 186–98, eds R. Money-Kyrle, B. Joseph, E. O'Shaughnessy and H. Segal, London: Hogarth Press (1975).

—— (1930) 'The importance of symbol-formation in the development of the ego', *The Writings of Melanie Klein*, vol. I: 219–32, eds R. Money-Kyrle, B. Joseph, E. O'Shaughnessy and H. Segal, London: Hogarth Press (1975).

—— (1932) *The Psychoanalysis of Children*, *The Writings of Melanie Klein*, vol. II, eds R. Money-Kyrle, B. Joseph, E. O'Shaughnessy and H. Segal, London: Hogarth Press (1975).

—— (1945) 'The Oedipus complex in the light of early anxieties', *The Writings of Melanie Klein*, vol. I: 370–419, eds R. Money-Kyrle, B. Joseph, E. O'Shaughnessy and H. Segal, London: Hogarth Press (1975).

—— (1952) 'Some theoretical conclusions regarding the emotional life of the infant', *The Writings of Melanie Klein*, vol. III: 61–93, eds R. Money-Kyrle, B. Joseph, E. O'Shaughnessy and H. Segal, London: Hogarth Press (1975).

—— (1957) 'Envy and gratitude', *The Writings of Melanie Klein*, vol. III: 176–235, eds R. Money-Kyrle, B. Joseph, E. O'Shaughnessy and H. Segal, London: Hogarth Press (1975).

Kohon, G. (1999) *No Lost Certainties to be Recovered*, London: Karnac Books.

Kris, E. (1952) *Psychoanalytic Explorations in Art*, New York: International Universities Press.

Kristeva, J. (1987) *Tales of Love*, New York: Columbia.

Kuhn, T.S. (1962) *The Structure of Scientific Revolutions*, 2nd edn, University of Chicago Press (1970).

Lacan, J. (1977) *The Four Fundamental Concepts of Psychoanalysis*, London: Hogarth Press.

Lakatos, I. (1974) 'Falsification and the methodology of scientific research programmes', in I. Lakatos and A. Musgrave eds, *Criticism and the Growth of Knowledge*: 91–196, Cambridge: Cambridge University Press.

Lao Tsu (1972) *Tao Te Ching*, trans. Gia-Fu Feng and J. English, London: Wildwood House.

Lao Tzu (1985) *Tao Te Ching: The Richard Wilhelm Edition*, London: Arkana.

Laplanche, J. and Pontalis, J.-B. (1973) *The Language of Psychoanalysis*, London: Hogarth Press.

Lear, J. (1998) *Open Minded: Working Out the Logic of the Soul*, Cambridge, Mass.: Harvard University Press.

Lebovici, S. (1982) 'The origins and development of the Oedipus complex', *International Journal of Psychoanalysis* 63: 201–15.

Leggett, T. (1978) *Zen and the Ways*, London: Routledge and Kegan Paul.

Lewin, B. (1955) 'Dream psychology and the analytic situation', *Psychoanalytic Quarterly* 24: 169–99.

Liang, T.T. (1977) *T'ai Chi Ch'uan for Health and Self-defence*, New York: Random House.

Lifton, R.J. (1961) *Thought Reform and the Psychology of Totalism*, London: Gollancz.

Limentani, A. (1995) 'Creativity and the third age', *International Journal of Psychoanalysis* 76: 825–33.

Loewald, H. (1979) 'The waning of the Oedipus complex', *Papers on Psychoanalysis*: 384–404, New Haven, Conn.: Yale University Press (1980).

Lohser, B. and Newton, P. (1996) *Unorthodox Freud: the View from the Couch*, New York: Guilford.

Lomas, P. (1981) *The Case for a Personal Psychotherapy*, Oxford: Oxford University Press.

McLaughlin, J. (1987) 'The play of transference: some reflections on enactment in the psychoanalytic situation', *Journal of the American Psychoanalytic Association* 35: 557–82.

Mack Brunswick, R. (1940) 'The pre-Oedipal phase of the libido development', *Psychoanalytic Quarterly* 9: 293–319.

Makari, G. (1998) Letter to the Editor, *International Journal of Psychoanalysis* 79: 1004–5.

Mannoni, M. (1970) *The Child, his 'Illness' and the Others*, London: Tavistock Publications.

Markillie, R. (1996) 'Some personal recollections and impressions of Harry Guntrip', *International Journal of Psychoanalysis* 77: 763–71.

Maslow, A. (1954) 'Self-actualizing people: a study of psychological health', *Motivation and Personality*, 2nd edn: 149–80, New York: Harper and Row (1970).

—— (1967) 'A theory of meta-motivation: the biological rooting of the value-life', *The Farther Reaches of Human Nature*: 313–57, London: Pelican (1971).

Masson, J. (1985) *The Complete Letters of Sigmund Freud to Wilhelm Fliess 1887–1904*, Cambridge, Mass.: Harvard.

Matte Blanco, I. (1975) *The Unconscious as Infinite Sets*, London: Duckworth.

—— (1988) *Thinking, Feeling and Being: Clinical Reflections on the Fundamental Antinomy of Human Beings and the World*, London: Routledge.

Meissner, W. (1984) *Psychoanalysis and Religious Experience*, New Haven, Conn.: Yale University Press.

Meng, H. and Freud, E.L., eds (1963) *Psychoanalysis and Faith: The Letters of Sigmund Freud and Oskar Pfister*, trans. E. Mosbacher, London: Hogarth Press.

Menninger, K. (1963) *The Vital Balance: The Life Process in Mental Health and Illness*, New York: Viking.

Milne A.A. (1926) *Winnie-the-Pooh*, London: Methuen.

Milner, M. (as Joanna Field) (1934) *A Life of One's Own*, London: Virago (1986).

—— (as Joanna Field) (1937) *An Experiment in Leisure*, London: Virago (1986).

—— (1950) *On Not Being Able to Paint*, 2nd edn, London: Heinemann (1957).

—— (1952) 'The role of illusion in symbol formation', *The Suppressed Madness of Sane Men: Forty-Four Years of Exploring Psychoanalysis*: 83–113, London: Tavistock Publications. (Originally published as 'Aspects of symbolism in comprehension of the Not-Self', *International Journal of Psychoanalysis* 33: 181–95.)

—— (1969) *The Hands of the Living God: An Account of a Psychoanalytic Treatment*, London: Hogarth.

—— (1987a) *Eternity's Sunrise: a Way of Keeping a Diary*, London: Virago.

—— (1987b) *The Suppressed Madness of Sane Men: Forty-Four Years of Exploring Psychoanalysis*, London: Tavistock Publications.

Mitchell, J. (1974) *Psychoanalysis and Feminism*, London: Allen Lane.

Modell, A.H. (1981) 'Does metapsychology still exist?', *International Journal of Psychoanalysis* 62: 391–402.

Moran, G. (1987) 'Some functions of play and playfulness: a developmental perspective', *Psychoanalytic Study of the Child* 42: 11–29.

Musashi, M. (1645) *A Book of Five Rings*, trans. V. Harris, London: Allison and Busby (1974).

Nacht, S. (1962) 'The Curative Factors in Psychoanalyis', *International Journal of Psychoanalysis* 43: 206–11.

Newton, P. and Lohser, B. (1998) Letter to the Editor, *International Journal of Psychoanalysis* 79: 1003–4.

Nicol, C.W. (1975) *Moving Zen: Karate as a Way to Gentleness*, London: Bodley Head.

Nissim Momigliano, L. (1992) *Continuity and Change in Psychoanalysis: Letters from Milan*, London: Karnac Books.

Ohi, T. (1997) 'History of Ohi ware', Kanazawa: Ohi Museum.

Oremland, J. (1997) *The Origins and Dynamics of Creativity*, Madison, Wis.: International Universities Press.

Padel, J. (1985) 'Ego in current thinking', *International Review of Psycho-Analysis* 12: 273–83.

—— (1996) 'The case of Harry Guntrip', *International Journal of Psychoanalysis* 77: 755–61.

Parris, L. and Fleming-Williams, I. (1991) *Constable*, London: Tate Gallery.

Pasquali, G. (1987) 'Some notes on humour in psychoanalysis', *International Review of Psycho-Analysis* 14: 231–6.

Pedder, J. (1977) 'The role of space and location in psychotherapy, play and theatre', *International Review of Psycho-Analysis* 4: 215–23.

—— (1979) 'Transitional space in psychotherapy and theatre', *British Journal of Medical Psychology* 52: 377–84.

Perloff, C. (1997) 'A director responds', in J. Oremland, *The Origins and Dynamics of Creativity*: 131–40, Madison, Wis.: International Universities Press.

Perlow, M. (1995) *Understanding Mental Objects*, London: Routledge.

Polanyi, M. (1962) *Personal Knowledge: Towards a Post-Critical Philosophy*, London: Routledge and Kegan Paul.

Pollock, G. (1982) 'The mourning–liberation process and creativity', *Annual of Psychoanalysis* 10: 333–53.

Popper, K. (1934) *The Logic of Scientific Discovery*, 10th (revised) impression, London: Hutchinson (1980).

Quine, W. van O. (1961) 'Two dogmas of empiricism', *From a Logical Point of View*, 2nd edn: 20–46, New York, Harper and Row (1963).

Rank, O. (1924) *The Trauma of Birth and its Meaning for Psychoanalysis*, London: Paul Trench and Trubner (1929).

—— (1929–31) *Will Therapy and Truth and Reality*, New York: Knopf (1950).

—— (1932) *Art and Artist: Creative Urge and Personality Development*, New York: Knopf.

Rayner, E. (1981) 'Infinite experiences, affects and the characteristics of the unconscious', *International Journal of Psychoanalysis* 62: 403–12.

—— (1995) *Unconscious Logic: An Introduction to Matte Blanco's Bi-Logic and its Uses*, London: Routledge.

Rey, H. (1976) 'Review of *The Unconscious as Infinite Sets* by I. Matte Blanco', *International Journal of Psychoanalysis* 57: 491–95.

Roudinesco, E. (1986) *Jacques Lacan and Co.: A History of Psychoanalysis in France*, trans. J. Mehlmann, London: Free Association Books (1990).

Rudnytsky, P.L. (1991) *The Psychoanalytic Vocation: Rank, Winnicott and the Legacy of Freud*, New Haven, Conn.: Yale.

—— ed. (1993) *Transitional Objects and Potential Spaces: Literary Uses of D.W. Winnicott*, New York: Columbia.

Sandler, A.-M. (1982) 'The selection and function of the training analyst in Europe', *International Review of Psychoanalysis* 9: 386–98.

Sandler, J. (1983) 'Reflections on some relations between psychoanalytic concepts and psychoanalytic practice', *International Journal of Psychoanalysis* 64: 35–45.

—— (1987) *From Safety to Superego*, London: Karnac Books.

Sanville, J. (1991) *The Playground of Psychoanalytic Therapy*, Hillsdale, N.J.: Analytic Press.

Schafer, R. (1976) 'The psychoanalytic vision of reality', *A New Language for Psychoanalysis*: 22–56, New Haven, Conn.: Yale University Press.

Schecter, D.E. (1983) 'Notes on the development of creativity', *Contemporary Psychoanalysis* 19: 193–9.

Schiller, F. (1795) *On the Aesthetic Education of Man in a Series of Letters*, trans. and ed. E.M. Wilkinson and L.A. Willoughby, Oxford: Clarendon Press (1967).

Schwaber, E. (1983) 'Psychoanalytic listening and psychic reality', *International Review of Psycho-Analysis* 10: 379–92.

Searles, H. (1975) 'The patient as therapist to his analyst', *Countertransference and Related Subjects: Selected Papers*: 380–459, New York: Jason Aronson (1979).

Segal, H. (1952) 'A psycho-analytical approach to aesthetics', *The Work of Hanna Segal*: 185–206, New York: Jason Aronson (1981).

—— (1957) 'Notes on symbol formation', *The Work of Hanna Segal*: 49–65, New York: Jason Aronson (1981).

—— (1962) 'The curative factors in psychoanalysis', *The Work of Hanna Segal*: 69–79, New York: Jason Aronson (1981).

—— (1974) 'Delusion and artistic creativity: some reflexions on reading *The Spire* by William Golding', *International Review of Psycho-Analysis* 1: 135–41.

—— (1979) 'Postscript to "The curative factors in psychoanalysis"', *The Work of Hanna Segal*: 79–80, New York: Jason Aronson (1981).

—— (1984) 'Joseph Conrad and the mid-life crisis', *Psychoanalysis, Literature and War*: 123–32, London: Routledge (1997).

Sharpe, E.F. (1943) 'Concerning the problem of technique and training', in P. King and R. Steiner, eds, *The Freud–Klein Controversies 1941–5*, London: Routledge (1991).

Simon, B. (1988) 'The imaginary twins: the case of Beckett and Bion', *International Review of Psycho-Analysis* 15: 331–52.

Sliding Doors (1998) Paramount Pictures.

Solnit, A. (1987) 'A psychoanalytic view of play', *Psychoanalytic Study of the Child* 42: 205–19.

Spitz, R.A. (1956) 'Countertransference', *Journal of the American Psychoanalytic Association* 4: 256–65.

Stewart, H. (1992) 'Interpretation and other agents for psychic change', *Psychic Experience and Problems of Technique*: 127–40, London: Routledge.

Strachey, J. (1953) Editorial introduction to S. Freud, *The Interpretation of Dreams*, *The Standard Edition of the Complete Works of Sigmund Freud*, vol. IV: xi–xxii, London: Hogarth Press (1950–74).

—— (1961) Editorial footnote to S. Freud, 'The dissolution of the Oedipus complex', *The Standard Edition of the Complete Works of Sigmund Freud*, vol. XIX: 173, London: Hogarth Press (1950–74).

Symington, N. (1985) 'Fantasy effects that which it represents', *International Journal of Psychoanalysis* 66: 349–57.

—— (1986) *The Analytic Experience: Lectures from the Tavistock*, London: Free Association Books.

Symposium (1962) 'The curative factors in psychoanalyis', *International Journal of Psychoanalysis* 43: 194–234.

Tomin, J. (1980) 'Inside the security state', *New Statesman* (London) no. 2555, 7 March: 350–3.

Trilling, L. (1951) *The Liberal Imagination: Essays on Literature and Society*, London: Secker and Warburg.

Turkle, S. (1992) *Psychoanalytic Politics*, 2nd edn, London: Free Association Books.

Verrall, A.W. (1910) *The Bacchants of Euripides, and Other Essays*, Cambridge: Cambridge University Press.

Wallerstein, R.S. (1988) 'One psychoanalysis or many?', *International Journal of Psychoanalysis* 69: 5–21.

—— (1995) *The Talking Cures*, New Haven, Conn.: Yale.

—— (1997) 'Merton Gill, psychotherapy and psychoanalysis: a personal dialogue', *Journal of the American Psychoanalytical Association* 45: 233–56.

Weil, S. (1947) *Gravity and Grace*, trans. E. Craufurd, London: Routledge and Kegan Paul (1952).

Wilden, A. (1968) *The Language of the Self*, Baltimore, Md.: Johns Hopkins.

Winnicott, D.W. (1941) 'The observation of infants in a set situation', *Collected Papers: Through Paediatrics to Psychoanalysis*: 52–69, London: Hogarth Press (1975).

—— (1952) 'Anxiety associated with insecurity', *Collected Papers: Through Paediatrics to Psychoanalysis*: 97–100, London: Hogarth Press (1975).

—— (1956) 'Primary maternal preoccupation', *Collected Papers: Through Paediatrics to Psychoanalysis*: 300–5, London: Hogarth Press (1975).

—— (1960) 'Ego distortion in terms of true and false self', *The Maturational Processes and the Facilitating Environment: Studies in the Theory of Emotional Development*: 140–52, London: Hogarth (1965).

—— (1971) *Playing and Reality*, London: Tavistock Publications.

Winnington-Ingram, R.P. (1948) *Euripides and Dionysos*, Cambridge: Cambridge University Press.

Wordsworth, W. (1810) *Essays upon Epitaphs III*, in W.J.B. Owen and Jane Worthington-Sayer, eds, *The Prose Works of William Wordsworth*, vol. II, Oxford: Clarendon Press (1974).

Wright, K. (1991) *Vision and Separation: Between Mother and Baby*, London: Free Association Books.

Wyndham, J. (1956) 'Opposite number', *The Seeds of Time*, London: Michael Joseph.

Yeats, W.B. (1921) 'The second coming', *Collected Poems*, London: Macmillan (1950).

—— (1936–9) 'Long-legged fly', *Collected Poems*, London: Macmillan (1950).

Name index

Abraham 33, 44–5
Achelous 116, 118–20
Actaeon 94fn
Aegeus 100, 101fn
Aeschylus 103, 119
Agave 90–5
Ahumada, Jorge 136
Alcmena 115–16
Antigone 90–1
Anzieu, Didier 25, 53
Aphrodite 94, 97, 117, 119
Apollo 121
Arden, Margaret 47, 49fn, 136
Arlow, J. 139, 174
Ares 97
Ariadne 101fn
Arieti, Silvano 158
Aristotle 36, 78
Arjuna 47
Artemis 94fn, 121
Arvanitakis, K.I. 99
Athens 90, 100, 101fn
Augustine, St. 26
Autonoë 94fn

Bach 61–2, 151
Bacon, Francis 197
Bakan, D. 10
Baker, P. 53
Baker, Ronald 136–8, 145
Balint, Enid 75
Balint, Michael 157
Bao Ruo-Wang 85fn
Barratt, Barnaby 190
Bateman, Anthony 134–5
Bateson, Gregory 133–6, 176
Beckett, R.B. 168

Beckett, Samuel 102; analysis with Bion
  53
Berlin, I. 69
Bermingham, Ann 163fn
Bernardi, Ricardo 189–90
Bettelheim, Bruno 84–6
Bion, Wilfred 3, 6, 25, 29, 47–9, 67, 174,
  184, 191, 197–8, 200; Beckett's analyis
  with 53; evolution of analytic identity
  3, 76–7
Birksted-Breen Dana 106
Black, D. 47
Bollas, Christopher 33, 161
Bonaparte, Marie 79
Borges, Jorge Luis 83
Braunschweig, Denise 113
Brenman Pick, I. 42
Brentano, Franz 78
Breuer, J. 37
Britton, R. 110

Cadmus 90, 92–3, 97
Caesar 129
Caper, Robert 84, 130
Cardinal, Marie 11–12
Carroll, Lewis 35
Carpy, Denis 134–5
Caruth, E. 142
Cavafy, C.P. 88
Chase, Karen 103
Chasseguet-Smirgel, Janine 81–2
Chelminski, R. 85 fn
Christie, George 138
Cithaeron, Mount 90
Clytaemnestra 103
Colonus 90–1, 99
Coltart, Nina 23, 25, 34, 47, 191, 193fn

215

Subject index

219